...an Viner's weekly dispatches from the country ...
...nost popular features in the *Independent* newspaper. He
...so a sports writer and columnist for the same newspaper,
...is the author of two previous books: *Tales of the Country*
...a sporting memoir, *Ali, Pelé, Lillee and Me*, both pub-
...d by Simon & Schuster/Pocket. He lives with his family in
...fordshire.

Also by Brian Viner

TALES OF THE COUNTRY
ALI, PELÉ, LILLEE AND ME

The Pheasants' Revolt

More Tales of the Country

BRIAN VINER

POCKET
BOOKS

London • New York • Toronto • Sydney

For Nancy, John, John, Shelagh and Jim,
who know that there is no such thing
as a dull lunch

First published in Great Britain in 2007
by Simon & Schuster UK Ltd
This edition first published by Pocket Books, 2008
An imprint of Simon & Schuster UK Ltd
A CBS COMPANY

1 3 5 7 9 10 8 6 4 2

Simon & Schuster UK Ltd
Africa House
64–78 Kingsway
London WC2B 6AH

www.simonsays.co.uk

Simon & Schuster Australia
Sydney

A CIP catalogue for this book is available
from the British Library

ISBN 978-1-41652-776-3

Typeset by Rowland Phototypesetting Ltd, Bury St Edmunds, Suffolk
Printed and bound in Great Britain by Cox & Wyman Ltd, Reading, Berks

Contents

1

Madeleine, and the Red Nose

We had lived in the country for a year before Madeleine entered our lives.

An attractive strawberry blonde of indeterminate years and a larger-than-average bust measurement, Madeleine was also slightly cross-eyed. My wife Jane's late grandmother, Nellie, a daughter of South Yorkshire with an inexhaustible repertoire of euphemisms, would have described her as having 'one eye in t'pot, other up t'chimney'. But it was not Madeleine's unfortunate strabismus that caught one's attention so much as her calm, almost beatific smile. She had about her an authoritative air, which was reinforced by a startlingly erect posture despite the considerable bust, yet softened by the lovely smile.

Indeed, it was a winning smile in more ways than one, for after several minutes of careful deliberation, the judges of the Yarpole village fête scarecrow competition awarded Madeleine first prize in the form of a flamboyant red rosette, which we excitedly pinned to her ample, dishcloth-stuffed bosom.

We'd been a little worried when we entered her, having propped her up awkwardly alongside a much more conventional scarecrow, with a carrot for a nose, and bits of straw bursting out of his tunic, Worzel Gummidge-style. However, the Yarpole judges had obviously been swayed by Madeleine's uncommon beauty, and the carrot-nosed scarecrow had to settle for second place. This was not well received by his patrons, a small boy wearing an England football shirt and the boy's stout, ruddy-cheeked mother. They both looked ready to cry.

Village fêtes, and their Best Scarecrow competitions, or Largest Marrow competitions, or Dog with the Waggiest Tail competitions, are taken with deadly seriousness in the country. We had discovered this the summer before, when we – Jane and I, and our children Eleanor, Joseph and Jacob – settled in rural north Herefordshire after living in Crouch End, north London, for eight years. In fact, keen to immerse ourselves in country ways, we had quickly become connoisseurs of the country show in all its manifestations, from the tiniest village fête to 2003's biggest, most razzlesome, dazzlesome production of all, namely the Autumn Garden and Country Show at the vast Three Counties Showground in Malvern, about half an hour's drive from our house.

Docklow, the small village on the Leominster to Bromyard road that we now called home, would have fitted at least fifty times into the Malvern Autumn Garden and Country Show.

Eleanor, then aged ten, said it was 'like a town' and so it was: a town with boulevards and crossroads and even gyratory systems. There was a bewildering array of tents and stalls, showcasing a certain kind of Middle Englishness at its most engaging. Behind the Vintage Horticultural and Garden Machinery Club (Eastern District) stall, for example, there were people dressed in period clothing to match their vintage horticultural and garden machinery, and although I at first studied them with bemusement, after a while I began to understand exactly why the man with the cloth cap and the pencil moustache looked so lovingly at his 1961 Villiers mk15 series 3. Not, I should add, that I was at all sure what it was, and I didn't want to offend him by asking. I thought it was probably a lawnmower, but it might have been a chainsaw, or a contraption to scare away pigeons, or to core apples.

From the vintage garden machinery stand we moved on to the harvest tent, where we passed a pleasant five minutes talking to a couple from the Herb Society – I like to think that they were called Basil and Rosemary, or perhaps it was Herb himself, and Lavender – who happened to mention in a marvellously casual way that horse chestnut extracts are excellent for treating varicose veins. It's not every day that someone gives you a piece of information as useful as that.

We also bonded with a jolly woman from the Swindon Fuchsia and Pelargonium Society, I remember. It's not something you forget. But the most fun we had was with the giant vegetables. We laughed liked drains at a carrot that looked spookily like John Hurt in *The Elephant Man*, and at leeks the size of cricket bats, and at pumpkins the size of small cars. So fascinated was I by the outsized pumpkins, in fact, that I made a note of the website where you can learn more about them, and only later realized how fortuitous it was that Jane was with me. I wouldn't have wanted her finding a scrap of paper in my pocket bearing the hastily scribbled words 'bigpumpkins.com'.

Whatever, this was an England – an England of big pumpkins and horse chestnut extracts and 1961 Villiers mk15 series 3s – of which we had never really been aware in London. We liked it very much. And by the start of our second year in Herefordshire, while still some distance short of putting on a flat cap to exhibit my 1961 Villiers mk15 series 3 or even one of the more racy mk15 series 4s, I felt sufficiently confident in my new status as a countryman to enter the Yarpole fête tug-of-war.

The contest, between two teams of eight, was decided by the best of three tugs, and our team, remarkably, won the first and last of them. I wasn't really sure how much I contributed to victory. If grotesque grimacing and sudden bursts of phut-phut-phutting flatulence helped the cause, then I helped a lot. But behind me there was an eighteen-stone farmhand with forearms like hams, and his contribution was almost certainly the telling one. Still, my children treated me with considerable respect for almost ten minutes afterwards.

Later that afternoon, back at home, they helped me erect the victorious Madeleine in our vegetable garden. We left her with her broomstick arms outstretched over the cabbages and the purple-sprouting broccoli. After all, there seemed little point in having an award-winning scarecrow if we didn't set her to work, but equally we wanted her to keep her aura of superiority, so we left her winner's rosette on, as well as her wig, a battered straw hat, a blue apron and a funky pair of pink suede gardening gloves that I'd given Jane for her birthday.

We stood Madeleine with her back to the fence dividing our

vegetable plot from the back garden of our neighbours Carl and Sian, and the following morning Carl reported that he'd gone out for some evening air at twilight, and for a minute or two had pursued an inevitably rather one-sided conversation with Madeleine before realising that the figure in the gloaming with arms outstretched wasn't, in fact, Jane doing t'ai chi. Even if my wife did t'ai chi, which she doesn't, I couldn't imagine why she would have been doing it in the semi-darkness wearing gardening gloves, a blue apron and a battered straw hat, in the middle of a bed of cabbages. All the same, it was nice to know that Madeleine could pass for a human being, an essential faculty in a scarecrow.

Madeleine stands in our vegetable garden to this day, but regrettably has never really fooled the birds like she fleetingly fooled Carl. Also, the seasons have rather taken their toll. Her beatific smile, drawn on her pillow-case head with a purple marker pen, has been all but erased by the rain that drives in from the Black Mountains in the west. And she has a tendency to lean, sometimes to the left, sometimes to the right and sometimes slightly forward, as if she has had one damson gin too many. But we leave her there because she reminds us of our first full summer as country folk.

We also find it reassuring to think that just as Madeleine has weathered in the country, so have we. For example, the first time one of our chickens needed killing, I could not bring myself to do it. This was partly because we had unwisely anthropomorphised the wretched creature by calling it Mrs Doubtfire, and partly because I still had townie sensibilities, which did not extend to slaughtering poultry despite Jane's suggestion that I do it in a townie way, by running over it in the Volvo. We had to call in a hitman – Malcolm, from four fields away – to carry out the dreadful deed. But now, whenever a chicken of ours is manifestly on its last legs, I am able to rise to the occasion like some horny-handed son of the soil.

The story of my stuttering metamorphosis from city-dweller to countryman began in my book *Tales of the Country*, and continues here. It is a tale of laughter and pain, of savagery and sensitivity, and I'm not just talking about my vasectomy, which was carried out in a small hospital in mid-Wales, deep in sheep-farming country, much to the amusement of my old London friends who wondered whether the operation might perchance be performed with a pair of shearing scissors.

We had taken the decision to move out of London in part to assuage a vague mid-life desire for change, a need to shake things up, to experience something new. People deal with this need in many different ways; by taking a lover, by buying a sports car, by learning to scuba-dive, by having the silhouette of a leaping dolphin tattooed on an ankle or even a buttock. We moved to Herefordshire. As for the vasectomy, that too tends to be a mid-life phenomenon, and by the time we had settled in to our new rural lifestyle I felt I was ready. I went to see my GP, Dr Senior, in the small market town of Leominster. He said he would add me to the NHS waiting-list.

A few months later I received details of my appointment and was surprised to find that they came from the Bwrdd Iechyd Lleol, Ysbyty Llandrindod ac Ysbyty Coffa Rhyfel Sirol, which was either some approximation of the noise made by post-vasectomy patients getting out of bed in the morning, or Welsh meaning the Local Health Board office at Llandrindod Wells War Memorial Hospital. It turned out to be the latter.

Like many men of my age – forty-three – I had quite a few friends who'd experienced the procedure already. I found it amazing that so straightforward an operation had produced so many anecdotes, most of them concerning the specimen of sperm that is routinely examined twelve weeks or so after the operation to determine whether it has been successful. One friend was ushered into a small room by a stern nurse who gestured to a table and told him matter-of-factly that there was a pile of magazines to peruse should he need some help ejaculating: once she was safely out of the room he looked at them and was understandably bemused to find that the magazine on top of the pile was *Caravanning Monthly*.

Another friend opted to do the necessary at home, but then had a limited amount of time to get it to St Mary's Hospital, Paddington. He'd had the operation there because at the time he lived nearby, in north Kensington, but then he moved to Muswell Hill, which is at least two complicated bus journeys from St Mary's. His account of trying to keep his little jar warm while changing London buses may well be exaggerated for comic effect, but it rarely fails to bring the house down.

For me it was different. I knew, for example, that on the day of the operation I wouldn't be using public transport to get to Llandrindod Wells, known in these parts as Llandod. To get to Llandod by bus from our house in Docklow is the kind of challenge that might be set by the organizers of the Duke of Edinburgh's award scheme (gold category). No, I would have to go by car, and Jane would have to come with me to drive me home. The advice leaflet sent by the Bwrdd Iechyd Lleol strongly recommended that a post-operative vasectomy patient should not drive himself (I nearly added 'or herself', which would, in that well-worn early twenty-first-century phrase, have been political correctness gone mad).

Just to add to my apprehension, the cruel syringe of fate had given me my appointment on Red Nose Day. When Jane realized this, she had practically needed hospital treatment herself, to repair a split side, and I nursed a strong suspicion that, when finally the operation had been carried out, I would walk gingerly back to the car to find that Jane had fitted a plastic red cone to the front bumper. But in a way I was quite pleased to be having the snip on Red Nose Day, taking the view that vasectomies seem to be inherently funny anyway, so why not make the most of the unfortunate clash with Comic Relief and milk it, figuratively speaking, for all it was worth? I made sure that I was the first to suggest that the surgeon and nurse dealing with my (formerly) private parts might be sporting plastic red noses over their surgical masks.

They weren't, as it turned out, and of course my own jollity had diminished somewhat by the time I stood in the bathroom at home on the appointed morning, carefully shaving. This may have been because what I was carefully shaving, as requested by the hospital, was my scrotum. None of my friends who'd had the op had said anything about shaving the scrotum, so you will understand my relief when, while walking the aisles at Boots in Leominster the day before this intricate exercise, I found that Gillette produced a shaving foam, designed for men with sensitive skin, that was 'specially formulated with soothing aloe'. If you had to shave your scrotum, I reckoned, it might as well be with soothing aloe.

The journey to Llandod took about an hour and a quarter, which coincidentally was the same length of time I had spent in the bathroom. Applying a razor blade to one's scrotum is not a job anyone should do in a hurry. We had a coffee in the town centre and then, while Jane took our dog Milo for a walk in the park, I went to see whether a vasectomy, too, would be a walk in the park. I had been assured by one or two of my mates that it was almost a pleasant way of spending a morning, while one or two others had enthusiastically furnished me with horror stories about nasty infections, terrible bruising and excruciating pain. One reader of my 'Country Life' column in the *Independent* – where I had aired my preoperative concerns – thoughtfully likened the sensation to having a donkey tap-dancing on his testicles. Yet I was reassured as soon as I arrived at the hospital. My only previous dealings with hospitals had been in London, where the staff were far too busy to dispense the milk of human kindness. Out in the sticks, things work differently. Not necessarily better, but certainly with more time for social niceties.

Of course, there is a flip side to living in the middle of nowhere, medically speaking. In May 2006 I was visiting my octogenarian mother and stepfather at their flat in London when my stepfather collapsed with what sadly turned out to be a fatal pulmonary embolism. While my mum briefly resuscitated him – remarkably calling on techniques that she had learnt in the Girl Guides seventy years earlier – I called an ambulance, and there were two paramedics actually in the room with him within five minutes of my dialling 999. When it comes to matters of life or death, who needs social niceties? When it comes to having one's vas deferens cut, however, it's rather reassuring to have a friendly natter beforehand with a motherly matron, and the surgeon who performed my vasectomy, plus the two nurses who assisted him, really could not have been sweeter. ''Allo,' said the surgeon, when I was shown into the operating theatre. ''Allo,' said both nurses, smiling at me. Only later did it occur to me that perhaps they had caught a whiff of my scrotum.

2

Owen, and the Comanches

Whether the doctor and nurses had caught a whiff of my aloe-scented scrotum or not, I must say that when I started writing this book, I didn't expect to embark quite so soon on the story of my snip in Llandrindod Wells. But then this is nothing if not the story of a middle-aged man, with middle-aged concerns, and the experiences, both good and bad, that he and his family would never have had if they had stayed in the city. It is not intended as a how-to manual for all those metropolitan folk who wonder whether they should swap mean streets for leafy lanes; in some ways it might qualify more as a how-not-to manual.

But let me return to our first full summer in the country, the summer of 2003. On the Saturday after the Yarpole fête, we attended our own village fête, which was held in the grounds of a large house called Broadland. In terms of our assimilation into country life, that Docklow fête was a small rite of passage. Twelve months earlier, we had turned up hardly knowing a soul, and although everyone was perfectly charming and friendly, it perhaps didn't help that we had arrived in a gang of nine with my sister-in-law Jackie, her husband Tony and their daughters Rachel and Hannah, who were visiting from Wimbledon. Nor did it help when 11-year-old Hannah caused a minor sensation by being stung by a wasp and shrieking in shock and pain. I have no doubt that beefy Herefordshire farmers on occasion get stung by wasps too, and possibly even shriek, yet the fuss somehow compounded our status as outsiders, unacquainted with country ways.

At our second Docklow fête, by contrast, we knew just about everyone and just about everyone knew us. We were not so naive as to think that a mere twelve months had fully initiated us as country folk in the eyes of our neighbours; we would always be what some people round here know as 'buggers-from-off' and what others know as 'blow-ins'. I must add, incidentally, that I was happier to be a blow-in than a bugger-from-off. Moreover, 'blow-in' rather caught the arbitrary nature of our move to Herefordshire for, having decided that we wanted to leave London – and with me able to pursue my day job as a national newspaper columnist from just about anywhere – we had whimsically picked three quite different regions of England and received a bombardment of estate agents' details from each of them until we found a house we all liked.

That house was Docklow Grange, a rambling, early Victorian house of local red sandstone, standing at the centre of a cluster of eleven former farmworkers' cottages. We were pleased to find that we were not the only blow-ins there. For example, Ingemar and Kerstin, who rented one of the cottages from Mr and Mrs Openshaw, the couple from whom we had bought Docklow Grange, had blown in from considerably more distant parts than we had. They were from Gothenburg in Sweden, where Ingemar had been a shipping executive, and Kerstin a headmistress. Their strategy in retirement was to spend the autumn, winter and early spring in England before returning to Sweden for late spring and summer.

I was beguiled by the idea that someone might come to Herefordshire to escape a winter. During our first winter here we had been besieged by dreadful weather, suffering a series of power cuts including one lasting four days. And even with power it had been impossible, with temperatures plummeting outside, to heat Docklow Grange's large, high-ceilinged rooms. I thought of Ingemar and Kerstin stepping gaily out into the icy winds, perhaps bantering in Swedish about how warm and toasty they felt, and remembered a former convict once telling me that it had been a relief being transferred to Wormwood Scrubs because it meant leaving Parkhurst. Ingemar and Kerstin's annual migration seemed a comparable phenomenon. I also remembered a Yorkshire friend of mine, a man square of jaw and blunt of manner, being described by a Glaswegian as a 'southern poofter'. In other words, everything's relative.

Ingemar and Kerstin told me that their friends back in Gothenburg could quite understand the move south for part of the year, but had been alarmed to learn that the destination was rural England. 'Haven't you seen *Midsomer Murders*?' one friend asked them, in all sincerity. 'In the English countryside everyone keeps getting killed.'

Our own friends had been less gloomy about our prospects of surviving in the countryside, but only just. Some of them thought we were brave to move somewhere as remote as Docklow, others that we were plain mad. And some of their concerns on our behalf were concerns we shared. We, too, thought we might miss the cosmopolitanism of the city, yet Docklow, in its somewhat smaller way, had proved just as cosmopolitan as Crouch End. Yes, there were people there who had lived in the parish all their lives. But there were others who were considerably more worldly than we were, not least Ingemar and Kerstin. And as Swedes they had a far more interesting perspective on English rusticity, and indeed on Englishness, than we did.

I asked them once whether they missed anything about Sweden, thinking that they might have a yearning for thirty different styles of herring or neutrality or Pippi Longstocking or something, but they said no, not a thing. So I invited them to make some observations on the English, and they said, slightly disconcertingly, that they considered us a lot friendlier and more open than the people of Sweden, but had found a lot of that friendliness to be merely on the surface. Oddly, this is precisely what English people say about Americans, and almost exactly the opposite of what Americans say about us, which is that superficially we are reserved and formal, but with hidden reserves of warmth and kindness. I suppose national characteristics are entirely in the eye of the beholder, like-wise regional characteristics, which reminds me again of my 'southern poofter' mate, the rugged Yorkshireman.

To return to the interesting social mix of Docklow and its

environs, another of the more intriguing of our new near-neighbours was a woman with several aliases but once known fondly by the tabloid press as Miss Whiplash. She had been a madam in London, whose clients included several high-ranking politicians, and she had settled in bucolic bliss partly on the proceeds of selling her fascinating story. Somewhat incongruously, she now seemed to make her living by breeding ducks, hundreds of them of all shapes and sizes. She lived just over the hill from us, and one afternoon, our friend Jane – whom we had got to know because her two children went to the same school as our three – called in on her way home from buying a pair of mallards there. But she didn't know that she had dealt with Miss Whiplash until we told her, and naturally she was astounded. Our 9-year-old son Joseph overheard the two Janes discussing the whole faintly surreal business. 'What's a dominatrix?' he duly asked.

While Jane, my wife, dithered, Jane, our friend, rose brilliantly to the occasion. 'It's someone who plays lots of dominoes,' she said. Joseph went away entirely satisfied, although possibly with a nasty surprise stored up for him later in life.

Regrettably, Miss Whiplash didn't make an appearance at the Docklow fête in the summer of 2003 – I was all for asking her to open it, or at the very least for asking her to donate a pair of nipple clamps for the tombola – but there was no shortage of fascinating characters there, including Owen, a farm labourer in his sixties, whose claim to local fame was that he had once come second in the Strongest Man in Herefordshire contest and still looked as if he could overturn a tractor with one twitch of his massive shoulders.

Owen had made no attempt to hide his suspicion of us when

we arrived, and in particular his suspicion of me: a bugger from London was bad enough; a bugger from London who made a living from writing newspaper articles, including one called 'Country Life' written as if he had discovered this small patch of Herefordshire where Owen had spent his entire life, was highly suspect. But over the course of twelve months we had supped enough beer together in our local pub, the King's Head, to develop what amounted almost to a friendship. And, he had been thrilled, rather touchingly, to be invited to the house-warming party we had thrown on the first anniversary of our move from Crouch End, a party to which we had also invited lots of our old mates from London N8. For Jane and me, the spectacle of Owen – shaven-headed, tattooed and with the broadest of Herefordshire accents – deep in conversation with our friend Simon – Toni & Guy haircut, slightly effete, and public school-educated – had been one of the highlights of the evening.

'What were you talking to Owen about,' I asked Simon the following morning.

'Fuck knows,' he said. 'And I don't think he understood me any more than I understood him. But he seemed like a great bloke.'

He was, once you'd found the warm heart behind his sledgehammer wit, and while I knew that he would always look on me as an outsider, I cherished his almost-friendship rather in the way that as a first-former at grammar school in Lancashire in 1974 I had cherished the almost-friendship of bigger boys who knew me because they lived in my street, or because their parents knew my parents. When they nodded and said hello, or better still asked me how I was getting on, I felt a rush of pleasure and security coursing through my veins.

16

Slightly pathetically, given that I was now a grown man with children, a mortgage and even a vasectomy, I felt the same rush on being greeted warmly by Owen.

'All right, Bri,' he roared, when we arrived at our second Docklow fête. He was carrying four full trays of beer – ninety-six cans – from the back of a truck to the refreshments tent and the only sign that it involved any kind of physical strain was a gleaming film of sweat over his bulldog tattoo. At every local event at which anything needed lifting or hauling, Owen was a fixture, as was his close friend Georgie, also a farmhand and if not quite the Wise to Owen's Morecambe, then certainly the Little to his Large. In Docklow, just as in Crouch End and doubtless everywhere else in the world, there is a pretty much fixed equation that 90 per cent of work for the community is carried out by 10 per cent of the community. Owen and Georgie were diehard members of the 10 per cent.

I should add that I am not. I'm one of those who turns up an hour beforehand or stays for an hour afterwards, unfolding a few chairs or collapsing a few trestle tables, and hopes that everyone has felt the weight of my contribution. I always intend to give up some serious man-hours, but then find that a column needs writing or a child needs taking to a guitar lesson, and when next I look, the bouncy castle is up and the bunting is out. To make up for this, I always buy lots of raffle tickets, although then there's the danger that you'll win the first three raffle prizes and folk will think 'Jammy bastard – it's not as though he's helped much, and now he's won the giant teddy, the fruit basket, *and* the framed print of Symond's Yat.' So then you ask for the fruit basket and the framed print of Symond's Yat to be redrawn, and either your tickets come up again, or your magnanimity is interpreted as condescension. Raffles can be strangely tense affairs.

At the Docklow fête, the mastermind behind the raffle and much else was Robert Hanson, the chairman of the parish council, who ran a thriving Land Rover repairs business from a barn at the farm where he had always lived. Actually, he wasn't quite Docklow born-and-bred, having spent his first twenty-four hours in hospital in Hereford, but nobody knew the parish better. It was more or less true to say that if Rob saw so much as a squirrel that he didn't recognize, then it meant the squirrel was only passing through.

'Hiya, Bri,' called Rob, from underneath a trestle table that needed fixing; he appeared to know me even from my tread. I liked the fact that he called me 'Bri', not least because early in our acquaintance he had called me 'squire', and while it was true that we had bought the big house in the neighbourhood, I certainly didn't want to be anybody's squire. In the books I had read, and the Catherine Cookson adaptations I had seen on television, squires were old buffers with gout and W. C. Fields noses, who had invariably taken advantage of a pretty scullery maid and fathered her illegitimate child. I reckoned I needed a good few more years in the country before I qualified as an old buffer with gout and a W. C. Fields nose. Five, at least. And we didn't have a scullery maid.

'Hello, Rob,' I replied, and complimented him on his efforts in organising the fête.

'It's just nice to see the village come together,' he said, humbly.

I had noticed that there was a lot of humility in Herefordshire. It seemed to grow in the hedgerows, sending spores through the air. To offer a further example, one of the attractions at that year's summer fête was a lesson in clay-pigeon shooting, being given by another of our neighbours, David. We'd known David for twelve months but it wasn't until Owen told us that we realized he was a former all-England clay pigeon shooting champion. His speciality, apparently, had been the Double Rise, where two clays go wanging off in different directions at once. I asked him whether he had hit them all?

'No, I just didn't miss as many as everyone else,' he said, modestly.

The truth of the matter was that he was a brilliant shot and, safely installed in an adjoining field, he gave tuition for hours, long after the fête had formally finished, to a succession of shooting novices. I had a go myself, and with his calm expertise at my shoulder – 'weight on the front foot, feel as though the back foot's almost lifting' – very quickly felt like John Wayne picking off attacking Comanches, if that's not too non-PC a description of a perfectly PC enterprise; the clays, I hardly need add, were fully biodegradable.

Whatever, dead-eye David with his shotgun, Rob the grand panjandrum of the parish council, Owen with his mile-wide shoulders, Madeleine the listing scarecrow, Ingemar and Kerstin the Swedes, and Miss Whiplash the duck-breeder, are just a few of the dramatis personae featuring in this book. But what good are dramatis personae without a back-drop? I wouldn't want to come over too Judith Chalmers, but Herefordshire is England's most rural county and in my humble opinion its most beautiful. Or better still, let me quote others, starting with Arthur Mee, whose epic 'King's England' series of books about every English county, written in the 1930s and 1940s, was presented by its publisher, Hodder &

Stoughton, as 'the indispensable companion of the Motor Age', and is still full of interesting information even in the Ant and Dec Age.

Cynicism, admittedly, was not old Arthur's thing. He conceived and edited a worthy publication called the *Children's Encyclopedia*, and later the *Children's Newspaper*, and practically everything he set eyes on seems to have delighted him. Victor Meldrew he wasn't. He even wrote a book unambiguously entitled *One Thousand Beautiful Things*, recording in the introduction, bless him, that 'everywhere around us beauty lies, spreading itself about the Earth, working its way into human life, sinking for ever into the hearts of men. All through the year, all round the world, all down the ages we find it. Oft we have travelled in this realm of gold; some of us have been travelling through it ten years, twenty years, fifty years, and the farther we go, the older, the more beautiful is Life's Garden. Here, in these pages, are some of its fruits.'

Perversely, I rather like to think of Arthur hunched at his typewriter reading over the line about beauty sinking for ever into the hearts of men, then spilling his tea and saying 'Oh shit!' In fact, I'm quite sure that such an obscenity never passed his lips, although I'm not the first person to take his name in vain. The Monty Python team once wrote a sketch that was notably bizarre even by their own glorious standards, called the 'All-England Summarize Proust Competition'. Contestants had to summarize Proust's *À la recherche du temps perdu* once in bathing costume and once in full evening dress, in front of a judging panel that comprised cardboard cut-outs of various Surrey cricketers and the violin virtuoso Yehudi Menuhin. The compère, played by Terry Jones in what was surely a

Pythonesque nod of homage to the creator of the *Children's Encyclopedia*, was called Arthur Mee.

To return to the King's England series, there was not a single county that failed to move Mee to lyricism. His book on Devon, first published in 1938, begins with the memorable *cri de cœur*: 'What do they know of England who do not Devon know?' And his 1941 book on the West Riding of Yorkshire unsurprisingly picks out the legacies of the Industrial Revolution as the only blots on a God-kissed landscape. 'It must be said,' he wrote, 'that William Blake's satanic mills keep company with his green and pleasant land in the county of broad acres. It has some of the ugliest towns ever seen in this world, heartbreaking to a traveller who rides through them in his car and realizes that these long depressing streets are England. But they are not the true Yorkshire.'

He was wrong, of course. Those 'ugliest towns ever seen in this world' were, and are, every bit as much the 'true Yorkshire' as his beloved Swaledale and York Minster. But I will forgive him his blinkered viewpoint, for what he writes in the introduction to his volume on Herefordshire, also published in 1938, was, and is, unassailably accurate.

It is Middle England's farthest west, a noble piece of our Motherland far too little known . . . It has much that most of us look for in countryside, the natural glory of the hills and valleys and rivers, and it has its fair share of the glory man has made. A little of the Roman and the Saxon still lingers for those who seek, and much of the visible grandeur of the Normans and the Tudors – the Norman mostly indoors, as in the majestic arches of the great cathedral, the Tudor in and out of doors, in churches and little houses and long streets, the exquisite craftsmanship in wood and stone and the black and white beauty that can never lose its charm.

It may be said perhaps that there are few counties so countrified as Herefordshire from the townsman's point of view, for its 842 square miles (with about 120,000 people on them) have almost everything we associate with English country life – woodland, orchards, clear running rivers, hedges rich in bird life and wild flowers, long views down valleys, distant heights challenging the sky, a warm and genial climate and (above all in the appeal to the eye) that rich green in grassy field and leafy tree which is eloquent of a fertile soil made rich by rain and sun.

I really can't put it any better than that, and although Herefordshire's 120,000 population has expanded since 1938 to around 180,000, and although it is slightly over-generous to write of a warm and genial climate (though the migrating Swedes Ingemar and Kerstin would surely concur), I doubt whether there is any county that Arthur Mee described in all his books that has changed so little in the subsequent seven decades. And while I'm quoting the encomia of others, another great chronicler of England, the famous architectural historian Nikolaus Pevsner, also got rather excited about the county I now call home.

Pevsner began the Herefordshire edition of his celebrated series 'The Buildings of England', published in 1963, with the observation that there

 ... are not many counties of England of which it can be said that, wherever one goes, there will not be a mile which is visually unrewarding or painful ... Herefordshire has an infinite number of rivers, streams and brooks, and unusually large areas still or again covered by woods – still, where the venerable oaks and elms and the tangled undergrowth line the serpentines of the river Wye from Ross down into Monmouthshire; again, where the Forestry Commission has planted its conifers which go so well with the calm outlines of the ancient hills towards Radnor and Brecknock. And how pleasant is the contrast of mood between them – the one picturesquely romantic, the other romantic in a deeper sense – and the orchards laden with fruit and the serried ranks of hop-poles with the joyous trails of the hops. No one can say that variety is lacking in Herefordshire.

And no one can say that old Pevsner didn't go on a bit, but at least he evoked an image which, like Arthur Mee's, applies as much now as it did then. Moreover, I have another reason for quoting Pevsner, because by the end of our first twelve months in Docklow we had befriended a wonderful woman called Shelagh Snell, a huge personality, who with her much quieter but charming husband Jim had in turn introduced us to their cherished friends John and John, and Nancy. All seven of us had lunch every couple of months on a Friday and duly formed what we grandly called the Friday Luncheon Club.

Readers of *Tales of the Country* have met the Luncheon Club already. The Johns were a couple, and Nancy was fairly recently widowed, and all except the younger John, who was sixtysomething, were seventy-plus. Before we moved to Herefordshire, a friend of mine had told me that, in her experience of moving from mid-Chiswick to mid-Gloucestershire, friendships in the country evolve entirely differently from friendships in the capital, in the sense that they are less influenced by one's age. In the city, where there are lots of people, one tends to choose friends from the same generation bracket. In the sticks, where there are few people, your friends are the people you like, irrespective of years. The Luncheon Club showed the truth of her theory. With the Snells, the Johns and Nancy, we had as many laughs as we had ever had with our contemporaries. Rarely did a Friday lunch or any other gathering go by without a great deal of uproariousness.

I doubt whether the words 'Pevsner' and 'uproariousness' rub shoulders too often, but one Friday Shelagh told us that, decades earlier, she had gone to hear the old boy speak at Cheltenham Town Hall. He was manifestly rather unused to what then seemed like the decidedly hi-tech accessories of a microphone and a slide projector, and apparently had to delay his speech for several minutes while he bad-temperedly grappled with unwieldy lengths of wiring, whereupon Shelagh got the giggles. Eventually, he began his address, but after ten minutes or so his projector overheated, just as he was referring to a slide of a Slavic, onion-domed church. Before an astonished audience's very eyes, the onion dome initially lost its sharp definition and then began slowly to subside, as the celluloid slide melted. By now Shelagh could scarcely contain her mirth. And when it occurred to her how marvellous it would be if Pevsner's voice, already slow, guttural and Germanic, also started to melt, like that of a robot with the battery removed, she had to stuff a handkerchief into her mouth to maintain what remained of her dignity.

So there you are, if this book is unique for nothing else, it at least tells a rib-tickling story about the late Sir Nikolaus Pevsner. There can't be too many of those. But I must apologize for gently poking fun at him, for in his entry on Docklow, he managed to enthuse about our fifteenth-century church, St Bartholomew's, which apparently sports a 'shingled truncated pyramid roof' of no mean architectural merit. He was kinder about Docklow than Arthur Mee, anyway. For Arthur it was 'a viewpoint and little else'. The miserable old sod.

3

John, and the Mothballs

While it was slightly unfair of Arthur Mee to dismiss Docklow as a viewpoint and little else, it was indubitably true to say that after a year of living there, we knew the place did not exactly throb with excitement, except, of course, on the days when we had our septic tank emptied.

Apart from the church and the King's Head, Docklow was more or less defined by a scattering of houses along the A44. Only at the end of our drive was there anything like a concentration of dwellings, dwellings which I will come to later in this story, but first I want to tell you about the drive.

I had never lived in a house with a drive before. Not a proper drive, anyway. I grew up in Southport, Lancashire, in a three-bedroomed, between-the-wars semi backing on to the Southport-to-Liverpool railway line. There was just room on our drive for my dad to park the car. And when the car wasn't there, or when my dad deigned to park it on the road, there was just room for my friend Andy Boothman and me to play a constricted game of cricket, which all too often ended in the ball getting an edge off the shoulder of the bat into the garden of Mrs Evans and Miss Oddy, the elderly sisters who lived next door.

Even after I had grown up and left Southport, I never lived anywhere with a proper drive, let alone a drive with a gravel turning-circle at the end of it. But Docklow Grange had both the drive and the gravel turning-circle, and twelve months after moving in I still felt a mild frisson of pleasure every time I turned off the main road on the last leg of the journey home, especially if I'd been away for a while on some kind of writing assignment. It was a wonderful place to return to, and the happy anticipation of seeing Jane and the kids again always intensified at the point at which I turned into the drive. My drive.

Over the course of our first year in Docklow I had watched the drive changing character with the seasons. It was lined with snowdrops and daffodils in the winter and early spring, and with rhododendron, hydrangea and tiny wild cyclamen in the late spring and summer. It also had a striking Monkey Puzzle tree, planted in Victorian times when the Monkey Puzzle was considered to be something of a status symbol. It was not, in truth, a drive that encouraged games of cricket, owing to the uneven bounce and the likelihood of losing the ball after every other shot. But it was still the drive for which, as a child, I would have traded practically anything, perhaps even my cherished collection of programmes from Everton FC's 1976–7 season.

Then, one morning in the late summer of 2003, after we had lived at Docklow for a little over twelve months, our neighbour Carl – the man who had mistaken a scarecrow for my wife – knocked on our back door. He was wearing a broad grin and clearly had some interesting news to impart.

The night before, he told me, he had been walking home from the King's Head when he noticed a Ford Sierra parked on the wild cyclamen about fifty yards along our drive. This, he thought, was curious, so he wandered over and shone his torch in, revealing a man sitting in the fully reclined driving seat being orally pleasured by a woman crouching over the handbrake. Carl, I should add, is a keen potholer, and has a torch of startling brightness. If Hereford United's floodlights ever fail, they phone Carl and ask to borrow his torch. In the unlikely event of Carl ever standing at the top of a cliff with his torch in his hand, turning round and round, he could easily be mistaken for a lighthouse. So the couple in the car, pursuing their amorous activities under the convenient cover of darkness, suddenly found themselves illuminated like Flanagan and Allen at the London Palladium.

The ferocious beam of Carl's torch understandably put this pair of lovebirds – if love is what it was – right off their stroke, whereupon the man hurriedly reversed the Sierra up the drive and made good his escape along the A44 even before, so far as Carl could tell, he had manoeuvred his seat back to an upright position or even tucked everything away.

This was the story that Carl told me. He thought it hilarious, but hard though I tried, I found myself unable to find the funny side. I wasn't sure whether this was sheer prudishness on my part. There was certainly a different moral code in the country, and perhaps it was growing on me. I'd recently met a woman called Helen who three years earlier had moved with her boyfriend from London to Dorset. She and her boyfriend had just decided to get married, and so booked a number of local B&Bs for friends travelling down for the ceremony. A woman who owned one of the B&Bs asked whether they were having a celebration.?

'Yes,' Helen said. 'Peter and I are getting married.'

'Oh, I'm so pleased,' the woman cried. 'Everyone in the village has been hoping you would.'

But I decided that I hadn't started to subscribe to the country's moral code. Unlike Carl, I just wasn't amused. After all, they weren't his wild cyclamen that had been flattened and it wasn't his precious drive. I wondered whether I should erect a sign alongside the one that said 'Slow Down for Children and Animals'. But what would it say? 'No Blowjobs'? Anyway, I confessed my concern in my newspaper column and a few days later got an e-mail from a reader called Gordon Cummings, who asked whether I knew a poem by Alan Brownjohn called 'Farmer's Point of View', which I didn't, and which goes as follows:

I own certain acre-scraps of woodland, scattered
On undulating ground; enough to lie hidden in. So,

About three times a year, and usually August,
Pairs of people come to one or another patch. They stray

Around the edges first, plainly wanting some excuse
To go on in; then talking, as if not concerned,

And always of something else, not what they intend,
They find their way, by one or another approach,

To conducting sexual liaisons – on my land.
I've tried to be careful, I haven't mentioned 'love'

Or any idea of passion or consummation;
And I won't call them 'lovers' because I can't say

If they come from affection, or lust, or blackmail,
Or if what they do has any particular point

For either or both (and who can say what 'love' means?)
So what am I saying? I'd like to see people pondering

What unalterable acts they might be committing
When they step down, full of plans, from their trains or cars.

I am not just recording their tragic, or comic, emotions,
Or even the subtler hazards of owning land –

I am honestly concerned. I want to say, politely,
That I worry when I think what they're about:
I want them to explain themselves before they use my woods.

Someone once told me that a piece of poetry can always
be found that will perfectly encapsulate any mood and any
circumstance, but I must say that I never expected to find a
poem perfectly encapsulating my indignation, following the
discovery of a woman fellating the driver of a Ford Sierra
halfway down my drive. So hats off to Mr Brownjohn, and

while I'm on the subject of taking things off, let me share with you an item in the *Hereford Times*, our excellent local newspaper, which appeared a year or so later, in October 2004.

It was headlined 'If you go down to the woods, you're sure of a surprise', which rather suggested that the story below was a frivolous one. But the opening sentence read: 'A Herefordshire mountain biker was left shocked and disgusted when he saw two pensioners in a compromising position in Haugh Wood.'

I wasn't entirely sure whether or not this was an amusing story worthy of a chirpy headline – and I don't think the *Hereford Times* was, either. I can see that encountering a couple energetically having alfresco sex when you're out riding your bike might be distressing, whether it's Romeo and Juliet going at it hammer and tongs, or Darby and Joan. On the other hand, the fact that the 'shocked and disgusted' witness was twenty-five, and the libidinous pair 'about sixty-five or maybe even older' according to his description, had to be worth a titter, if not a round of applause. After all, the boot is often enough on the other foot, and I thought of the story again about a week later when I found myself in Stoke-on-Trent one lunchtime, having soup and a sandwich in a hotel opposite the station. There was a group of young people at the next table, all of whom had taken drink and were fairly boisterous, but at one point one of the men, who can't have been more than about twenty-three years old, glanced out of the window at a statue of one of the region's most famous sons, and erupted in genuine outrage. 'Bloody hell,' he spluttered. 'Some moron's gone and stuck a traffic cone on Josiah Wedgwood's head.'

I smirked into my leek and potato soup and decided that if the *Hereford Times* story was anything to go by, it was probably a late-night prank by a senior citizen on his way home from the British Legion with a bunch of mates.

But the Haugh Wood story was worrying as well as amusing and uplifting (and here let me take the briefest of diversions to tell you the story of the elderly woman who goes into the pharmacy and asks if they stock Viagra, which she wants for her husband. 'Yes we do,' says the pharmacist. 'Can you get it over the counter?' the woman asks. 'Only if I take six,' replies the pharmacist). For one thing, it was laced with the ageist assumption that older people publicly having sex is somehow less acceptable than younger people doing it, and as I was myself chugging towards the mid-forties, I had my own reasons for finding such a notion offensive. Not that Jane and I were ever likely to be spotted in flagrante delicto by a passing cyclist, except in the improbable event of him cycling through our bedroom late at night, but you know what I mean. I felt a little aggrieved on behalf of the over-forties that the mountain-biker, James Taylor, was quite as horrified as he was. 'I have mountain-biked in Brazil, Laos and Cambodia,' he told the *Hereford Times*, 'but I have never seen anything like this.'

The *Hereford Times* itself, I decided, was not guilty of ageism. Obviously it would not have given the same prominence to the story had it been a pensioner shocked and disgusted to stumble across a pair of thrashing 25-year-olds. But every journalist is trained to know that a predictable tale turned on its head has news value; that 'dog bites man' is not a story, whereas 'man bites dog' is.

And while I'm on the subject of dogs, the *Hereford Times* had also reported, just a few months previously, that this same Haugh Wood featured on a website recommending places to watch other people conspicuously having sex – the practice known as 'dogging'.

I've never quite understood why anyone would wish to go dogging, although the subject always reminds of my old schoolfriend Jonny, who told me years ago that from the kitchen window of his flat in Balham, south London, a couple in a neighbouring flat could frequently be seen making love rampantly. Indeed, they seemed to invite the voyeurism, keeping the lights on and the curtains open.

By chance, when Jane and I were round at Jonny's place for dinner one evening, we were sitting at the dining table waiting expectantly for our spaghetti with meatballs when he called excitedly from the kitchen to tell us that the couple were, at that very moment, at it. To our eternal shame we made our way to the kitchen with what can only be described as haste, and peered out of the window.

'I can't see anything,' I said.

'No,' said Jonny. 'You need to stand on the draining board, hold on to the extractor fan, lean out as far as you can, and kind of twist your head to the right.'

How he first happened on the spectacle, I never did find out. I must ask him sometime. But I did learn from our friend John H, one of the Friday Luncheon Club stalwarts, that 'dogging' is by no means a modern phenomenon. When the subject cropped up at one of our lunches, John became positively misty-eyed with nostalgia and informed me that for him and his three best friends growing up in the Worcestershire village of Ombersley during the Second World War, dogging had been a regular Sunday afternoon pursuit. Like many other leisure activities in Britain during the war, however, it only really gathered pace once the Americans arrived. According to John, there was a copse at the top of Turnmill Lane to which the young women of the village were regularly escorted by GIs from the nearby US Army base.

Then in his early teens, and with a strong Worcestershire accent of which there is no longer any trace, John used to ask his friends whether they fancied 'goin' doggin''. They would identify a likely pair, follow them to the copse and watch the proceedings. 'Always from a safe distance,' John told me, 'although I'm not sure how discreet we really were. I suspect that in many cases they were well aware they were being spied on. Afterwards, we used to collect the discarded French letters, as they were called then, and keep them as trophies.'

One of this teenage quartet who spent the war dogging at the top of Turnmill Lane later became a very senior police officer, while John H joined the clergy and for many years served the Church of England with singular charisma and broad-mindedness, a practice that I suppose might be called Goddin'. After he retired, and to celebrate his seventy-fifth birthday, he and his partner John C invited Jane, me and our fellow Luncheon Clubbers across the Worcestershire border to Ombersley, not to take a tour of the copse and look for John's long-hidden cache of used French letters, I'm slightly disappointed to say, but to have lunch in a restaurant charmingly, if tweely, called the Venture In.

We sat in what John had known, more than sixty years earlier, as Mr Morrison's bicycle shop, where local children were given an ice cream every Wednesday. Whether or not the strange business of getting ice cream from a bike shop was something to do with there being a war on, I'm not sure. Even now we sometimes get fish from the butcher and jam from the ironmonger, so maybe it was a country thing, more than a war thing.

Very much a war thing, however, was the presence in the stables at Ombersley Court, the local big 'ouse, of Britain's ceremonial state carriages. They had been moved from London for safekeeping; indeed, Worcestershire and Herefordshire were chosen as safe havens for all sorts of priceless royal artefacts during the war, up to and including the Royal Family themselves. Had the King and Queen not stoically insisted on staying in London when German bombs were dropping, they would apparently have been rehoused in a stately pile near Malvern – if 'rehoused' is not too common a term for their Majestys.

The stately pile, incidentally, was called Madresfield Court, the home of the Earls of Beauchamp, whose family name was Lygon. It was apparently on life at Madresfield that Evelyn Waugh based his great novel *Brideshead Revisited*, with the Hon. Hugh Lygon, among Waugh's closest friends at Oxford, as the model for Anthony Andrews. Which is to say, Sebastian Flyte.

According to a once-obscure essay called 'Evelyn Waugh and the Origins of Brideshead Revisited', first published in *Gay Community News* in 1982 but now readily accessible, such are the wonders of the Internet, most of the major characters in Brideshead are based on members of Madresfield's Lygon family, with the seventh Earl Beauchamp evidently the inspiration for Lord Marchmain, played by Laurence Olivier in the celebrated 1981 TV version. Where the seventh Earl was concerned, however, Waugh did not need to deploy novelist's licence. If anything, he had to rein it in.

The leader of the Liberal Party in the House of Lords,

Beauchamp was also, by the 1920s, Lord Lieutenant of Worcestershire, Lord Warden of the Cinque Ports, Chancellor of London University and a Knight of the Garter. That he was also enthusiastically bisexual was fairly well known in political circles, although this did not on its own expose him to political attack by the Conservatives, who had quite enough skeletons in their own closet; indeed there was also room in the closet for their own former leader, Lord Balfour, known to his friends as Betty.

It was Beauchamp's wife's brother, the Duke of Westminster (described by *Gay Community News* with no bias whatever as 'the dissolute and bigoted head of a family of virulently Tory nouveaux riches, the Grosvenors'), who landed him in hot water. In 1931, seeking to ruin both Beauchamp and the Liberal Party, Westminster let King George V know of his brother-in-law's sexual proclivities. Worse, he told Lady Beauchamp, who promptly suffered a nervous breakdown. The King prevailed upon Beauchamp to resign his various offices, and according to *Gay Community News* 'He considered suicide, but was dissuaded by his son Hugh, instead emigrating to Venice, where he lived, like Lord Marchmain, in lonely splendour in a crumbling palazzo.' I love the notion of a chap considering suicide but being persuaded instead to emigrate to Venice. It's not the most obvious either/or scenario. Anyway, it's a jolly fascinating story and makes me wish that King George VI and Queen Elizabeth *had* relocated to Madresfield during the Blitz; it might have made them more interesting. As for the royal carriages, if the people who moved them had known what would become of them at Ombersley Court, they might very well have chosen to risk whatever the Luftwaffe could throw their way.

As a short aside on the subject of the Luftwaffe, my friend Angus MacLeod once stopped at a motorway service station where an elderly Welshman in uniform was selling poppies. In the broadest of Glamorgan accents he told Angus that he had just button-holed, more or less literally, a coachload of German tourists. Almost all of them had bought poppies and gone away cheerfully wearing them in their lapels. 'They asked me which branch of the services I was in,' the old Welshman told Angus. 'I told them the RAF but they looked blank. I said, "You know your Luftwaffe? Well it was like that, only better."' I love that story. But you've got to read it in a Welsh accent.

To return to John, he told us that his father had been chauffeur to Lord Sandys, the noble owner of Ombersley Court, and that he and his sisters had grown up in a flat above the stables. When the royal carriages arrived, the potential for imaginative games-playing increased considerably. John spent several happy years having fun in the royal carriages, years that also coincided with the onset of adolescence. At the Venture In, in a stage whisper that might have been heard several miles away in Droitwich, he announced: 'I had my first sexual experience in Queen Victoria's funeral coach.' As a conversation stopper, that took some beating. 'I remember that the interior was all black and purple,' he boomed. 'And I still get excited when I smell mothballs.'

It's not everyone who can top a story about heavy petting in Queen Victoria's funeral coach, but our friend Shelagh promptly came close. The subject of the ceremonial carriages reminded her, she said, of the state banquet held at Buckingham Palace during Harold Macmillan's time as Prime Minister, a banquet honouring General and Madame de Gaulle.

Conversation between the snooty Macmillans and the even

snootier De Gaulles did not exactly flow, apparently, so in a rather desperate gambit, Lady Dorothy Macmillan turned to Mme de Gaulle and said, haughtily: 'If there were one thing in the world you could have, what might it be?'

The people around them fell silent, while Mme de Gaulle considered the question for a moment. Finally, she smiled. 'A penis,' she declared loudly, plainly rather pleased with her command of the English language.

Appalled glances were exchanged, until the uncomfortable silence was broken by General de Gaulle. 'Non, non,' he said, correcting his wife's pronunciation. "Appiness! 'Appiness!'

At the Venture In we all roared at Shelagh's tale, but John, who'd had not one or two but three successful careers, as an actor, a teacher and a clergyman, had never been a man to relinquish attention once he had grabbed it so thrillingly. He went on to tell us that he bore no resemblance whatever to his late father, the chauffeur, but enjoyed the distinctive features of one of Britain's most prominent aristocratic families. He told us which one, too, but swore me to secrecy. I'll call them the Earls of X. He had once seen a portrait of the 11th Earl of X, he added, who had been a friend of Lord Sandys and on whom his highly attractive, rather flighty mother used to wait at shooting parties. The portrait, apparently, could easily have been of him. Amid the delighted laughter that followed this disclosure, I looked at him and saw that his patrician features were, plainly, not those of a chauffeur's son.

All of which has taken me a long way from the spectacle that had so tickled Carl on the way back from the pub, and more significantly, a long way from Docklow Grange. It was not only our burgeoning friendships that convinced us we had done the right thing by moving from London, but the house itself. During our first year in the country, it had been primarily a project, but by our second year it had become, unequivocally, a home. Our youngest son Jacob had spent the first twelve months after we moved referring to the house by name, asking on long car journeys: 'When will we get to Docklow Grange?' But gradually, imperceptibly almost, that became: 'When will we get home?'

We all felt the same. Moreover, Jane and I were beginning to get a grip on the holiday cottage business that we had fallen into almost accidentally, simply because the house had come with three cottages attached. Our cottages were beginning to turn a small profit, and were rewarding in other ways, too. One very engaging family from Telford booked a weekend with us because their daughter Aishling, bless her, wanted to wake up on her eighth birthday in a cottage in the country.

My own 8-year-old, Joseph, who was by now used to waking up in the country, thought this not much of a birthday treat. 'A trip to Legoland is a treat,' he said. Jane and I smiled weakly. We had indeed taken Joe to Legoland for his birthday, during the Easter holidays, but it hadn't been a treat for us; it had seemed more like a penance. We could only hope that Aishling's parents felt otherwise about their weekend in Woodlands Cottage.

4

Roz, and the Raspberries

From the start we had found the holiday cottage business endlessly fascinating. Some of the people who stayed with us were deliciously vivacious, others were pathologically shy; some were utterly charming, others were downright rude; some were irreproachably normal, others were decidedly weird. All of which, of course, applies to the human race as a whole, and that's what we had holidaying at Docklow: a microcosm of humanity.

This book could be about nothing other than our holiday cottage guests, and it would still have plenty of variety. Let's take Mr Usher, who phoned to make a reservation one evening, sounding exactly like Peter Cook's raincoated nerd, EL Wisty.

'Good day to you,' he said. 'My name is Usher. That's U-S-H-E-R. As in the man who shows you to your seat at a wedding, if you grasp my meaning. Mrs Usher and I would very much like to stay in Manor Cottage from 16 September to 23 September next year, if that would be possible. And we see from your website that you do evening meals. We would like to have an evening meal on the night of our arrival, but may I point out that Mrs Usher is allergic to rhubarb.'

He sounded so much like EL Wisty that at first we assumed that it had to be one of our friends winding us up. But it wasn't. Mr and Mrs Usher, whose first names we never discovered, duly arrived the following September. He was a small, dapper man of about sixty-five, with a thin moustache and a disconcertingly direct gaze. She was similarly small and dapper, with the gaze but without the moustache. We delivered dinner on their first night as requested, having irreverently toyed with the idea of giving them chicken braised over a bed of rhubarb followed by rhubarb crumble, along with the apologetic explanation that by stipulating their dietary restrictions only fourteen months ahead, they hadn't given us quite enough notice of the rhubarb allergy. But we didn't. And the following day they expressed great satisfaction with their dinner.

'It was most delicious,' said Mr Usher, EL Wistily. 'Most delicious indeed. Pray do tell me, what did you put in the beef to make it taste so good?'

'Lamb,' said Jane.

Mr Usher laughed, his laugh emerging as a series of staccato barks. 'Ha! Ha! Ha! Ha! Ha! Ha!'

A few moments later, through the wall separating our kitchen from Manor Cottage, Jane heard the bark again, as Mr Usher told Mrs Usher that what they had thought was beef had in fact been lamb. She felt certain that the lamb/beef mix-up would remain a favourite anecdote of Mr Usher's for years, if not decades, to come.

Not all our guests gave Jane's cooking such enthusiastic feedback, alas. For example, there was Mr and Mrs Frankland, an elderly couple from Coventry who stayed with us in October 2003 and asked us to supply them with dinner every night. It was true that our home-cooked meals, delivered to the cottages at a charge of £9.50 a head, represented quite a bargain, but we assumed that if guests availed themselves of this service, they would probably only want it on one evening, two at the most. Herefordshire, after all, is a notably marvellous part of the country both for eating out in pubs, and, with dozens of farm shops offering produce of superb quality, for fending for oneself. Yet Mr and Mrs Frankland in Manor Cottage wanted a tray delivered every night of the week, Meals on Wheels-fashion.

This was a tricky challenge for Jane, who had numerous other creatures, both two-legged and four-legged, to feed in her own home every evening. But it is the holiday cottage proprietor's duty to oblige at every turn, and she duly agreed to supply seven two-course dinners for two. Mr Frankland subsequently appeared on our back doorstep every morning, unceremoniously dumping the previous night's dishes, un-washed. This came as a shock. Everyone else we'd cooked for had taken it upon themselves to wash the dishes. It wasn't a spoken arrangement, nor did we request it anywhere in writing, it just seemed like the decent, civilized thing to do. After all, we weren't a hotel, just a holiday let business offering a service intended mainly for those who might want a hot meal on their night of arrival, after a long and tiresome motorway journey.

But in the case of the Franklands, either Jane or I would trot round to Manor Cottage every night with a tray bearing a delicious lamb hotpot and a hearty apple crumble, or a sumptuous chicken casserole and a mouthwatering treacle sponge, which was received either silently or with the curtest of acknowledgements. And by the time we picked up the dishes the next morning, their leftovers were already congealing. Maybe it was feedback in the sense that they were proudly showing us how much they'd eaten. Or maybe their idea of a week's holiday simply didn't involve Fairy Liquid. Or maybe they thought that £19 for two absolved them of washing-up responsibilities. Maybe it did. Maybe we had no right to expect them to wash up.

Whatever, one of the conclusions we have reached after a few years running holiday cottages is that appearances are often highly deceptive. Mr and Mrs Frankland, white-haired and pink-cheeked, looked pretty well scrubbed themselves. It was only their dishes that weren't. By contrast, we once had a troupe of sullen Eastern European acrobats staying in Woodlands Cottage, and just looking at them filled us with dread as to what state we might find the cottage in when they left. There were two peroxided women and four heavily tattooed, crew-cutted men, all in their early twenties, and while I hate to come over all Hyacinth Bucket, judging by appearances we felt certain that they would trash the joint, especially when we saw them disappear inside with an industrial-sized bottle of vodka. Yet they left the place sparkling. Perhaps it wasn't vodka; perhaps it was Windowlene.

We were also suspicious of Mr and Mrs Hastings, who were coming from Australia for a niece's wedding in Hereford, and had booked to stay in Yew Tree Cottage. Our suspicion was based, slightly unfairly, on an experience we'd had with another Aussie couple entirely, the seemingly deranged Mr and Mrs Price, which was chronicled in all its painful detail in my book *Tales of the Country*. But it was also true that Mrs Hastings had sounded a little fussy on the phone from Adelaide, asking searching questions about the beds, the bathroom, the television, even about the cutlery. So we thought they, too, might be trouble.

As it turned out, Mr Hastings – 'mate, you can call me Topper, everyone else does' – and Mrs Hastings – 'call me Roz' – were a genial pair. We liked them, and invited them, as we do all guests, to wander around our garden whenever they liked. But I didn't expect to find them, and two other Aussie couples also in Herefordshire for the wedding, who were staying in a nearby B&B, in my fruit cage one morning enthusiastically picking my carefully cultivated raspberries. Still less did I expect them to look not the slightest bit sheepish when I approached.

'G'day, mate, we're just stealing some of your raspberries,' called out Topper, beaming broadly at me.

'So I see,' I said, in what I hoped was a waspish tone.

'They're really delicious,' added Roz, brightly, popping one into her mouth.

Their sunniness stopped me remonstrating further, and made me wonder whether it was perhaps mean-spirited of me not to want them to pick my precious raspberries. Perhaps it was a deliberate tactic on their part, having been caught quite literally red-handed, to disarm me with good cheer. This was what I called the Lewin ploy: taking the wind out of someone's sails by responding to their anger in disconcerting, disarming fashion. I'd named it after Matthew Lewin, who'd been news editor at the *Hampstead & Highgate Express* in the late 1980s and early 1990s when I was a humble news reporter there, and who once saved both my fortunes and the paper's following a spectacular and potentially ruinous mistake.

It had been my job the week before to compile the newspaper's television listings, and I had to write a few explanatory words to accompany a listing for a documentary about a round-the-world yachtswoman, to whom for the purposes of this book I had better give a pseudonym; let's call her Virginia Cargill.

For some inexplicable reason I had it in my head that Virgina Cargill had once been a man! I don't much like exclamation marks but I think that misconception deserves one. I thought I remembered reading something about it, and was 99.99 per cent convinced that she was a transsexual. But even in my certitude I realized it was a fact I could not afford to get wrong. So I checked – albeit in a way that would probably not pass muster with the famously scrupulous fact-checkers on litigation-obsessed American publications such as the *New Yorker* – by asking Sue, who sat next to me.

'You know the yachtswoman Virginia Cargill,' I said. 'Isn't she a transsexual?'

Sue looked pensive. 'Yes, that seems to ring a bell,' she said.

Sue's response ramped up my certitude from 99.99 per cent to 100 per cent, and was all the proof I required before describing the programme thus: 'A documentary about the round-the-world yachtswoman Virginia Cargill who would have been a round-the-world yachtsman until her (or should it be his?) sex-change operation.'

And that was it, an innocent TV listing in a local newspaper, which would have been perfectly innocuous except for the fact that it was completely wrong. Virginia Cargill had always been entirely and unequivocally female, indeed she had given birth to two children. I had made – again, quite literally – a huge cock-up. Whether I was confusing her with someone else, I still don't know, but having cheerfully filed my listings I then went on holiday before that week's edition of the paper was published.

Jane and I were taking the train from London to Prague, a holiday which remains memorable to both of us for all sorts of reasons. One reason was that Jane then worked as a news and current affairs producer for BBC Radio 4, and our first night away was the night that Margaret Thatcher was toppled as leader of the Conservative Party. It was the biggest and most exciting political story for decades and Jane was not at her desk on *The World at One* high on adrenaline, frantically trying to get Ted Heath or Roy Jenkins into the studio, but with me on a train rumbling through the German countryside, eating stale bratwurst sandwiches.

We had arranged to stay in the Prague apartment of a man called Jaros, the BBC's stringer in the newborn Czech Republic, and he it was, a few days later, who told us that Thatcher's successor as the British Prime Minister was the comparatively little-known Chancellor of the Exchequer, John Major. Jane smiled thinly. She wasn't a news junkie like some of her BBC colleagues, nor was she as ferociously ambitious as many of them, but it still seemed decidedly unfortunate to have chosen that week, of all weeks, for a holiday. She steeled herself for a round of ironic applause as soon as she got back to *The World at One* office, while I felt grateful that Thatcher's downfall and its repercussions fell way outside my reporting orbit on the *Hampstead & Highgate Express*.

Yet I was the one welcomed back to work with ironic

applause, not Jane. I found that the shit – or ordure as it is known in Hampstead and Highgate – had well and truly hit the fan on the day of publication, when a friend of Virginia Cargill's, scarcely able to believe her eyes, had phoned the office to point out that her dear old mate Ginny was most certainly not a transsexual. Mrs Cargill herself lived in west Wales, a part of the world that not even the paper's bullish circulation manager, who liked to refer to Hendon as north Hampstead and Hornsey as east Hampstead, could claim fell within our circulation area. But it wasn't long before she, too, was on the phone. Matthew Lewin took the call.

'This is Virginia Cargill,' she said, shortly.

'Oh my God, I'm so sorry,' shrieked Matthew. 'We've been expecting your call and there is simply nothing I can say that can adequately convey how dreadful we all feel about this horrendous mistake.'

'Well, yes, I can assure you that I feel dreadful too,' she said. 'My friend in Hampstead has faxed me the page, and what this idiot has written is outrageously defamatory.'

'I know, I know,' cried Matthew. 'And you are perfectly entitled to sue us, and we have no defence. It is absolutely appalling. Appalling. This idiot, as you call him, although I can think of some much stronger words, has gone away on holiday but when he comes back I promise you he will be given a terrible tongue-lashing. Maybe even a real lashing. It is an inexcusable mistake. Unforgivable.'

'Well, yes it is—' she said, but Matthew interrupted her to lament that nothing this terrible had ever happened in his entire career, nor in the entire history of the newspaper, and that he would always have to live with the fact that it occurred on his watch.

There was a pause. 'Well, maybe it's not quite that bad,' she said, sympathetically.

'Oh yes it is,' he wailed.

And so the conversation continued, with Virginia Cargill becoming incrementally less angry, and Matthew becoming more and more outraged on her behalf, until she started trying to appease him, assuring him that instead of engaging a libel lawyer she would settle for a prominent apology.

Which is what duly happened, and I was reminded of Matthew's clever strategy, little though they knew it, by Topper and Roz Hastings from Adelaide. When you're cornered, always do the thing that's least predictable. And that applies to all sorts of situations, from being caught pinching raspberries, to being threatened with a law suit, even to being attacked by a lion. I was once told, by a safari ranger in Kruger National Park in South Africa, that anyone who finds themselves in the tricky predicament of being charged by a lion should not turn and scarper, but should charge directly towards it, the logic being that nothing on the African plains ever charges at a lion, that being charged falls entirely outside the compass of his experience, and he is therefore so disconcerted by this unprecedented spectacle that he will stop in his tracks and slink away.

I can't imagine having the bottle to try this myself in the unlikely event of needing to, and even if I did I expect my assailant would be the one lion that would accelerate towards me, thinking 'what kind of nutter is this?' Yet this ranger guy swore that he'd done it himself on more than one occasion, and I had no reason to doubt him for he was memorably square-jawed and macho, with no need whatever to invent stories either to impress me or to pull the one notably attractive and unattached young woman in our party, both of which he managed to do with consummate ease. Still, I was pleased to hear him add that he had once been to London and had suffered the most traumatic experience of his life trying to cross Piccadilly Circus. Knowing what to do in the face of a lion's charge wasn't much use to him surrounded by snarling traffic in the shadow of Eros.

He was the first man I had ever met, now that I think about it, who was preternaturally capable in more or less any outdoorsy situation, yet all at sea in the city. Since moving to Herefordshire, however, I have met many such men. Owen the farmhand, for one, can tie just about any kind of knot, can catch a runaway bullock and wrestle it to the ground, can dismantle a wasps' nest without wearing protective clothing, can tell you what the weather is going to be like for the next four days more accurately than anyone at the Met Office just by glancing at the horizon, and can rescue a drowning sheep from a stagnant pond, all of which I have witnessed with my own eyes, yet in terms of worldly sophistication he makes Crocodile Dundee look like Alan Whicker. When I first met him and told him I'd moved up from London, he said he'd only been to the city once, to the main shopping street whatever it was bloody called, and didn't much like it. I made sympathetic noises and said that it was called Oxford Street and I didn't care much for it either, that it was my least favourite thoroughfare in London. He looked at me as if I were some kind of simpleton. 'I don't mean bloody London,' he said. 'I ain't never been there and never bloody will. I'm talking about 'Ereford.'

For much of our first year of living in the country I had frankly found it difficult not to feel slightly superior to Owen, with his suspicion of the teeming metropolis that is Hereford.

But by our second year I had realized how misplaced, patronising and downright delusional this feeling of superiority was. Here was a man who could turn his hand to almost any rural task required of him, while my own proficiency in the fields around our house did not extend much beyond the ability to step over cowpats.

On the other hand, I was at least making some more metaphorical strides in the business of handling dead mammals, many different varieties of which seemed to wind up on our back doorstep, deposited by our cats Tiger and Sooty, practically on a daily basis. Our growing country menagerie is the subject of the next chapter, but for now let me record that after a year of confronting the half-eaten remains of baby rabbits or even rats, I had conquered pretty much all of my urban squeamishness. Not so Jane, who continues to call me if there are entrails to deal with. Although having said that, there is a law that applies in our household, which is that the more I am needed around the house, if only to give Jane some moral support during a domestic crisis, the more likely I am to be away from home.

We had noticed this even when we lived in London. It wasn't that I was away from home all that much, just that crises seemed to erupt whenever I was. On one occasion I was in Los Angeles on reporting duty when Jane called to say that Eleanor and Joseph, aged about five and three, had been in the shower having great fun blocking the drain so that the water rose around them. It then seeped under the door, cascaded through the bathroom floorboards, and brought the hall ceiling crashing down below, causing some £4,000 worth of damage.

Then there was the time when she allowed 4-year-old Joe to wheel 1-year-old Jacob along the pavement in his pushchair, an innocuous enough scene, except that he suddenly decided it would be more fun to run. Before Jane could stop him, the pushchair hit an uneven paving stone, and both baby and toddler went flat on their faces, at speed. Jacob's teeth cut through his tongue, resulting in an extraordinarily bloody scene. I, meanwhile, was in Florida interviewing the golfer Arnold Palmer. The more glamorous my assignment, and the further away it was, the greater Jane's domestic hassles. Mercifully, Jacob turned out to be fine, but when I got home a few days later, young Joe was able to solemnly show me his brother's bloodstains on the pavement.

This same phenomenon continued in Docklow, never more dramatically than in July 2005, while I was away covering the Wimbledon tennis championships. It was a warm night, and Jane had left the bedroom window wide open. She was cheerfully reading a book when suddenly she became aware of a flapping sound in the room. She looked up to see a bat, in her perhaps melodramatic words, swooping 'menacingly' and 'repeatedly' towards her. I like to think that, had I been in the other half of the bed, I might have dealt with the matter in a manly way. Jane's response – and this is a woman, don't forget, who remains one of nature's BBC producers despite having long since left the BBC, in the sense that she is singularly resourceful in dealing with most of the situations life throws at her – was to pull the duvet over her head and scream.

Luckily, her parents were staying in the spare room, and Bob, her dad, having heard her screams, thundered gallantly to the rescue, his heroism not at all diminished by my mother-in-law Anne's anxious cry after him: 'Bob! Bob! Are you wearing your pants?'

He was, thankfully. Had he not been, the thought of him

grabbing one of the children's fishing nets from the landing cupboard and dashing round our bedroom trying to catch the bat while Jane cowered under the duvet, might have tickled me even more than it did when Jane phoned me next morning to fill me in on the adventure. I ventured that the bat had probably been even more terrified than she was. 'I can assure you it wasn't,' she said, sharply.

After I had stopped laughing at her story, my main concern was that if a bat could accidentally fly through an open window into our bedroom, perhaps our cottage guests could be similarly terrorized. Because we now had a reputation to protect, having received a 'commended' certificate in the self-catering holiday accommodation category of the 2004 Flavours of Herefordshire awards (and if you think that's prestigious, then be aware of this: it was followed, in 2005, by a 'highly commended').

Now, a 'commended' in the self-catering holiday accommodation category of the 2004 Flavours of Herefordshire competition was not exactly a Nobel Prize, but no Nobel laureate could have been more pleased with himself than I was when I stepped forward to receive it. It stood comparison with the August morning in 1980 when I went to my school to collect my A-level results, and nervously tore open the envelope to find, to my amazement, that I'd managed an A, two Bs and a C, which in these days of straight As all round would be considered a reason to sit in a corner and weep self-pityingly, but back then constituted a reason to kiss everyone in the room, which included the hirsute school secretary, Miss Norwood. That, too, was a thrill. Getting ABBC, I mean, not kissing Miss Norwood. But I was no more thrilled that day than I was years later to get that first 'commended' certificate for the cottages on which we had lavished much thought, attention and, indeed, money since taking up residence in Docklow Grange.

The certificate was presented to me at a lunch organized by the estimable Jane Lewis of the Herefordshire tourism department of the county council, in the village of Much Marcle. This I mention for two reasons. One, because Jane Lewis will crop up again in this story; I later engaged her help when I stood up in much less congenial circumstances than the Much Marcle lunch, before the Hereford magistrates. And two, because I had always wanted to go to Much Marcle, even before we moved to Herefordshire. It was a name, like Nether Wallop and Broadwoodwidger, that seemed almost to smell of the English countryside. In fact, long before I ever dreamt that I would ever settle in the area, I had used it in my journalism to exemplify, in the nicest way, the sticks . . . the boondocks . . . the back of beyond. If London or Paris or New York represented all that was glitzy and excitingly metropolitan, their antithesis, it had always seemed to me, had to be this place called Much Marcle, an image compounded in a rather more negative way by the unfortunate fact that the serial killer Fred West had grown up there raping his sister and generally establishing the template for the screwed-up, inbred, *Deliverance*-style hick. But I didn't want to dwell too much on that thought.

I had been meaning to go ever since we moved to Docklow, but the exigencies of everyday life kept stopping me, so it was with a song in my heart (possibly 'I've Got A Brand New Combine Harvester') that I aimed my little VW Polo along the narrow country lanes that day of the Flavours of Herefordshire awards. Jane couldn't come for the prosaic reason that she had to pick up the kids from school, and in any case we didn't think that we would win anything. But as I tootled happily through the early-autumnal countryside, the fact that I was on my way to

Much Marcle, of all places, seemed somehow to symbolise our new life. And it still seemed new, even after a couple of years.

My long-cherished image of Much Marcle was compounded, as I neared my destination, by a sign to Little Marcle, Pixley and Trumpet. It occurred to me (obviously I didn't have anything of even middling importance to think about that day) that if ever I attempted to write a children's book, then Little Marcle, Pixley and Trumpet would have to be my protagonists. All I would have to decide was whether to make them elves or bunnies, but either way, it was quite clear that brave Little Marcle and clever Pixley would in some way come to the rescue of accident-prone Trumpet.

Later, indulging this flight of whimsy even further, I realised that Herefordshire had some of England's best place names for such a purpose. So if I decided against a children's book, but decided instead to write a historical novel about early American settlers, for example, then quite obviously it would concern the efforts of Moreton Jeffries to stir up his neighbours Munderfield Stocks, Edvin Loach and Edwyn Ralph into defending their land against the rapacious Stretton Grandison and his wily son-in-law Wormelow Tump. After examining my AA Road Map of Great Britain, I found that only East Anglia could give Herefordshire a run for its money in this respect. If I lived there, I decided that my children's book would be a little darker, featuring Shelfanger, Old Newton and Daffy Green, while my early American settlers would be Stratton Strawless, Monk Soham, Badwell Ash and Felixtowe Ferry.

All of this I rather self-indulgently recorded in my newspaper column, and was gratified to get a letter from a regular reader, David Gorvett, who said that he preferred to think of Edwyn Ralph and Edvin Loach as cousins, who fought each other to the death over a beautiful young woman. I wrote back, suggesting that the young woman in question might have been called Dilwyn Common. I also got an e-mail from Dave and Maggy Williams, hugely erudite *Independent* readers who had stayed several times in our holiday cottages, pointing out that my idea, of borrowing Herefordshire place names and giving them to fictional characters, was not unprecedented. They informed me – I wish I could say reminded me, it would make me sound so much better read – that Anthony Powell's *A Dance to the Music of Time* featured an Ada Leintwardine and a Lord Vowchurch, both named after settlements in Herefordshire.

By the time we had been at Docklow for a couple of years, we had quite a few repeat visitors, of whom Dave and Maggy were our most frequent. They came – and continue to come, bless their hearts – twice every year, once in the early summer and again in the autumn. Nevertheless, we needed to keep attracting new business, and to this end we repeatedly advertised in a small selection of magazines, the likes of *Woman & Home* and *Woman's Weekly*.

Once we had worked out which magazines did well for us, we were able to drop some and keep others, but if any of our adverts had yielded as much in the way of bookings as they did in the way of phone calls from advertising sales people from other magazines, we would have been Christmassing every year in Hawaii.

The most irritating were the sales operatives at a company called – I shall very generously protect what's left of their dignity by giving them a pseudonym – Barry Howard Media. They had a big stable of magazines, and we'd advertised in one or two, giving all the others in the stable the idea that we might hand over chunks of cash to them, too. For the best part of a year until we started getting stroppy, hardly a day went by without someone from Barry Howard Media giving us a call, which would have been more tolerable had their telesales staff not been trained to engage potential customers in small talk before cutting to the chase. If I heard Jane picking up the phone and saying 'Hi . . . yes, I'm fine thanks very much . . . yes, the weather's quite nice here too . . . no, the kids aren't back at school yet . . . no, I didn't catch *Coronation Street* last night . . .' then I knew for sure it was Cheryl or Charmian or Charlene from Barry Howard Media. And the pitch, once it began, rarely varied. It was always deadline day, they were always just about to close the issue, there was always one last six-by-two available, and because it was a last-minute offer, they could always give us the rock-bottom price of £150 plus VAT, whereas every other advertiser had been lumbered with the full whack of £225.

Moreover, the magazine's readership was always 'the perfect target audience' for us, according to Cheryl or Charlene or Charmian. 'Eighty per cent of them are young, affluent, urban professionals,' Charlene, Charmian or Cheryl would enthuse.

'Actually,' we'd say, 'we are trying to reach older, not necessarily affluent, provincial retired people.'

At the other end of the phone, Charmian, Cheryl or Charlene would scarcely miss a beat. 'Well, when I say young, I mean under the age of seventy-five. And when I say affluent, I mean with a combined income of more than £1,000 per annum, and when I say urban, I mean they probably live within 450 miles of Charing Cross. And when I say professional, I mean that they probably know a doctor or a dentist.'

That's exaggerating a little, but not very much. You got the sense, as so often with telesales people, that in front of them they had a list of responses for every eventuality. If I'd said, 'Please shove your six-by-four up your jacksy,' they would probably have responded, 'I will, sir, and thank you for the suggestion, but that leaves a very nice five-by-three, on a right-hand page.'

Still, in fairness, not all of them were that pushy. The people at the magazine publishers IPC, at least, got to the point immediately. Perhaps they realized that they were far more likely to get our business if they didn't express the slightest interest in the Herefordshire weather. But it still had to be the right kind of magazine. We had one pitch that tickled us no end. It started with all the usual guff about it being deadline day, with the very last five-by-one advertising space just begging to be taken, like the last puppy in the pet shop on Christmas Eve. And all for just £95 plus VAT, and a readership that could not have been a more obvious target for us had every reader sported concentric circles on his or her backside.

Jane listened to all this patiently. 'I'm sorry,' she said, 'but I missed the name of your publication.'

'Oh,' said the woman at the other end of the line, 'didn't I tell you? It's *Allergy*.'

Jane let her down gently, realising that it probably wasn't much fun trying to sell holiday cottage ads to run in the back of *Allergy* magazine. But afterwards we realized that we had missed a unique marketing opportunity by not snapping up the five-by-one and offering a welcome hamper containing half-a-dozen free-range eggs, a slab of Hereford Hop cheese, a bottle of local cider, a tube of Anthisan cream, a pack of Piriton tablets and a nasal spray.

In the holiday cottage game, you've got to drum up business however you can.

5

Zoe, and the Footballer

If you think the last chapter finished a little abruptly, then blame a woman called Wanda Renshaw. When I hit the word-count button on my computer and found that Chapter Four was getting a bit long, I thought how terribly irritated Mrs Renshaw would be, propped up on her pillow, and decided that I'd better push on with Chapter Five. Because, after reading *Tales of the Country*, Mrs Renshaw sent me the following e-mail.

Hi,
Have just finished and loved the book – we moved from
London to the country and I can identify with a lot of what

you wrote, situations and characters you describe.

To be really picky, why did you have such long chapters? As an insomniac, I often read in the middle of the night and allow myself one chapter at a time! My publisher daughter says long chapters happen when writers are prima donnas and can't be persuaded into bite-sized chunks.

Also, what happened to the pony? No mention of the children taking her to local shows – your record with animals was a little erratic.

All the very best, will come and stay one day, have looked at the website. Another book would be nice with chapters of about 10 pages please.

Wanda

I printed out her e-mail and still amuse myself by looking it at from time to time. She loved the book but considered me a prima donna! What kind of e-mail, I wondered, would she send someone whose book she didn't like? And I wasn't quite sure why it pained her so that there was no mention of the children taking the pony to local shows, nor why that demonstrated that my record with animals was 'a little erratic'. But it was undoubtedly true that as animal owners we had, since moving to the country, perhaps bitten off more than we could chew. On our last day in London we'd had just one pet, a hamster called Fizz, who seemed to catch hypothermia in our new house and only survived the move by a few weeks. Yet by the beginning of our second year in Docklow, we had eight chickens, a dog called Milo, a pair of cats called Tiger and Sooty, rabbits called Holly and Bramble, and the miniature Shetland pony, Zoe, whom our children – to Mrs Renshaw's unconcealed annoyance – did not take to local shows.

Over the next few years this menagerie would continue to expand, and at its most abundant we had twenty-one mouths to feed, not including ours or our children's. Of all these mouths, 7-year-old Zoe's was by far the most dangerous. She was a sweet-natured pony for much of the time, yet with an occasional alarming propensity for trying to chomp whatever was at head height. In my case this was a rather vulnerable set of genitals. I took to wearing three pairs of underpants whenever it was my turn to clean her hooves.

Zoe also systematically nibbled her way through the bark of several of the venerable apple trees in the orchard before we realized what was going on and defended them with a Maginot line of chicken wire. Our horsey friends had warned us that we were at best being naive by buying a pony. 'It's not like getting a hamster, you know,' one of them had said, condescendingly.

Jane, in particular, bridled at this, while I wondered whether our horsey friends might even question her right, as a non-horsewoman, to bridle. At any rate, to imply that we didn't have a clue what we were getting into, for Jane constituted, just to mix natural history metaphors, a red rag to a bull. We would show them. But as it turned out, Zoe showed us. After about a year of stubbornly refusing to admit it, we began to realize that our horsey friends had been right, and that as people whose equine experience amounted to little more than an annual bet on the Grand National, we had indeed been naive to think that we could easily get to grips with the needs of a strong-willed Shetland pony.

Apart from anything else, ponies are sociable creatures and it became clear that Zoe was lonely. When we bought her we assumed we had an inbuilt solution to this problem, because the breeder had assured us that Zoe was pregnant. But, as it turned out, she wasn't. Then someone told us that Shetland ponies get on well with goats. So we considered buying a goat, which would have had the twofold advantage of providing company for Zoe and giving me something truly bucolic to write about in my newspaper column, until someone else told us that goats are unbelievably destructive and will eat everything in front of them, including trees, sheds and wheelbarrows, moving on to Volvos. So we didn't get a goat, which at least saved us from the disapproving letter we would doubtless have received from the Goat Society of Great Britain, saying 'it's not like getting a pony, you know'.

Instead, we tried to give Zoe as much human company as we could, although the children, after the first throes of excitement, had rather lost interest in her. 'Ohhhh, do I have to?' was usually the response when we asked them to take her for a walk. And it wasn't as if they could even sit on her without her getting jumpy, because she hadn't been 'broken in'. At least if we had her broken in then Jacob, who by now was the only one of our children small enough to ride her, could do so.

Breaking in, for the benefit of those even less horsey than I, is the process of teaching a horse how to bear a saddle, and upon it, a human. Our vet, Mike Devoy, recommended a woman in Aymestrey, fifteen miles or so away, with whom Zoe could lodge for a week. 'She does need to be taught some manners,' Mike had told us, which at first seemed a rather severe, headmistressy choice of words, although we then discovered that teaching 'some manners' is horsey jargon too. However, it certainly encouraged the notion that Zoe would be going away to an equestrian version of Swiss finishing school. We decided that it would be a nice bonus if she came back knowing how to curtsy properly and fully au fait with the formal way of replying to a wedding invitation, but that we'd settle for her giving small children rides round the garden.

So, during one October half-term holiday, off went Zoe to Aymestrey. Jane and I had taken the kids for a holiday in Tobago, where we had generously been loaned the use of a villa for a week, and Anne and Bob, Jane's parents, were house-sitting while we were away. Anne was delighted that Zoe would not be among their charges. Much as she loved Milo, our devoted golden retriever, and had just about come to terms with the cats, she was properly and sensibly wary of Zoe.

A word here about house-sitting, something we'd never had to bother with in our previous life in Crouch End. There, we could leave our home empty without any qualms, at least once we'd set the burglar alarm, quadruple-locked the front door, and told the newsagent in a quiet voice – just in case that middle-aged woman with the child seemingly dithering between the Monster Munch and the Cheesy Wotsits was actually a burglar with a small accomplice straining to hear our address – that we wouldn't be requiring the papers until Saturday week. But leaving Docklow Grange was a different proposition altogether. The pets needed feeding and there had to be someone around to attend to the needs of our holiday cottage guests, as well as to deal with telephone enquiries.

That summer, before we went on our usual ten-day holiday with my parents-in-law to Cornwall, we'd had to find a professional house-sitter, an amiable woman called Pam, who did a perfectly good job but charged £30 per day plus travel expenses. That wasn't unreasonable, but did bump up the cost of the holiday by about £400. My in-laws, bless them, came cheaper. They bumped up the cost of our holiday in Tobago only by the price of a nice bongo drum – purchased on a beach after exciting negotiations with a man with wondrous dread-locks – which we thought would look fetching on their hearth back in Yorkshire. As, for that matter, would the man with the wondrous dreadlocks.

A few days after we got home, Zoe was returned to us fully broken in and 'bomb-proofed', meaning that she would not be startled if she heard a sudden loud noise. This was essential if she was to carry small children, not least because of the RAF Tornados that had a habit, three or four times a week, of zooming low over our house, so low sometimes that, if you were quick enough, you could see whether or not the pilot had shaved that morning.

For a while, Jacob was keen to ride Zoe. And from time to time we were also able to sit our smaller cottage guests on her, which pleased me greatly. It was nice to think that we could claim a proportion of her oats as a legitimate business expense. She also made a marvellous contribution to the well-being of the garden in the form of top-quality manure, as well as to my personal well-being in the form of the excellent exercise that a man in a largely sedentary job gets from shovelling shit. But we gradually came to the conclusion that Zoe, for her benefit as much as ours, would have to go. Our horse-loving friends had been wrong to doubt our ability to look after her responsibly – our vet said we'd kept her in fine fettle – but they'd been quite right to assume that we would tire of the responsibility. In May 2005, two years after buying her for £400, we advertised Zoe in the *Hereford Times* for a bargainous £200, making the classic part-time advertiser's mistake of assuming that something we very much wanted to sell would be something nobody would very much want to buy.

In fact, the first call came at 7.30 a.m. on the day of

publication and by lunchtime we could have sold Zoe fifty times over. But obviously we wanted her to go to an excellent home, and decided to sell her to the person who sounded nicest on the phone. Jane got the best vibes from a woman called Fiona, who lived just north of Leominster and could scarcely believe her luck in buying a pedigree Shetland mare for only £200. Fiona explained that she already had a male Shetland and was keen to give him a mate. That sounded perfect. Our only reservation, apart from the gradually dawning awareness that we could have sold Zoe for £500 or more, was that Fiona's Shetland was called Vinnie Jones after the hard-nut former Wimbledon footballer turned actor. We weren't at all sure that we wanted Zoe, a rather classy broad, to become a footballer's wife.

Still, Fiona arrived the following day with a horsebox and took Zoe away, followed by Jane and the kids, who wanted to see where she would be living. Their sadness at saying goodbye to their pony was dispelled as soon as they set eyes on her rolling new paddock in idyllic countryside, although it was Vinnie who was happiest of all with the new arrangement, thundering over and enthusiastically mounting Zoe even before they'd been formally introduced. Not that she seemed the slightest bit disconcerted at being rogered by a stranger. While Vinnie got his end away, she carried on contentedly munching grass. From now on, clearly, she was going to have a more enjoyable existence than the one she had endured in our orchard, with only chickens for company.

6

Miss Pepperpot, and the Fuzzies

The chickens, meanwhile, were proliferating. We'd started cautiously with four – three Buff Rock bantams and a Gold Sebright – but by our second autumn we'd added eight Marans and Warrens, and by the spring of 2004 we also had some Cuckoo Silkies, White Silkies and Cream Legbars. I even started chicken-related correspondence with an old acquaintance, a woman called Nicola, who like us had moved with her family to the country, in her case Somerset. She e-mailed one day to say that a fluffy yellow chick had recently emerged from beneath one of her broody Buff Orpingtons, although it had soon become clear that the mother was a middle-aged Light Sussex hen and the father a young Light Sussex cockerel, one of the hen's progeny from the year before, which of course meant, if you're still following me, that there had been sexual congress between mother and son, and that the mother of Nugget, the chick, was also her grandmother.

I replied, pointing out that this incestuous carry-on would be gravely frowned upon were it to happen between humans, and that I wasn't sure I approved of it even between chickens. Nicola assured me that, after some initial concerns, she had discovered that incest was perfectly acceptable in poultry circles. I later learnt, from the pages of *Practical Poultry* magazine, that it is known as line-breeding, and is a common way of producing purer versions of a single breed. Apparently, the offspring of an incestuous coupling between chickens are not born with extra limbs or anything, as might happen in the human world. Which is rather a shame, in a way, for those of us with three children who each prefer leg to breast.

It was in a newsagent's in Leominster, while searching the shelves for the *Spectator*, that I had come across the inaugural edition of *Practical Poultry*. The Pecktator, if you like. I was delighted.

When living in London, I would have offered long odds against my ever forking out for a magazine called *Practical Poultry*. But I'm almost embarrassed to admit that I actually felt a little surge of pleasure as I looked at the contents page. We had been wondering whether to buy some ducks, perhaps even from Miss Whiplash, and *Practical Poultry* had a feature addressing that very subject (alas, without the Miss Whiplash dimension). There was also an in-depth article about Marans, a breed that had originated in the French port of La Rochelle, I was interested to learn. That, I decided, explained why our Marans had that very morning been tucking with such enjoyment into some leftover potatoes dauphinoise. It was part of their heritage. I also learnt that the first Marans had arrived in Britain in the mid-1960s; the poultry-fancier Lord Greenway had spotted them at an agricultural show in Paris and imported 1,000 fertilized eggs, probably not in the pockets of his tweed jacket, although it's a pleasing thought.

Anyway, his lordship also favoured a bit of genetic modification, apparently, which ensured that the first crop of British Marans had no feathers on their legs, unlike their French cousins. Somehow, in the process, the dark-brown egg colour was altered, so that Marans on this side of the channel started producing medium-brown eggs the colour of beech, whereas the French oeufs were mahogany. I'm sorry if I'm boring you. Here in Herefordshire, there is scarcely anything less boring than the colour of eggs. Indeed, the day on which we collected our first Cream Legbar production was a truly exciting one, for Cream Legbar eggs are a beautiful bluey-green, a colour that even the celebrated paint-makers Mr Farrow and Mr Ball might struggle to reproduce.

I could comfortably fill the rest of this chapter with further reflections on poultry, although I have decided to spare you. Just another couple of pages should do it. Because, with no apologies for the pun, I have become quite an eggvangelist. I think everyone should be encouraged to keep chickens, as long as they can be given relative freedom to range. It doesn't even need to be a countryside pursuit any more; every summer during the Wimbledon tennis championships I stay with my sister-in-law Jackie and her family in a typical Wimbledon street of Edwardian terraced houses, and I find I am far more likely to be woken up there by cocks crowing in neighbouring gardens, not to mention the frantic flapping and squawking during a fox attack, than I am out here. Poultry-keeping has become quite the middle-class hobby in the city, in fact there is a modernist chicken coop called an Eglu which I am told is the last word in urban chic. It was invented by a chap called Johannes Paul, who at the time was studying industrial design at the Royal College of Art and probably expected to land a high-powered job with Unilever or Procter & Gamble, rather than an egg-powered job with three fellow-students, running a company they have very deliciously called Omlet.

It was Deborah Ross, a colleague on the *Independent* who lives close to where we used to live in Crouch End, who put me on to Omlet. Deborah is a fine comic writer who could wring laughs out of the most banal of domestic situations, and frequently does. Moreover, she's the last person anyone would expect to keep chickens, so she knew that a week living *The Good Life* would make a funny feature. She duly took delivery of an Eglu, and found that it considerably enhanced the look of her garden. It had, she reported, 'a privacy screen to shield the nesting box from the open-plan living space, as well as a slide-out droppings tray and a magnetized "eggport"'. She said she wished she could live in it herself. Here, with Deborah's blessing, is a short extract from her chicken-keeping diary:

Bank holiday. Pouring with rain. The chickens are coming today. What shall we call them? I want Margot and Jerry. But my pre-teen son has other ideas. He wants J-Lo and Beyoncé. 'How will you tell which is which?' I ask. 'J-Lo will have the bigger bottom, but Beyoncé will wiggle hers better,' he says. We prepare for J-Lo and Beyoncé. No lily-filled dressing rooms with white silk-draped sofas, alas, but we do chicken-proof the garden, securing the gaps in the fence with chicken wire. Chicken wire turns out to be miraculously ideal for the purpose.

'We're getting chickens,' my partner calls out to Peter, our neighbour on the other side.

'And they're called J-Lo and Beyoncé,' adds my son.

'They are prodigious shitters, chickens,' says Peter, darkly. We think he is just jealous.

Johannes Paul, one of the four designers behind the Eglu, arrives with ours. It is bright green. He also arrives with a carry-box that smells all farmy and is going 'blob-blob-blob-blob'. Our chickens? 'Yes. What are you going to call them?'

'Beyoncé and J-Lo,' says my son.'

'It'll make a change from Margot and Jerry,' he says. 'Everyone calls them Margot and Jerry.'

I laugh scornfully. 'Arses,' I say.

Johannes assembles the Eglu. And out come J-Lo and Beyoncé. Their breed is Marans noire cuivrée, both are about 25 weeks old, and one has started laying while the other is at-point-of-lay, which I'm guessing means she is about to. Which, though, is which? My son assesses their bottoms. They are similar sized. J-Lo, then, will be the one with the bigger, redder comb. J-Lo's bottom is immediately productive. Her poo is mustardy and runny.

'J-Lo,' says my son. 'You are no lady.'

'See, see!' shouts Peter from over the fence. 'Prodigious shitters!'

We leave them to peck and scratch and go blob-blob-blob in their run until dusk, when they go into the coop by themselves. I wish children were so easy to put to bed.

Day two: I go out first thing. No egg. Bloody, freeloading,

stinking, useless, blob-blob-blobbing chickens. So I go to work not on an egg and then, mid-morning, I get a panicky phone call. 'They can fly,' my partner hisses. 'I let them out and the cats had a go and now they've flown over the fence.'

I call Johannes. 'It seems they can fly.'

'Ohmigod,' he says. 'I forgot to clip their wings. But don't worry. They are ground dwellers, really. They can't fly far because they can't sustain the weight.'

I call home. 'Johannes forgot to clip their wings.'

'It's all right,' my partner says, 'they're back. They came in the kitchen, tried the cat food, had a crap and then another, then went out again.' We'd been told that cats are no threat to chickens, which I didn't really believe, but it's true. J-Lo and Beyoncé gang up, raise their blob-blob-blobbing a pitch or two, and see them off easily. The cats are terrified of the chickens. The cats are chicken whereas the chickens are not.

And so it went on, but I had no need to worry that my status as the newspaper's chief chicken correspondent was under threat. After a week, Deborah was more than happy for Johannes to collect J-Lo, Beyoncé and the Eglu, although I don't doubt that the loan had the intended effect, and that a number of city-dwelling readers of the *Independent* decided to give chicken-keeping a whirl. While I was working on this book I phoned Omlet and spoke to Johannes Paul, who informed me that his company had sold around 10,000 Eglus in the previous two years, 90 per cent of them to urban households. At the time of writing it costs £395 for the Eglu and two chickens, plus 20 kilos of organic feed. This would have them rolling in the aisles at the King's Head, if the King's Head had aisles. My own expenditure on chickens in the past few years is already considered a huge joke by Owen and his fellow farmworkers, although I make no apologies for shelling out, so to speak, on the more exotic members of our little farmyard, especially the White Silkies with their comical topknots. Sometimes I lean on the fence, next to Madeleine the listing scarecrow, just watching them. It can be oddly therapeutic, gazing at creatures whose biggest problems in life are deciding what to peck and where to crap. And actually they don't spend too much time thinking about that, either, or they wouldn't crap where they sleep. On which unedifying subject let me just tell you a little more about the holiday cottage business.

As we have established, Docklow amounts to very little indeed, apart from the pub, the church and a few houses. In fairness, Arthur Mee got it about right when he described it as a viewpoint and little else. And yet it is a meaningful name in coarse fishing circles, for it is also the home of Docklow Pools, a rather attractive self-contained hamlet with self-catering chalets, its own hostelry and several pools copiously stocked, so their website informs me, with carp, roach, rudd and bream. It made sense for us to tap into the popularity of Docklow Pools, especially as their own accommodation was often fully booked, so we considered advertising our cottages in various fishing magazines, but when we mentioned this to Mrs Openshaw, the previous owner of the Grange, she smiled sweetly and told us that in more than twenty years running holiday cottages, she only twice had to deal with soiled beds, and both times the guilty parties were groups of fishermen spending their days at Docklow Pools and their evenings getting paralytically drunk. Obviously, I wouldn't want to suggest that fishermen are in general prone to bouts of alcohol-related incontinence, but it was enough to put us right off the idea.

To return from fish to fowl, the chickens supplied by Omlet, Johannes Paul told me, were a Miss Pepperpot and a Gingernut Ranger, one of each. These were not breeds I knew, even though I fancied myself reasonably well informed on the subject, especially now that I was an occasional *Practical Poultry* reader – although not yet a regular subscriber. Keen as I was to enhance my credentials as a countryman, a subscription to *Practical Poultry* would have seemed slightly excessive.

As for my observations on the matter of urban chicken-keeping, while I'm all for everyone doing a Tom and Barbara Good and breakfasting on their own eggs, I feel that only in the countryside is chicken-keeping a pure exercise in self-sufficiency. In most cities and towns, if you find that you've run out of eggs then you simply walk to the corner shop. In the sticks, there's no corner shop, indeed no corner. Which is not to say that there aren't plenty of places within a short car journey selling eggs, but when you get used to eating your own it seems disloyal, somehow, to pay for them.

So when the nights draw in, and our egg assembly line slows right down, we simply eat fewer eggs. I know that we could maintain the supply by putting an electric light in the chicken-coop, replicating daylight, but to do that would feel vaguely industrial. Throughout the winter months we therefore try to make do with whatever they're laying, one or two eggs a day at the most. A fellow poultry-fancier once told me that in his experience, most hens stop laying on Bonfire Night and begin again on Easter Sunday. This struck me as improbably precise, as if they had collectively negotiated some union productivity agreement. I can almost hear the hard bargaining in a smoke-filled coop. 'If you think we're laying after 5 November and before Easter you're out of your clucking mind, pal.'

But although I scoff, it actually seems to be more or less true. Around the beginning of November our egg consumption as a family, having peaked in June and July, takes a sharp dip. During the summer months, the children eat a couple of boiled eggs each, or a plate of scrambled eggs, for breakfast. I quite often poach a couple for lunch. And whenever we have friends round, I like to knock up a frittata to slice into little squares and offer with drinks. With the regular Sunday-morning pancake frenzy, the occasional baking session and the odd omelette, I would estimate that from April to September we get through forty or fifty eggs a week between the five of us. But when production plummets, boiled-egg breakfasts give way to porridge, the frittata to crisps and nuts. As I said earlier, there is always the option of buying eggs, but neither Jane nor I can quite bring ourselves to put them in the shopping basket. Such are the perils of semi-self-sufficiency, and yet there is a certain pleasure even in the act of denial. We can't begin to claim that we live off the land, and even our dogs know the way – albeit backwards, looking out of the Volvo's rear window – to Somerfield in Leominster, Sainsbury's in Hereford, Tesco in Ludlow and Waitrose in Malvern, depending on how affluent we're feeling. Yet we embrace the principles of seasonal eating a lot more than we ever did in the city. And I have to say that it feels good.

Moving seamlessly on to the dogs, we had taken possession of Milo, the retriever, on 13 July 2002, the day after we arrived to live in Herefordshire. Three years later, almost to the day, we added a Jack Russell called Paddy to the household. Jane had been agitating for a Jack Russell for some time, an idea I resisted with my usual thunderous authority, which was how I came to spend much of July 2005 on my knees collecting Jack Russell poo from the hall floor. As Jane's fancy for a small dog grew, and my resistance increased, she had stitched me up like the proverbial kipper by asking at the dinner table one evening: 'who thinks we should have a Jack Russell puppy?' Naturally, the children's hands all shot into the air, and three pairs of guileless, pleading eyes, plus one pair of cunning, knowing eyes, turned on me. It would have been churlish and Victorian to say 'I absolutely forbid it!' So I said 'I absolutely forbid it!' But you don't get anywhere when you forbid things without being particularly forbidding. Jane duly answered an advert in the *Hereford Times*. Two days and £150 later, Paddy was ours.

He had already been christened Paddy, which was fortunate, because naming a pet hereabouts, or for that matter anywhere, can be a bit of a trial. Basically, I think the same rules should apply to naming a pet as apply to naming a child. Nobody names a child without giving the matter full and considered thought. A name might suit a sweet little baby, but will it suit a lumpen teenager, or someone staring into space in an old folks' home? It tickles me greatly that with the increasing vogue for old-fashioned Victorian names following on from a vogue for naming children after pop stars, there will come a time when bright young things called Edith, Agnes and Betty will visit their gnarled old grannies, whose names are Kylie, Shania and Britney. Oddly enough, the only people on whom these important considerations seem lost are pop stars themselves. Which reminds me that when we came back from our Cornish holiday one summer, we found that the water in our swimming pool (which in truth is more of a huge paddling pool) had turned green. So Jane got on the internet and found a website called PoolStore.co.uk, which listed 100 reasons why a pool might be cloudy, and offered 100 solutions, most of them costing £24.99. We decided that some of those solutions, Polyquat Algicide, Sparkle Granular Flocculant and Algae Water Clarifier, sounded very much like the stupid names rock stars give their kids. I could easily imagine Polyquat Algicide Geldof posing, in a *Hello!* magazine photoshoot, with Sparkle Granular Flocculant Bowie.

By contrast, when we pondered what names we should give our kids, we used what we called the Uncle Harry test. Jane's Uncle Harry, alas no longer with us, was a plain-speaking former village publican from South Yorkshire. Some of the more unorthodox possibilities we rejected purely because we could imagine Uncle Harry saying to Auntie Betty, 'You'll never guess what our Jane's called her baby!' So when we chose the name Eleanor for our firstborn we felt confident that it passed the Uncle Harry test, but then a card arrived from some other of Jane's Yorkshire relatives congratulating us on the safe arrival of Helena. On being told we'd called our baby Eleanor they merely assumed that we'd dropped the aspirate, Barnsley-style.

With animals' names, you have to take three things into consideration. One, do you know any humans called the same thing? When we named Milo Milo, we didn't know we were destined to become close to a woman called Avril, whose teenage son was also a Milo. This caused a certain amount of discomfort on Avril's part whenever she and Jane took Milo, and Avril's dog Hugo, for a walk. Because Jane would almost always yell: 'For God's sake Milo, stop rolling in that cowpat, you filthy beast!' Or something to that effect. And Avril would always give an involuntary wince. Not that her son Milo ever rolls in cowpats. Teenage boys have some unappealing habits, but I don't think that's one of them.

Avril's dog Hugo is a schnauzer, by the way, which enables me to tell the old story of the woman who shows her dog at Cruft's, and wins second prize. Afterwards, one of the judges informs her that it might have been first prize had not the dog's ears been considered slightly too hairy. So the next day she goes to her local pharmacy and asks for a tube of hair-removal cream. 'If it's for your armpits, then you probably shouldn't wear a silk shirt for a week,' says the pharmacist (very possibly the same one who was asked for Viagra in an earlier chapter), handing it over. 'And if it's for your legs, then you probably shouldn't wear stockings for a week.'

'No,' the woman says, 'it's for my schnauzer.'

'Oh,' says the pharmacist. 'In that case you probably shouldn't ride a bike for a week.'

Where was I? Oh yes, pets' names. You also need to consider what you will sound like when you call your pet's name repeatedly in Mortimer Forest, which covers hundreds of acres of north Herefordshire and south Shropshire and is one of our favourite places to walk. The best-known cry in Mortimer Forest is not that of a baby rabbit caught by a buzzard, nor that of a fawn stuck in some brambles, but of a woman calling 'Roger!' over and over again. Everyone who walks a dog in Mortimer Forest is familiar with the Roger cry. Were the bird and mammal impersonator Percy Edwards still alive, he would doubtless have perfected it, because it is an intrinsic part of the forest infrastructure.

However, whereas some human names work with dogs, some don't. I think Paddy works, as does Hugo, and of course everyone who grew up reading Enid Blyton's Famous Five books thinks of Timmy more as a dog name than a human one – a perception that the puppy-like children's TV presenter Timmy Mallett did very little to overcome. But Roger, like Keith, Colin and for that matter Brian, is all wrong. Still, I suppose there's always the chance that he was named Roger ironically, perhaps on account of his predilection for attempting to have sex with people's lower legs and small items of furniture. I don't know what kind of dog Roger is.

The third thing you need to consider when naming a pet is whether you will feel faintly or even extremely ridiculous in the reception area of the veterinary surgery. The BBC presenter and former tennis player Sue Barker once assured me that when Frank Bruno's ex-wife Laura took the family Rottweiler to see the vet, she was asked for her name and duly said Bruno. The receptionist gave a long-suffering sigh. 'No,' she said. 'I mean your name, not the dog's.' I should add that Barker, being the lovely person that she is, is even happier to tell stories at her own expense than at the expense of others. In the same conversation she gigglingly recalled the epic gaffe that she dropped on the day that Steffi Graf made her Wimbledon farewell. 'At least she leaves Centre Court with some great mammaries,' said Barker, a slip of the tongue cheerfully forgiven by the director, who moments later came bounding into the studio crying 'How right you were!'

Even when there is no misunderstanding concerning pets' names, they can still lead to stifled giggles. When Jane took Paddy in to be inoculated against something or other – me, probably – the vet came out and said matter-of-factly to a little old woman, 'Mrs Harrison, you can collect Big Daddy now.' Unfortunately, Jane was called by another vet before she got to see whether Big Daddy was a dog, a cat, a guinea pig, a rabbit or what, so it has remained a matter of family speculation ever since. Maybe it was something more exotic.

And speaking of exotic pets, in February 2005 we acquired one ourselves, in the thin and wriggly form of a snake called Nigel. I realize, of course, that it ill becomes someone with a snake called Nigel to poke gentle fun at someone for calling her dog Roger, but at least it was my 9-year-old son Joe who decided on Nigel, for the very good reason that the man who gave us Nigel, a friend of our neighbour Will, was also called Nigel.

Nigel was a baby corn snake, also known as a red rat snake, although in truth he was more orangey-yellow than red. Corn snakes are non-venomous constrictors and come from the south-eastern seaboard of the United States, where they tend to live in corn fields, although Nigel, slightly disappointingly, had spent all his life in a house in Ledbury. When we got him, Nigel (the man) told us it was actually a bit too early to determine the sex of Nigel (the snake), who was only six months old. So Joe accepted that he might have to be renamed Nigella, which Jane rather hoped would turn out to be the case, just because I once came back from interviewing Nigella Lawson full of what Jane considered to be rather unseemly enthusiasm for Nigella's velvety brown eyes, hourglass figure and air of vulnerability. To this day, whenever she catches me enthusing to someone about Nigella she rolls her eyes and says, 'Oh no, not Nigella and her air of bloody vulnerability again.'

Happily, it turned out in due course that Nigel was, indeed, a male of the species. He lived in a tank in Joe's bedroom and initially had one meal a week, which was no sight for the squeamish. Corn snakes eat dead rodents, so we had to keep a bag of dead baby mice in our freezer, which almost caused a terrible mix-up one weekend when Jane's parents were again looking after the house for us, and Bob came upon what he thought was a bag of frozen prawns. Anne shredded some lettuce and found some mayonnaise in the fridge before they discovered the error. They had come alarmingly close to sitting down to baby mice cocktail.

At Leominster Pet Supplies, the woman hadn't batted an eyelid when we asked her for a supply of frozen baby mice. She called them 'pinkies' and very cheerfully explained that when our snake got older, he would move on to 'fuzzies', which were slightly larger than pinkies with a slight covering of fur. She told us that she also sold frozen rats and even rabbits to people with bigger reptiles than Nigel.

Jane knew about all this because she had lived with a snake some years earlier in Tunbridge Wells, and I'm not making a husbandly crack at an ex-boyfriend. It was during her first job as a journalist, as a reporter for a fine organ called *Hardware Trade Journal*, long before she met me. She rented a room from a man called Ed who had asked her, when she first went round to check out the accommodation, whether she had any objection to sharing a house with a reptile. Picturing a lizard or two in a glass case she said no, then moved in to discover that the reptile in question was a ten-foot python called Grover.

In time, she grew reasonably used to Grover, and liked Ed a lot, although all hell – and more worryingly, Grover – broke loose one weekend when Ed was away. Jane came down for breakfast to find that Grover had dislodged the top of his tank and escaped, then she heard some angry banging coming from the pan cupboard in the kitchen. Understandably reluctant to deal with an enraged, escaped python on her own, she phoned a friend of Ed's called Liam, and asked as non-hysterically as she could, if he might come round and help her out of a little local difficulty.

Liam was a PE teacher, with a PE teacher's macho demeanour, and Jane reckoned, rightly, that he would not be able to refuse a damsel in distress. 'Right, I'll be over as soon as I can,' he said when she explained the problem, although she fancied that she recognized a faint hint of nervousness in his voice. When the bell rang forty-five minutes later Jane opened the door to find that Liam had come via the school PE equipment room. He was wearing cricket pads, wicket-keeping gloves and a fencing mask. 'OK, where is he?' he said boldly. Jane ushered him into the kitchen, where he boldly got hold of a by-now somewhat fatigued Grover and carried him through to his tank.

'Thanks very much,' said Jane. 'No problem,' said Liam. At no point did either of them acknowledge that he was rather unusually kitted out for a Saturday morning house visit in Tunbridge Wells.

I'm very fond of that story, and have listened appreciatively to it on many occasions, without ever dreaming that we, too, would one day own a snake. Not of course that Nigel was ever likely to be as problematic as Grover. He would only grow to about three feet, we learnt, and when we first got him he was no longer or thicker than a robust bootlace. Even Eleanor thought he was quite sweet, having initially been extremely dubious about sharing a roof with anything as slithery as a snake (which was ironic, because at the time there was actually nothing more slithery than our roof tiles).

When I wrote about Nigel in my newspaper column, I got a nice letter from a clergyman, the Reverend Alex Martin, who wrote to tell me that the story reminded him of a boa constrictor called Barnabas, which belonged in the early twentieth century to the chaplain of Trent College in Derbyshire, an eccentric but plainly rather wonderful cove nicknamed 'Daddy' Warner. When the Revd Martin became a chemistry master at the college, shortly after the Second World War, Daddy Warner was still the chaplain, and liked to tell the tale of how he had once been ill with a bad dose of flu, and feeling the need for company had sent for Barnabas to share his bed. The college had just got a new doctor, and when this chap later arrived to treat the chaplain, he drew back the sheet and was confronted by Barnabas rising towards him. Not unreasonably, he fled.

Daddy Warner also used to take Barnabas on long summer treks with his pupils. But one year, in the New Forest, Barnabas disappeared from the camp and couldn't be found anywhere. A day or two later, someone from the camp saw a headline on the front page of a local newspaper: 'Dangerous tropical snake found in New Forest'. Barnabas was duly reunited with Daddy.

Grateful as I was to the Revd Martin for sending me these wholesome snake stories, I rather hoped that Joe wouldn't become as attached to Nigel as Daddy Warner had been to Barnabas. We were also slightly disconcerted that Nigel (the man) had been nine years old when he was given his first snake, just as Joe was. Would Joe's interest develop into a passion, as Nigel's had? We hoped not, or at least that it might diminish by the time he reached courting age. 'Come upstairs and see my python' is really not a great chat-up line on any level.

Whatever, we knew that by moving to the country we had, for better or worse, furnished all our children with an altogether different set of interests, and with them a different destiny, than if we had stayed in London. On a basic level Joe would never have had a snake had we remained in Crouch End, not least because in London he shared a bedroom with his sister. Nor would he ever have gone beating on a pheasant shoot, pheasant shoots being relatively rare in north London. Living in Herefordshire had opened all our eyes on a different way of life.

It was a way of life we had embraced in some ways but not in others, although I thought it important to give everything a try, with the obvious exception of morris dancing. That's why I took Joe on the penultimate Docklow shoot of the 2004–5 pheasant season, on a clear but bitingly cold day in late January. We were both beaters, our job to wander through the woods making a racket, driving the birds into the range of the waiting guns. I was uneasy about this. I hadn't been born to country pursuits and it went rather against the grain to lure living creatures to their deaths. But I couldn't say that I felt strongly about it, and in truth I enjoy a pheasant casserole as much as the next man. Besides, I knew that at least the pheasants dispatched on our local shoot would be eaten, unlike the grotesque slaughter at some big country-house shoots where hundreds if not thousands of birds simply end up buried.

Joe and I enjoyed our debut as beaters. It started at a splendidly ramshackle shoot hut, where a fire blazed and industrial measures of port were handed round to the over-nines, to fortify us against the westerly wind. 'It's all very countryish,' Joe whispered to me, approvingly, and I knew what he meant. Living in a 'countryish' setting didn't necessarily make us countryish ourselves, so it was nice to feel immersed, just as I had while uncontrollably letting loose a succession of farts in the tug-of-war at Yarpole fête.

Once the port had been downed, the shoot got underway. I had to admit that it was exhilarating to hear a crack of a shotgun followed by a pheasant plummeting earthwards, although Joe and I irreverently – and silently – cheered to see others flying safely beyond the range of the guns.

We had been schooled in the art of beating by our neighbour Tracey, who was married to dead-eye David, the former clay-pigeon champion. But even Tracey admitted to us that she liked to see the handsome woodcock escape the guns. For one thing, they had flown all the way from Sweden, to escape the harsh Scandinavian winter. So too had Ingemar and Kerstin, yet nobody was roaming the English countryside trying to shoot them – except in the feverish imagination of their friends back in Gothenburg who watched *Midsomer Murders*. So it seemed a bit of a shame to shoot the woodcock. Especially when Tracey showed us the corpse of the only one gunned down that day. Removing the so-called pin feathers, she explained that they had been used to write the Bible. 'Cool,' cried Joe, and assured me that beating was at least as educational as going to school.

Apart from the woodcock, the tally on our shoot was 36 pheasant, 14 duck, a pigeon and a rabbit, which represented a haul almost as good as the one bagged at a ranch in Texas by US Vice-President Dick Cheney on 11 February 2006, which amounted to rather a lot of quail and his 78-year-old friend Harry Whittington. Like most people, I greatly enjoyed Cheney's embarrassment following that unfortunate episode, but barely eight months later we discovered for ourselves what it was like to be in the line of fire during a pheasant shoot, although it was not the bullets that hit us, but the pheasants.

A few days before Christmas, one of the mainstays of the

shoot, Richard, appeared at our kitchen window looking unusually agitated for a man who normally exudes reassuring calm. I was out at the time, but Jane let him in, and in due course phoned me to report a bizarre sequence of events. Richard first suggested that she might want to go upstairs with him, which was not the sort of offer she got every day, even from me. He led her to the westernmost room, which happened to be our bedroom, and gingerly opened the door. It was the gingerliness of a man who did not know what sort of dreadful scene might await him. And as he did so, a large male pheasant popped its head round the door, which gave Jane a considerable start. She did not expect to find big, handsomely plumed cocks in our bedroom. More's the pity.

Richard told her that there was a shoot going on in the neighbouring fields, and that having winged this particular bird he then watched it crash through our bedroom window. His reassuring calm had by now returned, and he said to Jane 'I'll just be a moment', before entering our bedroom to put the unfortunate wounded pheasant out of its misery. That left us with the lesser, although still substantial misery of having to clean up all the mess, which was unbelievable, as though a bomb had gone off in a poultry factory. There was glass, feathers and blood absolutely everywhere; I found a shard of glass and a speck of blood in my sock drawer, of all places, some three weeks after the event.

There was also, of course, a pheasant-sized hole where previously there had been a window pane. But the next day Richard, whose many talents included glazing, very decently returned and replaced the pane for us. Afterwards, over coffee, I expressed some surprise that the bird had been flying with sufficient velocity to burst through a window. But Richard explained that when you're shooting pheasants, you have to aim well ahead of them, such is the speed at which they fly. Especially, I ventured, when they're hurrying away from men with guns. He laughed, and added that he'd once been told by a former SAS soldier that even a sniper aiming at a man walking at a leisurely pace has to aim a metre or so ahead of his target, which, of course, begged the disturbing question: why should an SAS sniper have occasion to shoot a man walking along at a leisurely pace?

We downed our coffee and I cheerfully waved Richard off, then went back to my attic office, where not ten minutes later I was found by Joe, who said that he'd just been in the garden playing with the dogs and had seen a smashed upstairs window. I smilingly explained that the smashed window he'd seen had now been replaced. 'No, not your bedroom window,' he said. 'I think this might be a window in the spare bedroom.' My smile froze, and whereas lots of things were inclined to freeze in my office during the winter, including a cup of tea on one notable occasion, the reason had nothing to do with the temperature. Surely lightning had not struck twice?

Remarkably, it had. I opened the door of the spare bedroom to find precisely the same scene that had greeted Richard and Jane the day before, with the additional and plentiful bonus of pheasant poo to go with the glass, feathers and blood. Again, the creature was standing in the room, although this time not injured. It was standing under a chair looking rather proud of itself, but got predictably excited when I tried to catch it, so I used my hands more sensibly and phoned Richard. He thought that I was winding him up when I said that the same thing had happened again, although Jane and I later decided that perhaps the second pheasant had struck at more or less the same time as the first, during the panic of the shoot, and had simply spent the night in the spare room. That would explain the poo.

Whatever, it was an interesting reversal of the usual scheme of things in the country, humans feeling under attack from game birds. Perhaps the pheasants were revolting? After all, we had noticed a distinct rebelliousness on the part of our pet rabbits, Holly and Bramble, who had both escaped from their hutch and joined forces with their wild cousins in the surrounding fields, taunting us by appearing every now and then in our garden. The shoot regulars, too, had reported the occasional sighting of Holly and Bramble – who were conspicuously black and white and stood out rather impressively among the smaller grey wild rabbits – which for some reason always reminded me of the story of the performing bear that escaped some years ago from a circus in China.

It being China, circuses were not even remotely bound by the strictures of political correctness, and the bear had been trained to perform a full repertoire of tricks. I don't know how he escaped, but he was much missed by the circus owners, as well as by all the punters with whom he was a great favourite. Anyway, a few weeks later, 100 miles or so from where the bear had escaped, some deerhunters were in a forest when into the sights of their rifles cycled the missing bear, wearing a bowler hat. I know that's true, incidentally, because a friend of mine told me that it actually happened to the father of the brother-in-law of a Chinese friend of his cousin's, and you can't get a more reliable source than that.

Whatever, I quite shamelessly used the story in my column one week and was delighted to get another letter from David Gorvett, the *Independent* reader in Leominster who had been tickled by my flights of fancy concerning local place names.

This time, alerting me to a bear story closer to home than China, he sent me a booklet that he had himself written in 1987, a history of the Herefordshire village of Eardisley.

In late Victorian times, apparently, the Eardisley May Fair was a hugely popular event, with a circus as its centrepiece. In those days circuses had dancing bears, and sad old elephants which were sometimes compelled to walk dozens of miles from one showground to the next. While researching his text, Mr Gorvett found that on one occasion at the Eardisley Fair, a dancing bear had slipped its shackles and climbed to the top of a nearby poplar tree, where it stayed all day and well into the evening, resisting all blandishments to descend. 'Circumspectly gathered near the open doors of the two pubs,' Mr Gorvett wrote, 'many onlookers offered their advice, ranging from a swift use of Sir John Coke's elephant gun to the more hazardous employment of a two-handed saw from Powell's Spade Yard.' Fortunately, or maybe unfortunately given the wretched existence it was returning to, the bear eventually climbed down of its own accord.

Mr Gorvett also discovered details of a May Fair in the 1890s when the circus elephant caused a sensation by inconveniently dying on arrival in Eardisley. In warm weather a deceased elephant was only going to be an attraction for so long; after a while it would start to keep folk away. So negotiations were quickly begun with a local farmer, a John Edwards, who agreed that an exceedingly large grave could be dug on his land. There is still a mound showing where this interment took place, and I like to think of future archaeologists getting all excited over what they think is the skeleton of a young mammoth.

At any rate, it is clear that Nigel the corn snake was by no means the first exotic pet to arrive in Herefordshire. But he was the first to arrive in our house, and for a while was treated as a celebrity. Every visitor was solemnly taken up to Joseph's room to meet him, and the really lucky ones found themselves with a front-row seat at feeding time, watching, more often than not in appalled fascination, as Nigel dislocated his jaw to accommodate a pinkie.

Then, while Jane and I were in the kitchen reading the newspapers one Sunday morning in the early spring of 2005, a couple of months after Nigel had moved in, we heard a banshee-like wail from upstairs. It was Joe. Nigel had escaped.

We rushed upstairs to find Joe, sobbing inconsolably, on his hands and knees looking under pieces of furniture for his missing friend. Somehow, the lid of Nigel's tank had been dislodged, and Nigel had sssscarpered. We searched for him high and low – mainly low – but found no trace of him, no sloughed skin or even a pellet of snake poo. After a week or so we gave him up for dead. As natives of the southern states of America, even by way of Ledbury, corn snakes don't like the cold. His tank had had a heat mat underneath, replicating conditions in the corn fields of Georgia and South Carolina, but elsewhere in our house, even in early spring, conditions were more reminiscent of the Scandinavian tundra. And if the cold hadn't claimed Nigel, then one of the cats, Tiger or Sooty, surely had.

Occasionally, once Joe had stopped getting sniffly at the very mention of Nigel, we joked that he might be living under the floorboards, eating mice and steadily growing into the size of an anaconda. But we were all certain that he had slithered his last. My mother-in-law Anne was a little more circumspect for a while, and would gingerly pull the duvet back whenever she and Bob came to stay, but eventually even she forgot about Nigel.

Then, almost exactly a year later, I was doing some weeding in the back-garden border when a chocolate-brown rubber snake caught my eye. It was not unusual to find members of Jacob's extensive collection of rubber and plastic animals outside, usually carried in a dog's mouth and randomly deposited, and I stooped down to pick it up. As I made contact with this rubber snake, however, it rather unexpectedly reared its head. 'Fucking hell,' I said loudly, as I think even the Archbishop of Canterbury might have done in the same circumstances. Then I looked more closely. The chocolate brown was mostly soil. Underneath, the creature was orangey-yellow. It was like the scene in *The Good, the Bad and the Ugly* when Clint Eastwood gives himself up to fellow Confederate soldiers in grey, only for them to dust themslves down and reveal enemy uniforms of Union blue. Or maybe it wasn't much like that, but a classic film reference is apt, such was the drama of the moment. 'Nigel!' I cried. 'Nigel!'

My cries caused some bewilderment to our gardener, Alan, who was turning over some soil on the other side of the garden, in what we grandly call our spring border. From where Alan was standing, all he could see was me greeting what appeared to be, from the note of excitement in my voice, some long-lost relative. Yet I was looking closely at the ground, saying over and over again, 'Nigel! Bloody hell, Nigel!' Had I lost my marbles? It must have looked like that.

Alan came over, tentatively as if he half-feared that he might find me stary-eyed and frothing slightly at the mouth, to work out what on earth was going on. He was as taken aback as I had been, although for different reasons, to see a snake at my feet. A kind of snake which he knew, being a singularly knowledgeable fellow on all things outdoorsy, was not indigenous to the

British Isles. I explained the situation and he agreed that, yes, it was quite remarkable that Nigel should show up a whole year later, having apparently survived an entire winter in the open.

I returned Nigel to his tank, which we'd kept in the cellar in case we ever got round to replacing him, and waited excitedly for Jane and the kids to get home. They were as astonished and delighted as I was. A few days later Nigel (the man) came round to inspect his namesake. He found signs of attacks by predators – whether cat, a buzzard or even the lawnmower he wasn't sure – but said that Nigel seemed fundamentally to be in excellent shape, if a little wilder than he had been. The first few times he was picked up he rattled his tail, rattlesnake-like, which he had never done before, and which was more than a trifle disconcerting. Nigel, too, was surprised to hear that his reptilian namesake had reappeared after a year. He said he knew of one snake, a West African ball python, that had turned up after three whole years on the run, if 'run' is quite the right word. But how Nigel had got outside, and where he had spent the last twelve months, was as much a mystery to him as it was to us.

Whatever the explanation, Nigel was enthusiastically gathered back into the bosom of the family. And Jane went out to buy some fuzzies, making sure to keep the bag clearly marked, well away from the frozen prawns. And speaking of small pink things, it's regrettably about time I related the story of the day our roofing contractors saw me in the nude.

7

Kevin, and the Privies

We had fallen in love with Docklow Grange on the first day we saw it, and once we had arranged the industrial-sized mortgage we needed to buy the place, we didn't take much notice of petty things like full structural surveys. In fact, we didn't have one done; we just asked a surveyor, a friend of a friend, to come round and take an informal look.

The surveyor assured us that the roof looked in reasonably good shape, but after a few years of living under it, we knew that some remedial work was urgently needed. There were tiles missing, guttering that needed replacing, chimneys that needed repointing, and vegetation taking root in the eaves. All this we tried to ignore, even when a corner of the landing ceiling sprang a leak. For several months, whenever it rained, a succession of drips would plop down from an ever-expanding crack. Our solution to this, in the time-honoured fashion of people who live in old houses, can't quite afford the repair work, and think that the problem will eventually go away of its own accord, was to position a bucket strategically underneath it.

One day in March 2005, as was bound to happen sooner or later, part of the ceiling collapsed. A problem had become a crisis and we were forced to examine our options, which no longer meant repositioning the bucket, or even getting a bigger bucket, perhaps in a brighter colour. We found that our insurance policy would cover the cost of repairs to the ceiling, plus the fairly extensive redecorating required, but the assessor flatly refused to include the roof work. The scaffolding alone would cost thousands. We got a couple of estimates from local builders, both of whom made clear that if we wanted a comprehensive job, we could expect very little change out of £30,000.

Jane and I held a crisis summit at the kitchen table. There were really only two options that didn't involve buying more Lotto tickets: one was to sell up and move, the other was to sell an asset, which meant a holiday cottage. We decided on the second option and realized that the one to sell was Woodlands; it was the biggest of our three cottages, sleeping six, so it would fetch the most money, and yet we would miss it the least. Our customers were mostly couples, or occasionally couples with one or two children, so our smaller cottages – one-bedroomed Manor and two-bedroomed Yew Tree – were much more popular. We duly put Woodlands Cottage on the market.

In the meantime we took out a loan so that we could get the roofing work underway, and gave the job to a local company whose foreman was a lugubrious but highly capable man called

Kevin. We also asked Kevin and his gang to stabilize the bell tower. Much as we liked having something as stately sounding as a bell tower, the truth was that it was a rotting wooden structure with a galvanized tin lid, and the bell clearly hadn't been rung for years, possibly decades. Looking at it, we decided that the last time might well have been in celebration of Queen Victoria's Golden Jubilee, or possibly the 1918 Armistice. By the early twenty-first century, it looked as if a strong wind might just blow it off the roof altogether, which would be no fun at all for anyone beneath; they'd be in no condition to appreciate puns about dropping a clanger. So we were looking forward to the thing being made safe, and also to the Grange having a functioning bell again, although we couldn't quite decide whether we should press it into everyday use – perhaps to summon the children from the garden when it was time for their supper – or save it for landmark occasions, such as birthdays, anniversaries and, for that matter, armistices.

The work to the roof was to be carried out in three phases. But first, we needed scaffolding. So one drizzly Wednesday a team of six beefy scaffolders arrived and within three or four hours had covered the entire rear elevation of the house, a particularly tricky job because they had to get up and over the large Victorian conservatory. It was an impressive operation, only slightly diminished by the fact that they were meant to be scaffolding the side of the house, not the rear. Unfortunately, there was nobody around to point out the error. Jane was out and I was on my way back from an overnight stay in London. When I arrived home at about midday, the job was just about done. So I jovially offered them some coffee and biscuits, as a sweetener before dropping the bombshell that they would have to undo four hours' work, and start it all again somewhere else.

I went into the house, put the kettle on, and phoned the woman at the roofing company who listened in horror and admitted that the fault was hers for giving the scaffolders ambiguous instructions. I asked whether Kevin could start at the back rather than the side, so that the scaffolders could leave everything where it was, but she explained that the first phase of the work had to be the side, because of the particular materials Kevin had ordered. There was nothing for it; the scaffolding would have to be taken down.

I went outside. 'I've got some bad news,' I said. The foreman of the beefy scaffolding team was the beefiest of them, with a shock of grey hair and a spectacular set of Ken Dodd-style buck teeth. 'What's that, then?' he said cheerfully.

'I'm afraid you've put all this scaffolding up in the wrong place,' I said. 'It's meant to be round the side of the house.'

The foreman looked at me for a full sixty seconds without saying a word. His smile didn't falter. Finally he spoke.

'When you said you 'ad bad news,' he said slowly, 'I thought you was going to say you'd run out of coffee.'

He was looking down at me from a wooden platform, which made it gallows humour in an almost literal sense. But to his immense credit, he and his gang cracked on with the tiresome task of dismantling their morning's work with not the slightest complaint, even though the drizzle had now turned into a downpour. Some hours later, when the scaffolding had been re-erected where it should have been in the first place, our neighbour Carl emerged and quite reasonably asked why we were scaffolded up to the nines. 'We're getting their Christmas lights up early,' said the foreman. His wit and good humour were a credit to the scaffolding profession. It was March.

Anyway, once we were shrouded in scaffolding in the right

place, Kevin and his sidekick were able to get on with the job. I say 'we' when what I mean is 'our house' but it many ways it seemed like a disruption that we had to bear physically. If you've ever had major repairs done to the exterior of your home then you'll know that scaffolding seems to intrude even on life indoors, and one morning it did so all too literally when I stood in the altogether on the bathroom scales, having quite forgotten that there was planking just outside the window affording a rather graphic full-frontal. Who got the bigger shock – Kevin when he glanced through the window into the bathroom, or me when I glanced out – I wasn't sure. Either way, when he sheepishly told me later that day that he'd spotted some perished guttering that needed urgent replacing, I didn't know whether he was referring literally to the roof, or, more euphemistically, to me. He also said that he'd found one of the chimneys to be perilously close to collapse, just to put the galvanized tin lid on my day.

Our chimneys, too high to be accessed with even the longest of ladders, had been a headache since we moved in to the Grange, mainly because of the birds that took up residence there from early spring to late summer. Jackdaws were our main boarders, and although we considered asking our neighbour David, Docklow's answer to William Tell, to shoot them, we were put off the idea when someone told us that jackdaws mate for life. This was further proof that we could not yet call ourselves fully fledged country-dwellers; sentimentality towards animals tends to be a townie phenomenon, not a rural one. So it was clearly our lingering townie sensibilities that stopped us from ordering the assassination; we couldn't bear the thought of seeing a feathered widow or widower moping about the place.

Instead, we found ourselves waging an attritional battle of wills with the jackdaws, coming downstairs every day to find twigs in the grates, and every morning lighting fires which drove them away from the chimney pots and into the nearby lime tree, where they would perch looking very cross indeed. The following dawn, they cracked on with the job, until we got up and lit the fires again, and the £100 question every year was whether we would get fed up lighting fires before they got fed up with the smoke and heat, and decided to nest somewhere else. It was a £100 question because that's what it cost us to get the chimney sweep round when the nesting season was over, although the sweep's name was at least a source of comic relief and has already cropped up in a different context in this chapter: Ken Dodd. The only person this failed to tickle was the American friend we had staying with us one autumn. Having never heard of Ken Dodd he didn't understand what was so funny about the name, and he expressed further disappointment on meeting Ken, confessing that he had fully expected an English chimney sweep to be nine years old, wearing a battered top hat.

As for the rest of the roof, the repairs were eventually completed and we were able to tick the biggest box of all on the list of improvements we had made to the Grange since moving in. The only sizeable box remaining to be ticked was the septic tank, which overflowed a little too often for anybody's liking, especially the liking of David and his wife Tracey, who passed through our small wood, where the underground chamber was located, whenever they took their dogs for a walk.

I don't want to get too bogged down – unlike Tracey and David – in the troublesome matter of our septic tank. But it does move me to recall a marvellous book I was given for my forty-third birthday in October 2004, called *Herefordshire Privies*. I must admit that at first I had the book pegged as the kind of novelty present that a chap gets when he reaches the age of forty-three; I assumed that I would look at it once and never again. But a quick flick through its pages – while appropriately seated, of course – made me realize that it was far too interesting to be consigned to a bottom drawer along with the socks playing the *Match of the Day* theme tune (later to be joined by the shard of glass and speck of pheasant's blood). It was, in fact, a fascinating volume, written with a light touch and engaging wit by a respectable-looking, fairly elderly woman called Paddy Ariss who, in some of the photographs, stood proudly beside some of the county's more noteworthy outdoor toilets, with captions such as: 'Interior of the superb three-holer at Great Parton Farm. The author takes a pew!'

Interestingly enough, Mrs Ariss had discovered that the three-holer at Great Parton Farm once felt the weight of a famous posterior, that of Mrs Winston Churchill. Which reminded her of the old story about Winston himself being visited at home by the Lord Privy Seal, who had been disrespectful towards him that day in the House of Commons. The butler duly went to find Churchill, who happened to be on the loo. 'The Lord Privy Seal is here to see you, sir,' he called through the door. To which the great man supposedly responded: 'Tell the Lord Privy Seal that I am sealed to my privy, and can only deal with one shit at a time.' I hope that's true. Like the story of the missing circus bear cycling into the sights of the Chinese hunters, it deserves to be true.

Mrs Ariss didn't appear to have been remotely hampered by subject matter as seemingly restricted as privies and Herefordshire. Indeed, she found that the county has an honourable place in lavatorial evolution, for it was a Hereford firm, Saunders Valves, which designed the valve used to operate a flush loo in supersonic aircraft. Think of all those distinguished bottoms, on all those Concorde flights, which were able to let loose their contents thanks to Herefordshire ingenuity. It makes me proud to be an adopted Herefordian.

She even flushed out an old limerick connecting Hereford and privies, and whereas any three-syllabled town would fit, I like to think that Hereford was the original: A Hereford fellow named Hyde Fell into a privy and died. His unfortunate brother Fell into another, And now they're interred side by side.

I read on, fascinated, and found details of a venerable stone privy barely a couple of miles from my house, a two-holer – affording friends or lovers, or even brothers named Hyde – the opportunity to do their business in tandem. Apparently, it is built over the Whyle Brook near Pudleston, the neighbouring village to Docklow. 'I have recently learnt,' the intrepid Mrs Ariss wrote, 'that a running stream will break up faeces before it has travelled a dozen feet.' Which is well worth knowing, I'm sure you'll agree.

The book was full of interesting titbits of knowledge like that. Mrs Ariss found that three British kings died on the loo – the highly unfortunate Edmund Ironsides, James II of Scotland and George II – and also that Henry VIII's toilet seat was cushioned in velvet, which to adapt a venerable *Two Ronnies* joke, must have tickled his fancy. She was fuelled, I'm pleased to say, by an unashamedly childish sense of humour, and even included the following line from a book of Sophia Loren's favourite recipes: 'Eels have become one of my favourite meals after a tremendous experience I had with them on the Po.'

I enjoy the idea of a respectable-looking woman of advanced years sniggering at that one.

More relevantly, she discovered that privies in Herefordshire were often located under the county's many yew trees, apparently because flies dislike the smell of yew. Not that the flies could reliably be kept away. She related the delightful tale of a young fellow up from London to visit his uncle on a farm near Hereford, I suppose a century ago or more. The young man badly needed to exercise his bowels, so his uncle directed him to the privy, which was just past the pigsty. However, he soon returned, saying that, much as he needed a poo, he couldn't bear to sit among so many flies. The uncle consulted his pocket-watch. 'If you wait a few minutes,' he said, 'your aunt'll have the joint on the table and all the flies'll 'ave gone there.'

Much tickled by this and other stories, I decided to look up the author. Ariss is a pretty unusual name and Herefordshire is a sparsely populated county; I decided that it wouldn't be too hard. Sure enough, I found a single entry for Ariss and dialled the number. A man answered. 'Could I speak to Paddy Ariss?' I asked. There was a long pause. 'I wish you could,' he said, quietly. 'She died three years ago.'

I was mortified, as well as saddened. Her husband Peter, for he it was on the other end of the phone, told me that she had died of leukaemia, aged seventy-two, barely a year after finishing the book. But she'd had huge fun writing it, he added, and that I didn't doubt for a second. He explained that the book was one of a series about different counties and their privies, and that didn't surprise me either. That only Herefordshire might have privies worth writing about was really too much to hope for. Peter suggested that I call the publishers,

Countryside Books, which I did, and spoke to the owner, a Mrs Battle, who informed me that a woman called Mollie Harris, the actress who'd played Martha in *The Archers*, was a co-author of the original volume, *Cotswold Privies*. Mrs Battle also told me that the *Hertfordshire Privies* volume had been written by the former television newsreader Richard Whitmore. You can't say this book doesn't furnish you with conversation-stoppers.

There were over a dozen in the county privies series, apparently, of which by far the biggest seller was *East Anglian Privies*. 'The subject is a bit earthy for some counties,' Mrs Battle told me, 'but East Anglia embraced it with great excitement.'

I recorded this memorable line, and wrote about Mrs Ariss's book, in the *Independent*. That particular column quickly flushed more privy stories out of the closet than I would have thought possible, including one from a man who recalled an exchange between his father and his wife-to-be when she expressed concern that there was no lock on the door of the privy at the end of the garden. 'I don't think that matters,' he said, slowly. 'We've been here for thirty years and nobody's stolen a bucket of shit yet.'

It never fails to amuse me, incidentally, just how enthused by lavatorial matters the English are; it's really no wonder that the pioneering toilet designer Thomas Crapper was one of us. Another of the letters I received was from a Sally Hotson, who wrote that her mother had been with the Land Army during the Second World War and was billeted on a farm near Leominster. Having come from the indoor-loo belt of the Home Counties, Mrs Hotson's mother was horrified to find, in Herefordshire, widespread reliance on the outdoor privy. The farmer had a four-holer, apparently, which he and his wife always used to visit together. How sweet. I've heard the theory that all couples should have a bed too small to allow one partner to roll too far from the other, on the basis that you can't stay cross with someone whose bottom you touch every night, and defecating as a duet is perhaps a more extreme example of the same notion.

Mrs Hotson had kept most of her mother's wartime letters home, and one of them revealed her appalled fascination with this farm privy. 'It's a wooden building at the side of the garden which is separated from a field by a hedge and is also on a much higher level, so that there is a sheer drop from the garden to the field. A moat runs along the field by the hedge, and the building juts out over it in some way. Unfortunately, the moat does not run very swiftly and, extraordinarily, flows along the whole length of their garden – it must be pretty overpowering in hot weather.'

What the farmer could have done with, as I now know thanks to Paddy Ariss's splendid book, is a running stream to break up the faeces. That is another dose of knowledge I would almost certainly never have acquired had I never moved to Herefordshire. And although I can't envisage a situation in which a grasp of the mechanics of faecal disjunction might come to my aid, one can never be wholly sure. So I commend the book to you, or perhaps one of the others in the series more relevant to where you live. Every loo should have one.

To return to our own toiletry matters at Docklow Grange, I promised not to get too bogged down in the subject of our septic tank, and I won't, except to say that overwhelmingly, living in an old house in the country, it is what is beneath your bottom and what is above your head that create the most concern. Once you've got the roof and the waste disposal sorted, then you're more than halfway to a hassle-free existence, although there is always the possibility of a ghost or two generating some excitement.

8

Ralph, and the Poltergeist

As it happens, I have never been a believer in ghosts. In *Tales of the Country* I wrote flippantly that when I first set eyes on Docklow Grange, I felt sure that it would come with a resident ghost, but I didn't really think that it would. Nor has it, and here I'm touching wood because a chap's got to have some superstitions. But while I am yet to be woken up in the middle of the night by a headless man driving a coach and four through my bedroom wall, my scepticism has receded.

This is partly because of an edition of Michael Parkinson's chat show I watched a few years ago. Parky's guest was Joanna Lumley, a woman for whom I have the utmost admiration, and whom it was once my privilege to interview over lunch in

Holland Park. Her table manners are so exquisite that to have lunch with her is to feel more or less permanently that you have a piece of spinach stuck between your teeth, even if you are careful, as I was, not to order anything with spinach.

Anyway, on Parkinson she told a riveting story about an old house she and her husband once bought in Kent. When she was in the cellar one day she felt a chilling, other-worldly presence, followed by a rasping voice which said, fairly unequivocally, 'Leave this place!' Not surprisingly, they quickly sold up, and I can't say I blame them. Of course, Miss Lumley is a consummate actress, and I for one would cheerfully listen to her reading a railway timetable, so her ghost stories are bound to be irresistible.

But more significantly, when Eleanor went to secondary school in Hereford in 2004 we got to know the parents of her new classmate Hester, Ben and Penny, and in due course they became close enough friends to confide in us that their rambling sixteenth-century home, in rolling Herefordshire countryside near Ledbury, had been haunted until they engaged the services of a ghostbuster. We found it hard to disbelieve them. Neither of them was the slightest bit flaky, and they and their four lovely children seemed to be perfectly grounded in reality. Yet they assured us that when they moved into the house, around the time we moved into ours, strange things started happening in a former scullery that the previous occupants had converted into a family room, and in the spare bedroom directly above it.

They insisted that on more than one occasion, sometimes in front of the children, screwed-in lightbulbs had mysteriously detached themselves and shot across the room. Frequently, the television turned itself on. And once, when a friend of theirs was staying in the spare room, she woke up in the middle of the night to find something lying on top of her, and it wasn't Ben.

When she had calmed down she described it as 'an energy'. She then packed her bags rather hurriedly and left, unlike the energy, which continued to make its presence felt in all sorts of supernatural ways. So Ben and Penny phoned a woman called Ariel Warner, an American living in Ludlow, whom they had met a few times, and knew to be a self-proclaimed 'space-clearer'. She thought the term ghostbuster rather vulgar. And yet she had certainly busted Ben and Penny's ghost. Ever since she'd spent an afternoon there, the lightbulbs had stayed put, the television had behaved, and overnight guests had slept soundly. Ben gave me her number, and I called to ask her to tell me more. I admitted my scepticism towards the supernatural, although that didn't faze her in the slightest.

She told me about a woman in a town in north Wales who had hired her because she felt a malevolent presence in her house. It wasn't a 500-year-old house like Ben and Penny's, either. It was in a cul-de-sac built in the 1950s. Ghosts aren't that fussy, apparently. It turned out that this woman, whose eldest son had tragically died in a motorbike accident, had found out that there had been only two previous owners of the property and each had suffered the death of an eldest son. The woman wanted to sell the house but didn't want to pass on the curse, which is why she hired Ariel.

'She picked me up from the station,' Ariel recalled, 'and told me that she'd had a priest in the year before to bless the place. But as soon as I got there I realized the joint was still jumping. The CD player was on full blast, and she assured me that it hadn't been on when she left for the station. Moreover, the CD that was playing was her son's favourite band, Metallica.'

I said something appropriate, like 'blimey'. But Ariel wasn't finished. 'Her son was not the only presence there. There were others, not nice at all. It took me pretty much all day to get rid of them, and about six months later she called me and said that nothing had happened since, and she was now ready to put her house on the market.'

Ariel told this story matter-of-factly. She really didn't sound like a nutter. Which is not to say that I concluded the conversation believing implicitly in the afterlife, but when we both politely suggested that we should meet face to face sometime, I added that I'd rather she didn't come to Docklow Grange. I didn't want her seeing anything I couldn't. And actually, when I thought about it I could claim a possible encounter with a ghost myself, on the weekend that my close university friend Dominic and I attended a twenty-first birthday party in Gloucestershire, circa 1984.

We had been billeted out by the birthday boy's parents to some friends of theirs who lived in a creaky Jacobean manor house, and who kindly gave Dom and me the exclusive use of the west wing, for which the word 'characterful' is perhaps the best adjective. Before the party, Dom ran a bath for himself in a gloomy bathroom with original Victorian fixtures and fittings. I asked him to run a bath for me when he'd finished. Being wasteful students, and it being the Thatcher era of every-man-for-himself, I don't suppose the thought would have occurred to either of us that he might leave his bathwater in for me to use. And there was nothing as new-fangled as a shower. So when he returned to our twin bedroom he told me that he'd filled the bath again for me. Yet when I padded along the uneven corridor a few minutes later, the taps were closed tight and the elderly, cracked enamel was bone-dry. I went back to remonstrate with Dom but he assured me that there had been a full, steaming bath when he'd left the room. We laughed it off, I ran another bath and that was that. But here's the spooky thing: when I surfaced the next morning, predictably hung over, I stumbled along to the bathroom to find a bath full almost to the brim with hot water, the steam still rising. Dom, meanwhile, was fast asleep, gently snoring. So we later concluded that it could only have been a ghost, with an impish sense of humour.

By contrast, Docklow Grange, as I have said, seems undisturbed by ghosts, ghouls, banshees or poltergeists either with or without a sense of humour. Which is not to say that there is a total absence of creatures moving about unseen in the wee small hours. Like any big house in the country, we have a happy contingent of mice, with which we deal periodically by summoning the friendly neighbourhood pest control expert.

That used to be Maurice O'Grady, about whom I wrote affectionately in *Tales of the Country*, but between me finishing that book and starting this one, Maurice decided to hang up his rat poison and his mole traps. We miss him. He used to sit at the kitchen table clutching a mug of tea and telling us his latest infestation stories, which was always a happy way of passing a morning. The last time I saw him, in the street in Leominster one cold January day, he assured me that he was thoroughly enjoying his retirement. He was sporting an unseasonal tan, and explained that he and his wife had just spent a fortnight at a five-star hotel in Tunisia. 'We had a wonderful holiday,' he said, in a heartfelt kind of way. But was it the food he enthused about? No. Was it the service? No. The spa facilities? No. The weather? No. It was the cockroaches. In the hotel there had been an abundance of a sub-species known as the German cockroach, and he'd had a simply fabulous time watching them. He'd merrily pointed them out to the holiday rep, he told me, and she had clearly cursed her luck at having Maurice in the party, especially as the German cockroach, to the untutored eye, can pass for the common fly. 'She didn't seem to want to know,' he said, ruefully.

One interesting thing about moving to the country from the city is that what at first seems like a pest problem, after a while seems like no great reason to get your knickers in a twist. Thus it was with mice, as long as they didn't become too prolific, and I even became quite happy to tolerate the solitary bat that from time to time whizzed in a fast, tight circle around the lightbulb in the back cellar where I kept my wine. He minded his own business and I actually became quite fond of him. I even gave him a name: Hugh, after Hugh Johnson, the celebrated oenophile.

Mr and Mrs Openshaw, from whom we'd bought the Grange, had shown us the front cellar, which housed important things like the boiler and the coal shute, before we moved in. But we didn't even discover the back cellar until after we had been living here for several weeks. I was thrilled, especially to find three ancient wrought-iron wine racks. I had always fancied having a wine cellar. We'd had a low-ceilinged cellar in Crouch End in which we kept wine, but to get to it I needed to bend at the waist and perform a cautious forward shuffle, like the oldest man in the world.

It took me another year to get a serious wine collection going. Before we'd moved to Docklow there had been no room in either my house or my life for hobbies, and for the first twelve months I had other priorities. But gradually I began to see the charm of hobbies, a word I had regarded with great suspicion even as a child. Obsessed though I was with sport as a boy, making or collecting things never floated my boat. It would have been unfloatable anyway, had it been a model boat. I had friends with complicated Airfix models dangling from their bedroom ceilings, but I only ever made one and it was such a disaster that I never tried again. It was a Messerschmitt with an emphasis very much on the first syllable. Basically it ended up as a large ball of dried glue with a small propeller attached.

For a while, encouraged by my mother, I also collected stamps, but I wasn't much good at that, either. Those fiddly little hinges became the bane of my life, ending up everywhere except on the backs of the damn stamps. Gradually, however, I found that country living had hobbyfied me. You will learn in a later chapter about my growing passion for vegetable-gardening, but suffice to say here that it slowly became downright anal. Every year from early spring the conservatory was full of dozens of precisely labelled seed trays, and anyone who wanted to see the gentle, loving side of my nature could be sure to find it there. When I said 'How was your day, darling?' there was a good chance that I was talking to one of my children, but a similarly good chance that I was addressing a Little Gem lettuce seedling.

From the late autumn right through the winter, however, the vegetable garden was usurped in my affections by the wine cellar, and the fact that Hugh the bat was occasionally to be found down there effectively made it my own private sanctuary: everybody else in the family gave it a wide berth. I was reprimanded even by the children, by the way, for naming a bat Hugh, or indeed naming a bat anything. Jane, in particular, after her unpleasant encounter in the bedroom with one of Hugh's relatives, or possibly Hugh himself, felt that it was decidedly provocative, and didn't hesitate to celebrate one day a year or so later, when I announced, mournfully, that I had found Hugh dead on the cellar floor. Not that she understood at first who I was talking about.

'I've just found Hugh dead in the cellar,' I said.

'Who?' she said.

'Hugh.'

'Who's Hugh?'

'What do you mean, who's Hugh?'

An irritable sigh. 'OK, let me put it another way. Hugh who?'

'Who's Hugh? Hugh who? Hugh the bat, of course.'

'Oh, that Hugh. Hurrah!'

'Which Hugh did you think I might have found dead in the cellar?' I asked, slightly narkily. 'Hugh Grant? Hugh Fearnley-Whittingstall? The seventies porn star Hugh G. Rection? Huw Edwards? Hughie Green?'

It wouldn't, in fact, have been the first time there had been such a misunderstanding. For Christmas one year we had given Jacob a hamster, and felt certain that he would give it an embarrassingly corny name such as 'Hammy'. We were therefore highly delighted when he decided, for some curious reason, to call his hamster Ralph. Ralph, we felt, was a suitably ironic name for a hamster, and went nicely with Nigel, the snake, not that they were ever likely to meet. It was also, by chance, the name of Jane's mum's cousin, known fondly to Jane and the children as 'Uncle Ralph', and therefore failed one of our own rules of naming pets. Uncle Ralph was one of the children's favourite relatives, although that was largely if not entirely on account of the fact that he very thoughtfully sent each of them a fiver for their birthdays. We hardly ever saw him.

Anyway, in September 2006 I went overseas for a few days on a writing assignment. On the day I got home, Jane had gone to London to see a friend's new baby. Anne and Bob had come to look after the house and the children. And, of course, the pets.

Scarcely had I opened the door than Anne announced that she had some sad news. 'Ralph died earlier this week,' she said.

'Oh no,' I cried. 'Jane didn't say anything on the phone. Things like that always seem to happen when I go away.'

'Yes,' said Anne, looking at me slightly strangely. 'He was on holiday in Belgium.'

It must have been the jetlag, but I spent at least a couple of seconds attempting to work out why Jacob's hamster might have been on holiday in Belgium, before it dawned on me that she was talking about Uncle Ralph. Which was considerably sadder, of course, but at least stopped me worrying about how Jacob might have taken the news (as it turned out he had merely asked, in that unsentimental 8-year-old way, whether Uncle Ralph's demise meant that he would no longer be getting £5 for his birthday).

Just to return to hamster names for a moment, we found out after acquiring Ralph that our friends Steve and Joanna and their kids had had a whole series of hamsters down the years, all named after characters in either *Star Wars* or *Thunderbirds*. It was Brains who escaped from his cage one day and couldn't be found, much to everyone's distress. But in bed that night, Steve woke up to find Brains sitting quietly on his bottom. I suppose he could count himself lucky that he liked to sleep face down.

Almost everyone we knew seemed to have amusing hamster stories. Other friends, Ali and David, had a hamster called Sherlock who lived in their daughter Amy's bedroom. One day Amy reported tearfully that Sherlock seemed to be developing a growth, and sure enough there was a large round protuberance emerging from what Ali genteelly described to us as his rear end. An emergency appointment was made with the vet, and Sherlock was carried there in a box, but when Ali opened it, Sherlock's growth had miraculously gone. Like Basil Fawlty removing the silver dome to reveal his duck à la orange, only to find that it wasn't there, she did a bewildered double-take. But the vet calmly pressed Sherlock's little tummy and out popped the growth.

'Was this it?' he asked. Ali confirmed that it was. 'Those are his testicles,' explained the vet.

Apparently, Amy's bedroom was in the attic where in the summer it got rather warm, and male hamsters, when feeling a little overheated, have a tendency to drop their testicles, which helps them keep cool. We decided not to tell Jacob that, in case he put Ralph on the Aga to see whether it was true. But at least we could be sure that we wouldn't experience Ali's other hamster-related drama, because they also had a female, Clover, and when they went on holiday one year they asked some friends to look after Sherlock and Clover, who lived in separate cages. Unfortunately, their friend's daughter thought it might be nice to let the two hamsters play together, and a couple of days after they got home – on account of the fact that a hamster's gestation period is only slightly longer than the duration of a holiday on the Costa del Sol – they found that Clover was a mother of thirteen.

What on earth, I asked Ali, did they do with them all? 'We

kept three, found homes for nine, and she ate one,' came the matter-of-fact reply. I should have known that it wouldn't be an altogether happy ending. Keeping pets is an emotional rollercoaster.

Back to the wine cellar. With or without Hugh for company, I spent some happy hours down there devising a colourful labelling scheme so that I would know how long each bottle should be stored for. With the help of Jancis Robinson and the original Hugh, Johnson, or at least with the help of their books, I tried to teach myself more about wine, which is one of those mind-bogglingly vast fields of expertise that seem to stretch over the horizon. The more progress you make, the further you realize you have to go.

But at least we had our very own friendly neighbourhood vineyard as a further source of information. Broadfield Court vineyard, at Bodenham two or three miles south of Docklow, was owned by a lovely couple called Mark and Alexandra James, who were energetic producers of English wines with notably non-English names, like Reichensteiner. Alex had become a good friend and was able to shed further light on the mysteries of viticulture. I mentioned her in *Tales of the Country*, and she will pop up again in this book in the improbable context of me getting locked in her stable shortly before dawn with a pair of hysterical, slavering dogs. But for now let me merely say that it helped enormously, as I tried to educate myself about wine, to have someone to explain the actual practicalities of the business. For example, at Broadfield Court they still wince about the Great May Frost of 1982, when an unusually late and severe overnight frost wiped out their entire crop. These days, if they anticipate frost in May, they light fires around the vineyard so that a pall of smoke will act like a blanket over the vines. I dare say that grapes are protected with greater sophistication in the Medoc; maybe you have to come to north Herefordshire to find the primitive essence of wine-making.

With my slowly expanding viticultural knowledge, and my burgeoning interest in growing my own vegetables, I had to get in touch for just about the first time in my life with the practical side of my brain, which had always been singularly underdeveloped, hence the cack-handed efforts at making Airfix models and even sticking stamps into albums. It wasn't as though I was making my own wine, of course, but I reckoned that it wasn't enough merely to learn the difference between a Pouilly Fumé and a Pouilly Fuissé; I wanted to grasp the mechanics of manufacturing the stuff.

This was a curious turn of events. After comprehensively flunking my chemistry O level in 1978 I had rejoiced in the thought that I would never again have to worry about the fractional distillation of nitrogen, or care whether concentrated sulphuric acid could be used to dry ammonia. I seem to remember ritually burning my carefully drawn Periodic Table, with the same faintly sinister relish with which the good people of Lewes burn effigies of Guy Fawkes every Bonfire Night. Yet here I was enthusiastically teaching myself the meaning of terms such as malolactic fermentation, and once more, for the first time in almost thirty years, considering the pH of things. It was another way in which moving to the countryside had broadened my mind, a kind of chemical process in itself, and precisely the opposite effect to that which ardent metropolitans warn you about when you up sticks for the sticks. Away from the multicultural, cosmopolitan buzz of the city, your mind will wither, they say. Without the stimulation of all the museums, art galleries, theatres and art-house cinemas, your intellect will shrink like a woolly jumper in a hot wash, they imply. Well, I had only one word for those people, or actually two words: carbonic maceration. It's the way in which some early maturing red wines, notably Beaujolais, are made, by fermenting the grapes in sealed vats filled with carbon dioxide. So there.

There was, I should swiftly add, one area which remained immune to my new-found autodidacticism. I had never been able to grasp even the rudiments of DIY, as was understood very early on by my woodwork teacher at grammar school, the long-suffering Hubert Long, who thought I had made a stool when in fact it was supposed to be a bread-bin.

This was a shame, because by the time we had fully settled in at Docklow Grange, what the children coveted more than anything else was a treehouse. In our tiny garden in Crouch End we'd had a treehouse, yet, oddly, no tree. At the Grange we had at least 150 trees, yet no treehouse. Something had to be done, but plainly not by me. So we asked our joiner, Alan, if he'd have a go.

The children already had a rope swing, which to their great excitement had been installed in our small, three-acre wood by the strongest man in Herefordshire. This wasn't Owen, although he'd once finished second in the Strongest Man in Herefordshire competition, but a man called Nick, who'd won the thing outright in 1993 and was built like – I speak with a degree of authority having read Paddy Ariss's book – a three-hole outdoor privy. Since the competition had never been held since 1993, the title was technically still his.

Nick was a tree surgeon, one of the few jobs in which the feats required to win a Strongest Man competition actually come in useful. I suppose if you're an engine driver then it might on occasion be quite handy to be able to pull a train with your teeth, especially on the Hereford to Paddington line where it would probably speed the service up. But by and large there isn't much call for such skills in real life. For Nick, however, hardly a day went by without him having to toss the odd caber.

He seemed like a fine fellow, though I would say that, wouldn't I? A version of the old joke about the gorilla with the machine-gun comes to mind. What do you call the Strongest Man in Herefordshire carrying a chainsaw? Sir, although he didn't seem to mind 'Nick'. He had come to thin out the wood, which had become almost impenetrable, and we hoped that he might leave his charming signature, a tree stump carved into a handsome toadstool. There was a lot more to Nick than met the eye, although what did meet the eye pretty much filled the eye. When he'd finished clearing the wood I asked him to rig up a tyre swing for the kids, and he seemed pleased with the commission. He told me that he could get a type of rope used by the SAS, and also knew where to put his hands on a lorry tyre. I half-expected to drive along the A44 and find a juggernaut on its side, with one tyre missing. And perhaps a few SAS men trussed up nearby.

Alan, meanwhile, despite being to carpentry what his beloved Thierry Henry was to football, had never made a tree-house before. But that didn't faze him in the slightest. Alan is a man of perfect equilibrium, which I suppose makes sense for someone whose best friend is his spirit level. He calmly looked on the Internet for inspiration, although, as so often with the Internet, what he got was information overload. Do a Google search for treehouses and you'll see what I mean. Some of them are unbelievably sophisticated. The children had in mind a treehouse where they could hold a kind of Enid Blyton-style Secret Seven summit, but never mind the Secret Seven, what we found on the Internet were treehouses that could accommodate a G7 summit.

The other problem was finding a location for the thing. Paradoxically, the profusion of trees made it much harder than it had been in London to find the right spot. But eventually, in consultation with Alan, we chose a handsome old elm, and he was able to download from the Internet some pictures of the kind of structure he had in mind, one without a dining area for ten or a hot tub. He set to work with characteristic zeal and within a week it was finished, a spectacular treehouse twenty feet off the ground with a balcony and a fireman's pole designed for quick departures. It was wonderful. The kids really didn't know how lucky they were, which was not for want of me reminding them every few minutes. It was the sort of thing that at their age I would have killed for.

Very satisfyingly, though, they started making plans to sleep in there as soon as the weather got milder, and were further enthused by the idea of sleeping out of doors by a camping trip we made one weekend to the Brecon Beacons.

It was our first family camping expedition, which was perhaps why we chose the Brecon Beacons; it wasn't exactly invoking the spirit of Shackleton to choose a destination that we could see from our house. Nor was camping anything like I remembered it from my days as a student backpacking round Europe. It had become the new football, in the sense that the middle classes had claimed it as their own. During the weekend that we were there, at any rate, Pencelli Castle Caravan and Camping Park resounded to the merry sound of the bourgeoisie enjoying themselves, clinking champagne flutes in celebration of the altogether splendid idea to rough it under canvas for a couple of nights.

I confess that I was the one who took the champagne flutes. There is absolutely no need these days for a camping holiday to involve hardship. If you can drive right up to your pitch, then why not take real, breakable glassware? We even, on occasion, drove from the tent to the toilet block, which was entirely contrary to the spirit of camping but rather expedient given that the loo was a good 500 yards away. As for those words 'toilet block', they have a slightly penal ring and also evoke childhood memories of evil-smelling cesspits, but the toilet block at Pencelli Castle was a pleasure to visit. It would have been a bit weird to eat off the floor, but we certainly could have done.

As for the actual under-canvas experience, I had entirely forgotten, since my previous night in a tent circa 1984, that sensation of sliding slowly downhill in a sleeping bag. And when I last camped I was hardly more than a child myself, so had never faced the interesting challenge of letting a 9-year-old desperate for a pee out of a tent in the middle of the night. Which would have been a sight easier but for the fact that tents these days, or our Khyam Galaxy 600 anyway, have a bewildering array of zips. What unfolded at 3 a.m. was a scene not unlike the *Not the Nine O'Clock News* sketch with Rowan Atkinson as a punk standing at a urinal, frantically opening different zips to find his member.

The treehouse at least did not present that problem when the children finally got round to braving a night in there, which in fact didn't last beyond 11 p.m., the point at which they got scared. As they all trooped in I was reminded of my old university chum Mike, who had also had a night in a treehouse cut short, although through no fault of his own.

It happened in August 1978, when Mike was twelve and on an exchange visit to a French home. The French boy, Didier, had already spent a fortnight at Mike's parents' house in Surrey, and the two of them had got along well. So Mike was looking forward to visiting Didier's home, in the countryside not far from Lyons. He was met at Lyons airport by Didier and his parents, and the two boys instantly resumed their friendship of the summer before. When they got back to the house, late in the afternoon, Didier's mother suggested that they might like to spend the night in 'la cabane dans un arbre' – the rather unwieldy French expression for treehouse. Mike, when he learnt what was being suggested, was beside himself with excitement, especially when he saw that it was a storybook treehouse, in a wonderful gnarled old tree.

They even ate their supper in the treehouse, and then settled down for the night in their sleeping bags. But as darkness fell, there was a terrible wailing from the house, and Didier's mother came tearing down the garden in a state of great distress. 'Didier! Didier!' she cried, her words interspersed with huge racking sobs. 'Didier! C'est Papa. Papa est mort!'

Mike's French was good enough for him to understand the horrible meaning of this, and was not surprised to find that Didier responded to the news with anguish. He climbed down the steps of the treehouse into his mother's arms, and clutching each other for support, they made their way back up the garden, with a bewildered Mike following. Didier's father had looked fine just a couple of hours earlier.

But not only was there no way they could spend the night in 'la cabane'; when Didier's mother had pulled herself together sufficiently to talk without crying, she explained to Mike in English that, regrettably, he would have to go home the following day. She would phone his parents and make the due arrangements, and perhaps sometime in the future he could visit again. Mike then went to bed in the spare room, aware of Didier blubbing himself to sleep next door.

The following morning, he awoke to find that Didier's mum had phoned his mum, and had explained the tragic circumstances necessitating his premature departure so that the family could mourn Papa in private. She had booked Mike on to a flight from Lyons to London later that day. Mike and Didier then ate their breakfast *pains au chocolat*, Didier still demonstrably upset but not quite as devastated as he had been the night before. His mother, meanwhile, busied herself with mundane domestic tasks but occasionally the phone rang, and she would have an emotional conversation with someone, which would set off the tears again.

In the middle of this, Didier's father came down the stairs. Mike looked at him as if he had seen a ghost, which as far as he was concerned, he had. Didier, however, appeared not to have noticed his dad, so Mike thought that he should pass on the good, indeed miraculous news. He clutched his friend's arm. 'Didier,' he said, urgently. 'Regard. C'est ton papa. He's not dead. Il, erm, n'est pas mort.'

Didier looked at Mike, then turned to look at his father. His father was looking at Mike. So was his mother. None of them was the slightest bit amused by the realisation that Mike had, rather spectacularly, grabbed the wrong end of the stick. Instead, Didier's mother sat down at the table and earnestly explained that the Papa who had died was not Didier's father, or grandfather, nor any relative, but 80-year-old Paul VI, the Pope.

9

Boycie, and the Spam

Unlike Mike, and despite studying French until I was eighteen, I was never offered a sniff of an exchange visit to France. I'd have loved to, but the schools I went to simply didn't encourage such things. The closest thing to it was an organised penfriend scheme when I was at primary school, but my penfriend didn't live in France, he lived in Halifax. Still, at the time that seemed like a thrillingly long way away from Southport, and I can still remember the excitement with which, aged ten, in 1972, I opened my first trans-Pennine missive. The excitement faded quickly, however, when I found that my penfriend loved motorbikes and hated football. I mistrusted motorbikes (our 21-year-old next-door neighbour had been killed on one) and I loved football. After one letter each, our penfriendship unsurprisingly fizzled out.

These days, the ease of communication on the Internet has given even the word penfriend an old-fashioned glow, although Eleanor's French teacher, to her credit, did get her class to write to some children at a school in Normandy. And to our family's discredit, we all reacted with unseemly mirth when a reply duly arrived from 12-year-old Marguerite. 'I have the blue eyes and many of the brown hairs,' she wrote. Naturally, Jane and I tried to impress upon Eleanor that her efforts in French might cause at least as much hilarity across the Channel, but we had a good laugh, all the same.

Jane had never been on exchange visits, either, during her schooldays, but her sister Jackie had. Jackie once stayed with a German family near Munich, where every mealtime the father, an enormously fat guy with a bushy moustache, would rapidly finish his own food and then start spearing pieces of sausage and potato on all the other plates, including Jackie's. I love that image, although in fact it's only my second-favourite German mealtime story. Some years ago, a good friend of mine, Mark Sutcliffe, who was running a leisure centre in Warrington, took an under-12s football team on a tour to the Rhineland. These were tough kids from working-class families, most of whom had never been out of England before, and one or two of whom had never been out of Warrington before.

The German town hosting their visit made a huge effort to make them feel welcome, even laying on a sumptuous supper in the ornate town hall. As Mark described it, there was a long trestle table absolutely groaning with cold cuts of meat: thick slices of glistening Black Forest ham and every kind of sausage you could think of; Mettwurst, Bockwurst, Fleischwurst,

Rotwurst, Weisswurst and for all I know, Geoffwhurst. It was a magnificent spread, at which his boys gazed bemusedly. None of them had ever seen anything like it. But Mark had told them that they weren't to tuck in until the town's burgomeister had made a speech. The burgomeister's speech was then translated by an interpreter, an English teacher at the local high school. There was polite applause, followed by a second or two of resounding silence, which was shattered by a boy calling out in a loud, high-pitched and distinctly Warringtonian voice: 'Hey Jonesy, pass the spam!'

That tale makes me shudder to think of the culinary disappointments lying in wait for French kids, in particular, when they come on exchange visits to England. On the other hand, I'm quite sure that not all French mothers plonk down a rich, steaming cassoulet in front of their children every night. Yet when some friends of ours with children at a secondary school in rural Herefordshire were summoned to a meeting by the head of the modern languages department, ahead of a visit by some French kids from Toulouse, he solemnly told the assembled parents that they should avoid giving their French guests fizzy drinks, processed food or flavoured crisps, because back at home theirs was a diet of simple, nutritional fare. This turned out to be a preconception as erroneous as my own adolescent belief – encouraged by the hero of my school textbook, an eager lad called Gerard Vernier – that every French boy drove a *vélomoteur*. Their son's French friend loved crisps of all flavours, wouldn't touch fresh vegetables, formed a deep attachment while in Herefordshire to pork pies, and excitedly took home two bottles of sparkling Vimto for his family to try.

But if he had missed his *maman*'s home-cooking, then

there's every chance that he might have hungrily eyed up some of the local horseflesh. My friend Ian told me once that he went to Brecon horse fair, at which a sturdy young pony was introduced to potential buyers with the promise that he was 'absolutely bomb-proof'. As I knew from our experiences with Zoe, this referred to the pony's calmness in the face of sudden or loud noises. But Ian was amused to hear an old Welsh farmer, standing next to him, muttering dyspeptically: 'Never mind bloody bomb-proof, it's bloody bullet-proof he needs to be.' Several of the most enthusiastic buyers were there, as the old farmer well knew, to service the needs of the French horsemeat market.

That said, I find it amusing that we Brits recoil in such disgust at the notion of eating horses. Where's the moral difference between that and eating cows, sheep or pigs? It's not like we're talking about eating Best Mate, or Desert Orchid, or Mister Ed, just some anonymous nag. But, of course, a bit like cows in India, horses in Britain are revered. As are dogs. We could no sooner sit down to a horse steak than to a dog curry. And Johnny Foreigner does that too. The basic reason why we feel able to poke fun at the French for eating horse, and the Koreans for eating dog, is that we don't. But when you think about every 12 August, when mass slaughter commences on the grouse moors of northern England and Scotland, can we really claim the moral high ground? Not that I want to come over all righteous on the subject. Apart from anything else, righteousness ill suits a man who spent an afternoon beating pheasants out of woods for other men to shoot.

To mark the first day of the grouse-shooting season in 2005, the day known to huntin', shootin' and fishin' types as the Glorious Twelfth, and to grouse as 'Bollocks, Is It Already

That Time of Year Again?', the Radio 4 programme *The Message* decided to discuss the media's coverage of countryside issues. As I had by now been writing my country life column for almost three years, and had just had a book published about my family's move from London to Herefordshire, they thought I might like to be a guest on the programme along with the estimable editor of *Country Life*, Clive Aslet, and Tim Bonner, the publicity director of the Countryside Alliance.

I was already used to being given local platforms to air my views on country living. Even before I wrote the book, my newspaper column had imbued me with a tenuous celebrity in north Herefordshire, which led even to a couple of invitations to open village fêtes. You know you've made it in life when you're asked to open a village fête. Either that or you know that the fête organizers don't have a phone number for Monty Don of *Gardeners' World* or the actor John Challis, Boycie in *Only Fools and Horses*, who are the only two bona fide celebrities living in these parts. I might add, incidentally, that opening a village fête is not necessarily the straightforward operation you might expect. At any rate, I know now, even if I didn't before, that it is impossible to cut a ribbon with a pair of ceremonial garden shears, especially when there is a small crowd looking on, most of them helpless with laughter.

I also know – another of the many, many lessons I have learnt since moving to the English countryside – that the most formidable person in almost any community is the chairman of the local branch of the Women's Institute (not for them the politically correct 'chair', or 'chairperson', still less 'chairwoman', with its unfortunate resemblance to charwoman).

I learnt this the hard way when the secretary of the Ludlow WI contacted me to ask if, in principle, I would be willing to address one of their meetings. When I said that I would, she explained that the chairman would be in touch to determine the title and date of the talk. The call duly came, from a woman whom I subsequently found to be quite charming in person, but whose telephone manner was terrifyingly imperious.

'What fee will you require?' she asked.

I said I had no idea. What fee did the Ludlow WI normally offer?

'Normally something in the order of £25,' she said, briskly.

I said, in what I hoped was not a condescending way, that I couldn't take £25 from the WI. Had she said £250, I suppose that might have been a different matter. But then I had a flash of inspiration. 'How about giving me a cake, instead?'

'A cake?' she said, in exactly the same tone as Dame Edith Evans, as Lady Bracknell in *The Importance of Being Earnest*, once said 'A handbag?' It sounded as if her lorgnettes were rising with her eyebrows.

'Erm, yes,' I said, suddenly unsure of my ground.

There was a stern silence. 'What sort of cake?' she eventually enquired.

'Oh, I don't know. How about, erm, a chocolate cake?'

In my mind's eye, the lorgnettes were now being removed. 'A chocolate cake?'

'Yes.'

'The WI does more than make cakes, you know.'

I realized that she thought me patronising for asking for a cake. I gave silent thanks that I hadn't asked for a pot of damson jam, or apple chutney.

'Oh I know,' I said, wishing that I'd just settled for the twenty-five quid. 'I just . . .'

She cut me off. 'Very well,' she said, which was how I came

to address the Ludlow WI and receive my remuneration in edible form, although not as a single cake, as I'd expected, but a bagful of home-made cakes scrupulously valued at £25. I got a butter madeira cake, a spicy apple cake, a pineapple and cherry cake, a Dundee cake, a lemon cake, an almond cake, and a Bara Brith, a Welsh bread made with mixed fruit, and drove into the night wondering whether I should offer my agent 15 per cent.

However eccentric they must have thought me, the members of the Ludlow WI were all perfectly lovely to me that night, and I had a most convivial evening with them in a church hall. But I remained hopeless at negotiating fees, and so, when a perky production assistant called Sarah promised me a BBC cheque that I calculated would cover very nearly the entire cost of a ploughman's lunch, I agreed to be a panellist on *The Message*. I had dithered mainly because I wasn't sure whether I had enough robust opinions on the subject of the media's countryside coverage. Moreover, Sarah had told me that Clive would be in the Canterbury studio, Tim in the London studio, I'd be in Hereford, and the presenter Jenni Murray would be in Manchester. Round table discussions live on national radio are quite challenging enough without all being at separate round tables.

But in the end I agreed to take part not least because I'd had some traumatic experiences on the radio, and every appearance was a further step towards exorcising the memories. The most bruising experience came when I was talking on the *Johnnie Walker Show* on Radio 2 from our house in London. I was the *Mail on Sunday*'s television critic at the time, and a regular contributor in a slot on Johnnie Walker's show recommending the best things to watch on the telly that night, which could be done from the comfort of my little study. But I had scarcely got into my stride on the day in question when Joseph, then aged three, burst into the room to say, very loudly and insistently, that he needed his bottom wiping.

Unable to contain his amusement, Johnnie said that I perhaps ought to attend to my child's pressing lavatorial needs before treating Radio 2 listeners to my television recommendations. I came off the phone a few minutes later convinced that my broadcasting career, such as it was, had been flushed down the pan no less than Joseph's toilet paper, and spent the next few days in a state of great agitation, lest the snippet be broadcast again for the nation to laugh at on the review programme *Pick of the Week*. It wasn't, thank God. But my embarrassment was in no way diminished by a friend who said he happened to have been listening to Radio 2 in his car when I came on, and Joseph's demand for bottom-wiping assistance had nearly caused him to swerve off the A565.

That wasn't all. On the very day that *Tales of the Country* was published, I was interviewed by Sandi Toksvig on the London radio station LBC. Before we started talking about my book, she happened to ask me whether I had ever been to Disneyland Paris. I said that I had, with my wife and three kids when our third child was only six weeks old, and that it had been horrible. It peed with rain for the entire time we were there, and we lost our middle child (Joseph again) for ten agonising minutes, a Kafka nightmare of a trauma because although we had bought Joe a waterproof yellow poncho with Mickey Mouse on the back, which in an ordinary crowd might have made him easy to spot, every other child was wearing one too. And quite aside from all that, I told Sandi Toksvig, I could never really shake off the notion that behind every beaming Mickey and Minnie and Pluto mask there was a gloomy

Frenchman, probably reflecting on the finer points of existentialism or at the very least on the films of Jean-Luc Godard. Only America gets Disney right, I asserted, because at least in Florida or California you can be reasonably sure that behind every vacant plastic grin there is a vacant plastic grin.

Anyway, towards the end of this little rant I realized that perhaps I was saying something not altogether appropriate, since Sandi's bright smile had given way to a slight frown. 'Right,' she said, when I'd finished. 'We'll talk some more with Brian Viner in a moment, but now for our competition, to win a weekend for four at Disneyland Paris, courtesy of the Walt Disney Company.' Like the gaffe-prone character on *The Fast Show*, I thought that I should probably offer to get my coat.

10

Madge, and the Herbs

When I turned up at the BBC's studio in Hereford for *The Message*, it turned out that I had more opinions than I'd thought about the media's coverage of countryside issues. Indeed, I found myself being even more bullish than Tim Bonner, who reckoned that country matters were pretty well represented. My own view, once I was required to have one, was that there is an acute media bias towards London and the urban south-east at the expense of the countryside, and for that matter at the expense of more or less everywhere. Nothing summed this up, I said bolshily, more than the disproportionate number of column inches devoted to Ken Livingstone's congestion charge in the capital. The appalling inadequacy of public-transport provision in the sticks, by contrast, got scarcely any attention whatever. That it was a story affecting relatively few people didn't make it any less of a story, I said. Yet even in *The Archers*, which on the whole did a decent job of rasing consciousness of countryside concerns, everyone seemed to get, without any trouble at all, to wherever they wanted to go.

I was busking it dangerously there, in fact, because unlike my dear wife I never listened to The Archers. This had got me into trouble before, with Maurice O'Grady before his retirement from full-time pest control. Maurice considered it downright irresponsible to live in north Herefordshire and not listen to *The Archers*.

He had come round one day with a couple of traps for Holly and Bramble, the rabbits, who had escaped from their hutch after one of the children accidentally left the door open, and who were occasionally spotted by men with guns on the shoot. We hadn't phoned Maurice to tell him about the missing rabbits; he'd just found out. The countryside, we had discovered, was amazing like that. If we looked westwards through our living-room window we could see for forty miles without setting eyes on a single other house, yet gossip and rumour and titbits of information spread like wildfire. It turned out that Maurice had heard from our occasional gardener, Tom, about the rabbits going AWOL. They were members of the same shooting club. Maurice and Tom, that is, not the rabbits.

So Joseph put a carrot in one of the traps and left it on the bottom lawn overnight. And the next morning, there was Bramble. Holly was still nowhere to be seen, but when Maurice next came round he was amazed that we'd caught even one so quickly. 'If it'd been me setting that trap,' he said, 'I wouldn't have caught your rabbit for weeks. But your boy gets her first time.' Naturally, Joseph was thrilled. We started calling him 'Trapper Joe' and wondered whether there might be anywhere in Leominster where we could buy him a raccoon-fur hat.

When Maurice, who favoured the flat cap, dropped in to pick up the traps, we gave him a cup of coffee and talked infestation, as you do with a pest control specialist. A few years earlier, he told us, there had been a woolly bear epidemic in Herefordshire. We were agog, until he explained that woolly bear was the name given to the larvae of the carpet beetle. 'And it only eats natural fibres,' he added, with what sounded like admiration. He was less admiring of a badger in the neighbour-hood that had made a terrible mess of several gardens. I asked how he planned to deal with it. 'Badgers are protected,' he replied, sadly. 'Didn't you know that David was fined £400 with £200 costs for killing a badger?' Jane nodded solemnly, while I looked confused and asked who David was. David Archer from *The Archers*, she told me, in a tone that you might use towards a young child who had asked who the Queen was, or who Jesus was. Maurice, meanwhile, looked at me in absolute amazement. 'You don't listen to *The Archers*?' he said, incredulously. I fessed up.

So had he been listening to me on *The Message*, he would have known that I was bluffing. For all I knew there had been a story that very week about the unreliable bus service through Ambridge. But nobody took issue with me. Coincidentally, although not unpredictably, our discussion had itself been introduced with the theme tune of *The Archers*, which, in my best stab at an authoritative Radio 4 voice, I said was sig-nificant, because it was surely an indictment of newspapers and television news that the only regular in-depth coverage of certain rural issues was provided by a radio soap opera.

Two major concerns in north Herefordshire, I added, both tackled squarely by *The Archers* but only fitfully by the press, were bovine tuberculosis, said to be carried and spread by badgers, and industrial-scale strawberry farming. I had my own views on strawberry farming, in more ways than one, because from our house we could clearly see the acres of polytunnels under which the strawberries were grown to satisfy Britain's regrettable demand for year-round supply. A local farmer called John Davies had become Europe's largest strawberry producer by controversially shrouding the land-scape in plastic and importing cheap Eastern European labour to do his picking.

In fact, Jane had recently picked up two of his employees, a man and a woman in their early twenties, who were hitchhiking on the A49 from Leominster to Hereford. She knew that I wasn't hugely in favour of her picking up hitchhikers, but then if she wasn't by nature a kind, helpful person and a sucker for helping out those whom life has left by the side of the road then I probably wouldn't have married her, and more to the point, she probably wouldn't have married me.

Anyway, at the moment she pulled over she was listening to an item on Radio 4's *The World This Weekend* about the Polish economy, which was a remarkable coincidence because the young couple turned out to be a pair of economic migrants from Poland. 'I think this is Polish foreign minister on your radio,' said the man, in wide-eyed astonishment, as he settled into the passenger seat. The three of them then listened in rapt attention to the rest of the item, which, according to Jane, was one of the more curious situations in which she had found herself on the A49. When it had finished they talked about strawberry-picking. They told Jane that they were used to hard work but that it was much harder than they had expected, and that they were homesick and utterly miserable. She got the feeling that if the Polish foreign minister had been speaking in his native language, they might both have burst into tears.

So I had a genuine opinion on strawberries, but on bovine TB, by contrast, I had no thoughts whatsoever, so I phoned a farmer friend, Tim, to ask him his. Tim told me that the only regular media coverage the subject got was the odd forty-five-second slot on *Midlands Today*. He also complained that when the issue did get aired there was always an articulate, media-savvy spokesperson for badger conservation groups making rhetorical mincemeat of a ranting farmer such as him. And when it wasn't ranting farmers representing agricultural interests in the media, he added, it was professors with no practical experience of farming.

On the radio I shamelessly made Tim's opinions mine, although I forgot to pass on his teasing parting shot. 'Less than 2 per cent of the population work in agriculture, but everyone has a stake in it. What I always say is that people shouldn't complain about farmers with their mouths full.'

It's true enough, and the panic over bird flu, in the autumn of 2005, was another example of a general hypocrisy towards the countryside. Had the media been predicting merely a rural blight, reporting and opinion-airing would not have been half as extensive. But hell, this was something which could even kill people in our cities! So the thing got saturation coverage.

As you can see, my relatively brief domicile in the country-side has made a bitter man of me. But actually, the subject of bird flu is interesting. What became of that killer pandemic, considered by some of our most responsible journals to pose a danger to humanity practically on the scale of a nuclear holocaust? 'It's coming' was one banner headline at the height of the scare, and a year later, when it struck poor old Bernard Matthews, or at any rate his turkeys, you could almost sense an air of satisfaction in the media that it had, as predicted, come.

But whatever happened to the disease that some doom-mongers expected to kill up to a quarter of the population? As the estimable Simon Jenkins wrote in *The Guardian* on 14 February 2007, a phenomenon even scarier and more dangerous than bird flu is mad publicity disease.

Still, as a professional newspaperman I should probably not accuse the press of whipping up hysteria, nor, for that matter, should I have agreed with a theory floated by my brother-in-law Tony while he was staying with us over Christmas 2005. Yet I knew exactly what he meant.

Tony had volunteered to take charge of building and maintaining the open fires, which were a vital source of heat in the Grange's high-ceilinged rooms. He wandered into the kitchen one morning after taking what seemed to have been an inordinately long time to lay the fire in the living room. 'Have you ever noticed,' he ventured, 'that newspapers are never more interesting than when you're using them to make a fire?'

Tony was referring to the near-impossibility of scrunching up even a month-old paper without an article suddenly catching your eye. It might even be one that you had glanced at a month earlier and decided not to read, but now, sitting cross-legged on the floor with coal dust all over your hands, it seems imperative to read every word.

The accuracy of this theory struck me a few days later while I was mucking out the chickens, a task that required the removal of a layer of poo-encrusted newspaper. Suddenly, beneath the collective doings of our Warrens, Marans and Cream Legbars, I spotted an interview with George Clooney that I simply had to read. I stood there in the chicken run, on a chilly winter's day, and read the Clooney interview from beginning to end, guessing at the few words obliterated by particularly adhesive bits of chicken shit. Only afterwards did it occur to me how ridiculous this was, trying to read a paper that had passed through my hands several days earlier in pristine condition but had since been deployed as a lavatory for poultry. And that's when I realized that human beings, in many ways, are at least as stupid as chickens, a notion that the cartoonist in the *Daily Telegraph* seemed to be exploring when he drew a picture of one Neanderthal-looking man asking another whether he was worried about bird flu. 'No,' came the reply. "Cos I'm a bloke, aren't I?'

Even in the wake of the Matthews rumpus it seemed to me that the joke was on those who took avian flu too seriously, not those who were ignorant of its dangers. By then we had befriended a hugely engaging man called Stuart Mee, who with his father and brother ran one of England's most reputable, organic, free-range poultry farms just a couple of miles along the road from us. If ever there was a man who ought to be worried about the devastating likely impact of a disease carried and spread by chickens, that man was Stuart. Yet he was far more worried about the threat to his business posed by a hungry fox. Indeed, I was once with him when Rod, his dad, suggested that they upgrade the lighting system to discourage nocturnal visits, because a fox could easily cause £20,000-worth of damage in a night. It seemed remarkable that such a modern, well-run business could be so vulnerable to a peckish predator, yet Stuart told me that nothing, not even electrical fencing, could be wholly relied upon to keep the chickens safe. But no fox would ever attack in daylight, which powerful lighting would replicate.

Whatever, when people asked me whether, as the owner of a small flock of chickens, I was worried about bird flu, my answer was that I would start to worry when my friend Stuart did.

There was no panic, either, at the Wernlas Collection, the rare-breeds centre in Shropshire which sells upwards of 8,000 birds a year and where we had bought our more exotic hens for sums that caused Owen, supping in the King's Head when he heard, to laugh so much that he practically burst a blood vessel. When I phoned the owner of the Wernlas Collection at the height of the scare he told me that although he was taking it all very seriously, his health was more endangered by the possibility of damaging his back when lifting up the European Union directive on controlling avian influenza. It's a formidably hefty document, apparently.

He added that the threat of bird flu needed to be kept in perspective, which the papers had notably failed to do. He stopped short of suggesting that the press had been deliberately alarmist because it would sell more newspapers, but pointed out that bird flu was nothing new. It had been responsible for ninety-odd human deaths since 1988, which, while very bad news indeed for the ninety-odd, did not suggest that the world was about to be hit by a twenty-first century version of the Black Death. On the other hand, I suppose there was a point at which the Black Death, too, had caused only ninety deaths. Or just one, for that matter. Who was the first person to die of the Black Death? If I were to ask my children they would turn for the answer to the great Google, all-seeing and all-knowing, although I think even He might struggle.

I digress. The fact remains that most media organisations are inclined, from time to time, to over-egg the health scare pudding. That might be a clumsy metaphor, but at least it involves eggs, and I think you'll agree that it's rather satisfying to get egg metaphors into a discussion of bird flu. And looking back now to early 2006 and early 2007, there seems little doubt that the bird flu pudding was comprehensively over-egged. However, as a small gesture of solidarity with my birds, I did try not to line the henhouse with any front pages containing any stories about the disease. It would have seemed insensitive. And apart from anything else I reckoned that, as females given to occasional bouts of broodiness, they would far rather sit on George Clooney.

Now there's an A-list celebrity by any standards. The level of my own celebrity, as we have seen, was more in the environs of Z. And that only in north Herefordshire. On a good day. But it was nonetheless true that along with the request to talk on radio programmes such as *The Message*, invitations to open things such as the summer fête where I had struggled to cut the ribbon with the shears, speak at things, present things and judge things did start to plop, sporadically, on to the doormat.

Some of these invitations were odder than others. In August 2006 I got a call from a woman who asked if I would like to cut the first sod at the new Ludlow eco-park. 'A sod?' I said, probably sounding a little like the chairman of the WI on being asked for a fee in the form of a cake. I also wondered what an eco-park was, but didn't quite dare to ask. 'Yes, a sod,' said the cheerful woman at the other end of the phone. It turned out

that the sod-cutting ceremony was to be the culmination of
the 'magnalonga', a walk inspired by an annual event in
Ludlow's twin town of San Pietro, near Verona in Italy. The
idea is that the walkers stop every now and then at points
along the way, where they sample local food and drink. In 2006
the magnalonga was to finish at the eco-park, basically an
environmentally friendly business park, where I was to cut
the sod.

I turned up at the appointed hour, and tucked into some
of the local produce without the excuse of having participated
in the six-mile magnalonga. After a while, replete not only
with local raspberries, Little Hereford cheese and Butford
Farm cider but also a sense of my own importance, I got ready
for my big moment. I had expected to deliver a little speech
while standing with my foot on the ceremonial spade, and was
going to say that I hoped the honour of digging the first sod
might entitle me to consider myself the honorary 'First Sod'
of Ludlow.

That, I had felt sure, would get a nice titter and perhaps even
a round of applause. But with no microphone, and participants
in the magnalonga arriving in dribs and drabs, it quickly
became clear that my First Sod joke would be lost on the
breeze. Moreover, nobody was the slightest bit interested in
some fool digging a small square of turf, not when they'd just
walked up a few hills and worked up a serious thirst. I wasn't
even the only one cutting the sod. The Mayor of Ludlow had
also been invited, and had arrived looking most distinguished
in his splendid and historic ceremonial robes, which was how it
came to pass that one man looking like an eighteenth-century
alderman, and another man in faded jeans, stood looking
faintly bemused in a large field with a foot each on a spade,

while the only vague expression of interest came from a boy of about ten, who took our photograph with a disposable camera. I wasn't at all sure who the boy was. Eventually I concluded that, since he clearly wasn't with the *Shropshire Star*, he was probably with the Mayor.

Still, I was quite happy that the event was low-key. I didn't mind at all not being given an opportunity to speak, although it's always wise to be prepared on these occasions, as I tried to be on the occasion of the Red Carpet Awards, another nod to my entrance into the ranks of Z-list celebrity following the publication of *Tales of the Country*. And that was swiftly followed by an invitation to judge cider and perry, at the good old Three Counties Show in Malvern.

Let me tell you first about the 2005 Red Carpet Awards, dished out for particularly fine examples of carpet-related journalism. In truth, I owed my invitation entirely to the fact that my good friend Rupert Anton, with whom I had been at university and who had been the only person I knew within a fifty-mile radius when we moved to Herefordshire, was the sales and marketing director of the Carpet Foundation, an association of the country's major carpet manufacturers. Rupert, who organized and ran the Red Carpet Awards with singular diligence and enthusiasm, lived in Pudleston, a small village a couple of miles north of Docklow, and with which Docklow enjoyed a kind of umbilical attachment, in that we had a pub, which they didn't, and they had a village hall, which we didn't.

Despite being a tiny place, Pudleston was also, coincidentally, the home to several other movers and shakers in carpets, or movers and Shake-'n'-Vac-ers as I like to think of them. This was because Kidderminster, the nerve centre of the carpet industry, was not too far away.

Anyway, Rupert managed to gather a tremendously distinguished panel of judges for his awards, including the celebrated interior designer Nina Campbell, a magnificently imperious woman who let slip, without being remotely embarrassed when corrected, that she thought Kidderminster was somewhere in the north of England, 'like Carlisle'.

Among the other judges were the fabulously successful fabric and wallpaper entrepreneur Cath Kidston, the actress and former Bond girl Fiona Fullerton and the former editor of the *Daily Express*, Sir Nicholas Lloyd. I wasn't entirely sure what I was doing alongside them but it was nice to be asked. However, they had all done the job before and so knew their weaves from their tufts. I did not. But at least I knew about words. So I decided that if the opportunity arose, I would make an impassioned (if tongue-in-cheek) speech about how the Carpet Foundation needed to give the very word 'carpet' a positive spin, to counter its use in a whole load of negative metaphors, among them 'carpet-bombing', 'carpetbagging', 'to be swept under the carpet' and 'to receive a carpeting'. Not to mention carpet beetle, to which Maurice O'Grady had introduced us. If you think about it, it seems rather unfair that the poor old carpet, which has done so much to keep us warm and comfortable in our homes over the years, should be so abused.

It was probably for the best that the opportunity did not, in fact, arise. The formidable Nina Campbell would almost certainly have told me to sit down. We ended up having an extremely convivial lunch at a smart restaurant in central London, and I left knowing rather a lot more about carpets than when I arrived, my favourite titbit of information being that whenever the Carpet Foundation invites a comedian to speak at the actual awards ceremony, there is always a discreet sweepstake on how long it will take him to make a 'shag' joke. It's rarely more than twenty seconds, apparently.

As for the cider and perry competition at the Three Counties Show, despite my gradually burgeoning knowledge about wine, I was again very much a clueless amateur among highly educated professionals, keenly aware of my ignorance of the finer or even the blunter points of cider-making. My two fellow judges were a chap called Martin Rich, a cider-maker from Somerset, and Geoff Morris, who at the time ran an endearingly eccentric shop in Leominster specialising, for some reason I never managed to work out, in the wines of England and Greece, as well as beer and, of course, cider. In his shop one day I had introduced myself to Geoff as the chap he would be doing the judging with, and he told me earnestly that the last time he'd done it, some of the cider he tasted was a little bit 'mouse', some was a bit 'rope', some was acetic, and some was high on indoles. He clearly expected me to know what he was on about, but as there was nothing in my bible, Jancis Robinson's *Wine Course*, about mice or rope, I really didn't have a clue what he meant. So I laughed nervously and said that I wouldn't know a cider that was high on indoles from one that was high on LSD. It was his turn to laugh nervously.

A few weeks later, in a huge marquee at the Three Counties Show preparing to sample a bewildering array of alcoholic drinks, Geoff told me that he had once been a chemistry teacher. This gave me a slight funny turn. You'll recall that in *The Fall and Rise of Reginald Perrin*, the great Leonard Rossiter as Reggie used to visualise a marauding hippopotamus every time his mother-in-law was mentioned. Whenever I meet a chemistry teacher I get a similarly vivid and disconcerting picture of a laminated Periodic Table, a vision not exorcized, in fact possibly exacerbated, by my ceremonial burning of the horrible thing following my O levels.

But Geoff did not ask me any difficult questions about potassium permanganate, which is still my secret dread when I meet chemistry teachers, or even ex-chemistry teachers, despite the fact that I've reached my mid-forties. It is odd, the way we are sometimes reduced to our schoolboy or schoolgirl selves. In the mid-1990s, when I was writing for the *Mail on Sunday*, I was invited to address the annual dinner of my grammar school old boys' association, a function attended by several of the teachers who had once put the fear of God into me, not least the former headmaster, Geoffrey Dixon.

Mr Dixon – I could never in a million years have called him Geoffrey, still less Geoff – was by then well into his eighties, yet to me he looked exactly the same as he had two decades earlier when I was an impressionable fourth-former, and he a remote figure of almost godlike stature and unimpeachable authority. Yet here we were, sitting side by side at the top table eating overcooked beef, and suddenly my years of experience as a journalist, and my status as a husband and father, simply melted away. I felt throughout the dinner as if it were only a matter of time before another teacher, somewhere else in the room, bellowed: 'Viner, what the hell are you doing sitting next to the headmaster! Get over here, boy, and don't be so damned impertinent!'

But, of course, Geoff Morris (whom I was quite happy to call Geoff) did not ask me anything about potassium perman-ganate. Instead, he explained with great patience how exactly cider is made, information which I tried hard to absorb while also wondering how I was going to reach the fifth and last judging category (bottle-conditioned ciders and perries) without falling off my stool. Once again I left with more knowledge than I'd arrived with, even if the main two things I learnt were that, when you sample more than sixty ciders and perries on a warm day, you a) need someone to drive you home afterwards, and b) need a long lie-down when you get there, ideally with a cold compress on your forehead. Still, despite my increasingly woozy state, and despite the fact that Geoff had painstakingly explained to me that assessing the quality of cider is all about the pH level of your saliva, I had been gratified to find that, by and large, the stuff I liked was also the stuff that he and Martin liked. Oddly enough that had been the case with Cath Kidston, Nina Campbell and my fellow Red Carpet judges too. Sometimes in life, I have found, naive enthusiasm serves you just as well as sharp-eyed expertise.

The other interesting side-effect of having written about our experiences in Herefordshire was that, from time to time, letters arrived from readers keen either to upbraid me or compliment me. I once read something Laurence Olivier used to tell his acting protégés, to the effect that if they didn't sniff their bouquets too hard, then the brickbats wouldn't hurt too much. In other words, ignore the praise; that way it's easier to ignore the abuse.

It's sound advice, but of course much easier said than done: I don't seem to remember Olivier being exactly oblivious to all the flattery and adulation he received. Moreover, there is a third category: some people send bouquets, some send brickbats, but some send both at the same time, what you might call bouqbats, or better still, briquets.

The letter I'd had from Wanda Renshaw, the woman who enjoyed my book but considered me a prima donna for writing it in long chapters, was one example of this phenomenon.

Another was a letter I got from a man I'll call Mr Hall. He started off by saying how much he'd enjoyed my book, and how much it had made him laugh, so I settled down with a smile to read the rest of it. It's always nice to have your ego stroked, especially on a cold January morning, as this was. It quickly became clear, though, that stroking my ego was not Mr Hall's intention. He had some grievances to get off his chest, the most nagging of which concerned our decision to send our children not to the primary school nearest to our house, three miles or so away, but to another primary school, eleven miles away. It was no wonder, he thundered, that rural communities were losing facilities such as schools and shops. People like me were to blame, wanting – this was his phrase – to live 'in the country without being of the country'. His letter got nastier and nastier, as if in the process of writing it he got increasingly worked up. As in the case of Mrs Renshaw, I could only guess at the kind of letter he might have written if my book hadn't made him laugh so much.

I replied straight away. If you don't reply to unpleasant letters immediately, I have discovered from painful experience, then you find yourself composing responses at all hours of day and night, when your mind should be on other matters. 'Dear Mr Hall, thank you for your letter of 18 January' is not what you want to be thinking when you are helping your kids with their homework, for example, still less when you are enjoying a romantic moment with your wife. You can get into trouble if you start muttering something about a Mr Hall. No, better to get the thing written and dispatched, then you can forget about it.

I reiterated what I had in fact written in the book, if he'd taken the trouble to read it carefully enough, which was that we looked at the nearby primary school and would very much have liked to send the kids there, not least for our own convenience, but having taken them out of a large urban school in London, we felt strongly that it would intensify their feelings of dislocation suddenly to find themselves at a tiny village primary with only sixty pupils and a span of ages in each class. Therefore we looked for somewhere bigger, and were lucky enough to find a fine school a bit further away, another state primary, with places available. They had been extremely happy there, I added, not that I felt compelled to justify our educational choices to him. But then that is the problem when you write about your life; you positively invite judgemental-ism. And you can't have your cake and eat it. If you write a newspaper column about the way you live your life, and subsequently a couple of books, then you can't expect people not to make judgements about you. It's an occupational hazard.

Shortly after receiving the letter from Mr Hall – and there is a connection – I went with Jane and the kids to the Assembly Rooms in Ludlow to see the acclaimed film *March of the Penguins*. Afterwards, I couldn't really understand what all the acclaim was about – the film was fine enough, but it didn't seem to me any better than any old *Survival Special* or *Wildlife on One*. All the same, I realized that it was quite nice for the family to be forced to sit through a wildlife documentary from beginning to end, instead of us all gradually drifting off to make a cup of tea, or to phone a friend. But I hated Morgan Freeman's commentary, which was absurdly sugary and actu-ally rather insulting to those of us who know that penguins don't really fall in love, at least not with a forty-piece orchestra in attendance.

Which reminds me, just to go off on a tangent from what is

already a tangent, of a lovely story about Alfred Hitchcock, who objected, while he was making the film *Lifeboat*, to the rather intrusive background music. He therefore sent a stiff note to the studio's head of music, caustically asking where he thought all that orchestral music might be coming from in the middle of the ocean. The head of music read the note, screwed it up, and said to the messenger: 'You can tell Mr Hitchcock that I'll explain why there might be music in the middle of the ocean if he explains why there might be a camera.' Touché, I think is the word.

To return to *March of the Penguins* and the saccharine voiceover, Morgan Freeman's penguins didn't die, they simply 'faded away'. And sex was another unmentionable. I found myself eager to know where the male penguin's penis was, and I knew that David Attenborough would have given it to me straight. Nevertheless, it was sweet to see how much care penguins took of their young, without any other penguins bawling them out for making the wrong educational choices, come to think of it; although I mention the Assembly Rooms in connection with Mr Hall's angry letter not for that reason, but because he also took me to task for something I had written about our occasional family visits to the cinema in Worcester, twenty-odd miles from our house. Was I not aware, he raged, that there were cinemas in Hereford and Tenbury, much closer to where we lived? The more I thought about Mr Hall's letter, the more I reckoned he might be slightly deranged. Why should it matter to him where we go to the cinema? Besides, as it happened, the Assembly Rooms in Ludlow was our favourite place to see films. There's an extremely genteel man selling ice creams in the auditorium: it's frightfully civilized.

Happily, most of the letters I got from people who had read

about my experiences in Herefordshire were friendly ones, none more so than one from a 91-year-old woman called Madge Hooper, who said that she felt a kinship with us as incomers, because she had been an incomer herself, albeit in 1939. There was something so spirited about her letter that I knew I ought to meet her. Apart from anything else, she gave me her e-mail address, and any nonagenarian who gives you her e-mail address has to be worth meeting.

I called her, and she invited me over to her home in the nearby village of Stoke Lacy, for a late-morning sherry. She did not disappoint. I quickly realized that Madge was one of those extraordinary old people whose zest for life is undiminished by great age and increasing infirmity. To celebrate her ninetieth birthday, she told me, she had taken a ride from Worcester racecourse to Eastnor Castle near Ledbury, in a hot-air balloon. She had marked her eightieth by abseiling in the Brecon Beacons.

Madge had grown up on the Gower peninsula and remembered seeing a German Zeppelin flying over during the First World War, presumably on its way to, or from, a bombing raid on the docks in Cardiff. By the time of the Second World War she was married and living in Stoke Lacy.

'We recognized aircraft by sound,' she told me. 'That was how we could tell whether it was one of theirs or one of ours, by the sound of its engine. And one day, when I was mowing the lawn, I heard one of theirs. I suppose it was coming back from bombing Coventry or Birmingham, and had wandered off course. Not very cleverly, I took shelter under a young red may tree, which wouldn't have protected me from a bowl of porridge.'

A little later there was a distant explosion, which shook the windows of her house. It turned out that the Luftwaffe bomber had jettisoned its ammunition before the long journey back to Germany. Mercifully, the bombs dropped on farmland, not on Stoke Lacy itself, although there was still a good deal of local consternation when it was discovered that a cow had been blown high into the branches of a tree.

By then, Madge was a professional herb farmer. As a girl she had been greatly inspired by a book her father brought home one day, containing advice, obviously assembled by a proto-Hugh Fearnley-Whittingstall, on how to take culinary advantage of the meadows and hedgerows. So in 1935, when she was twenty, Madge enrolled on a four-year course taught near Sevenoaks in Kent by one of the pioneers of herb-gardening, Dorothy Hewer. Miss Hewer came from a distinguished medical family – Madge told me that her father was the royal obstetrician who in 1926 delivered the future Queen Elizabeth II – but presumably the conventions of the times dictated that she should do something more ladylike. She was also deaf, with a booming basso-profundo voice, and Madge put down her schooner of sherry to give me a memorable impression. 'She took six students a year, all girls of course, and worked us tirelessly, mostly harvesting peppermint and lavender to make oil. She used to come into the shed and say "Girls, something lamentable has happened." That was her favourite word, lamentable, although it was never anything very dire.'

Most of Madge's fellow students were simply filling in time before getting married, but for her, herb-growing became a vocation. In 1939, she and her husband rented Stoke House in Stoke Lacy, and started growing commercially. During the war they had to follow directives issued by the Ministry of

Agriculture – or 'the Ministry of Ag', as Madge called it – and grow only herbs required to help the war effort. But they developed a useful sideline sending pot pourri to America. Afterwards, they built up a flourishing business, which she ran on her own after she and her husband separated in 1952, and in 1954 she bought Stoke House – which she'd been renting from another well-connected Dorothy, Dorothy Morgan of the Morgan Cars dynasty – for £70 a year. The property came with six acres and cost her £1,400. Twenty years later she sold up and built herself a bungalow in the grounds, which was where I visited her. She told me that she had closed the herb business in 1992, when she was a stripling of 77. But her books on herb-growing are still considered to be definitive; Miss Hewer would have been proud of her protegée.

I love talking to people like Madge. They make local history come alive. She told me that when she arrived in Stoke Lacy, the entire village belonged to the Morgan family. Dorothy Morgan's father and grandfather had, between them, been rectors in the village for more than fifty years, and her brother Harry had built up the car-manufacturing business. Stoke House had been built for Dorothy on Flower Show Meadow, the site of a much-loved annual staple of the Herefordshire social calendar. 'Had the house not been for a Morgan daughter,' said Madge, 'I expect the locals would have torn it apart brick by brick. Another sherry?'

I left feeling that I had made a new friend, despite an age gap of nigh on half a century. It was further proof of the theory that to find kindred spirits when you move from the city to the country, it's sometimes necessary to look beyond your own generation. I'd had a similar feeling in June 2004 on the sixtieth anniversary of the Normandy Landings, when we opened the door to find an 82-year-old woman called Sylvia Coigley on the doorstep.

It turned out that Sylvia had been in the King's Head asking if anyone knew where I lived. Owen had cheerfully given her directions, possibly reasoning that she didn't look like someone who was bent on doing me harm, although knowing Owen, he would have readily dispensed the same information to a geezer in a balaclava carrying a shotgun. On which subject, a friend of mine – now quite a famous man, as it happens, although this was long before he became a celebrity – once heard that a stranger had been in his local pub asking where he lived. It turned out that the stranger was a hitman, engaged by my friend's lover's estranged husband. Fortunately, nobody in the pub gave him what he wanted, just discreetly phoned my friend and told him there was an exceedingly dodgy-looking character on his trail.

There was nothing dodgy-looking about Sylvia, who was short, immaculately dressed and utterly charming. She apologised profusely for interrupting our Sunday afternoon, but explained that she had lived in Docklow as a girl, and had therefore been reading my newspaper columns with great interest. As she was passing, she had decided to look me up.

The reason she was passing was that she had been to Berrington Hall, a stately pile between Leominster and Ludlow, for a ceremony to mark the D-Day anniversary. She had spent several years at Berrington as a nurse with the Red Cross, but left on the morning of D-Day itself – 6 June 1944 – to take up a job at St Thomas's Hospital in London. It was there that she met her husband, a doctor, and she told me that they were still happily married, living just outside Stratford-upon-Avon.

Is it just me who gets bored when some elderly members of my own family – notably Jane's uncle Gerald – start sharing their wartime memories, but captivated when others do so? I could have listened to Sylvia all afternoon, not because her experiences had been especially exciting, but because she, just like Madge Hooper, related them so vividly. She was recruited in Corn Square, Leominster, by the local Red Cross commandant, a woman she remembered only as Mrs Herbert Taylor, 'who had the smallest waist I've ever seen'.

Berrington Hall was the home of Lord and Lady Cawley who, undeterred by the fact that their house had been turned into a hospital, still dressed for dinner every night. Sylvia told me that Lady Cawley, who took charge of the nurses, was a fierce disciplinarian. 'She had to be. The army was in Leominster, the RAF was at Shobdon, and we were a gaggle of 18- and 19-year-old girls. We had a fine old time.'

Then the Americans arrived at Berrington. 'I felt so sorry for Lord and Lady Cawley,' Sylvia said. 'They loved their park and it got so churned up. But I liked having the Americans there. I became friendly with an officer who used to whistle up his jeep for me when I walked out of the gates, and instead of having to cycle home through Hamnish, I was given a lift.' If Sylvia had been as attractive and spirited then as she was by the time I met her, I should think that the Yanks were lining up to drive her home. Whether she and her nice officer stopped for any shenanigans on the way, she didn't say. Perhaps they took a little detour over the nearby border into Worcestershire. In which case I like to think that my friend John, who spent the war years dogging in Ombersley, might have been peeping.

11

Jane, and the Engine

John's memories of wartime – such as his sexual inauguration in Queen Victoria's funeral coach – were very different from those of Sylvia Coigley and Madge Hooper, but together they presented a fascinating picture of those years. The next time I went to Corn Square I could almost visualize the tiny-waisted Mrs Herbert Taylor recruiting girls – or more likely 'gels' – for the Red Cross. But it wasn't just the historical insight that our older friends gave us, it was also a useful perspective on our own lives.

Jim and Shelagh Snell invited us round for a drink one evening, and introduced us to some contemporaries of theirs called John and Mary who lived, like Madge, in Stoke Lacy.

I had been in London earlier that day, not long after the 7 July bombings of the London Underground, and I happened to mention how uneasy I had felt standing on a crowded Bakerloo Line train at rush hour, especially when the train lurched to a halt and, without the usual weary explanation from the driver, remained stationary in the tunnel for six minutes.

I knew, really, how irrational it was to be scared. On 12 September 2001 – the day after the terrorist attacks in America – I had been on a flight from Edinburgh to London and, absurdly, convinced myself that the Asian man alongside me was about to hijack the plane. As we took off he seemed nervous and was muttering a prayer, so I clutched a pen and prepared to drive it into his eye the second he stood up. But eventually we fell into polite conversation and it turned out that he was just a nervous flyer, and, of course, he, like me, had been greatly rattled by the events of the day before. He was no more a terrorist than I was. Yet the colour of his skin, alarmingly, had helped me to add two and two and make seven, and if he'd decided to go to the toilet, the poor man would have got my ballpoint in his eye.

I also recalled a story sent to me in 2003 by a reader of my newspaper column, Derek Hanlin. I had written about a hilarious misunderstanding which arose when the American secret services mistook a distillery on the remote Scottish island of Islay for a bomb factory. The whisky-making procedure is not unlike that used to make bombs, and the distillery's website had got the Americans decidedly hot under the collar. Mr Hanlin then wrote in to say that a few months earlier he had been working for his local authority, Rhondda Cynon Taff Borough Council, in South Wales, cutting grass outside the Royal Mint at Llantrisant. It was the job of one of his colleagues, a lad of eighteen, to blow the cut grass off the pavement, which he did with a three-foot tube attached to a blower strapped to his back. Needless to say, the lad was horrified suddenly to find himself surrounded by security guards and growling dogs; he had been spotted on the CCTV cameras and mistaken for a terrorist with a rocket-launcher.

So I knew, as I stood on the crowded tube, that it was paranoid of me to assume an imminent terrorist attack. And yet that didn't stop me getting more and more anxious as the minutes ticked by in the tunnel. At the Snells, everyone listened politely to my story, but then John recalled travelling on a main-line train with his mother, when he was a boy during the Second World War. The Luftwaffe had bombed the track ahead and the train was delayed for six hours while the track was repaired. Nobody complained, they just gave thanks that the bomb had landed ahead of the train and not on it. John didn't tell this story in the spirit of 'think yourself lucky, sonny, because when I was a lad . . .' but it had pretty much the same effect, again reinforcing how instructive it can be to have friends of pensionable age.

But we had also made some dear friends of our own age, I'm pleased to say, not least Jane, the woman who had advised our son Joe that a dominatrix is someone very good at dominoes, and Avril, whose son Milo confusingly shared a name with our dog, plus their respective partners, James and Ian. My Jane, the other Jane and Avril became regular dog-walking buddies, together with Joanna, whose husband Steve had woken up one night to find the family hamster, Brains, on his bottom. And rare was the day that Jane did not return with this or some other memorable story about one of them, or about their partners, or one of their children. It became clear, encouragingly, that we were not the only family to whom embarrasingly comical things happened. Besides, whereas Avril and her partner Ian were born-and-bred country folk, Jane and James, and Joanna and Steve, were like us; relocated townies. Which made them, as it made us, far more susceptible to the crazy vicissitudes of country life.

One Monday morning, for instance, Jane and James had a hysterically harrowing start to their week. Or to be more precise, it was harrowing for James, but hysterical for Jane. Even now, her eyes still moisten with mirth at the thought of it.

Like us, Jane and James lived on the edge of open country-side, where rodents were not uncommon. The fun had started when their cat Beano, who was a brother to our cat Tiger, brought a live mouse into their kitchen. Beano then dropped it, and the terrified creature shot behind the fridge. Jane told James, who was about to set off for work, that the job of catching and dispensing with it was his, to which end she handed him a pair of pink rubber gloves.

The sight of James trying to corner a mouse while dressed for work except for pink rubber gloves was funny enough in itself, but the spectacle became a sight funnier when a strange look came over James's face.

'It's just gone up my bloody trouser leg,' he cried.

'Oh, don't be ridiculous,' said Jane.

'No, it has, I can feel it,' James insisted, and ran out on to the decking outside their kitchen, where he whipped off his trousers and shook them frantically. So now he was standing outside in his underpants, in the rain, still wearing the pink gloves, shaking his trousers.

Events then took an even more comical turn when the doubtless terrified mouse came flying out of a fold in the trousers and, for a fleeting moment, clung on to the front of James's underpants, very much in the manner of a mountaineer tenaciously trying not to fall off the north face of the Eiger, before dropping on to the decking and scurrying off to the sanctuary of the orchard.

Jane, and their children Jack and Alice, who were also witness to this marvellous pantomime, spent the next ten minutes holding each other up while screaming with laughter. James, whose sense of humour is wonderful but bone-dry, laughed too, if with understandably less abandon. Later, when she had recovered some composure, Jane related the tale to an acquaintance in the village. He listened politely and then said: 'That's nothing, a bat once flew down my mother-in-law's nightie.' That's the danger with telling funny animal-related stories in the countryside; the person you're telling will invariably have a better one.

We knew nobody better than our friend Jane, however, for telling stories to sum up the indignities that arise from sharing your life with animals and children. If she was happy to tell the mouse story against James, she was equally happy to tell an excruciating Thomas the Tank Engine story against herself. It is my favourite example of what can go wrong when you're living in the middle of nowhere with a toddler.

One morning, after James had gone to work, she was playing with Jack – then aged two – on the kitchen floor. He was brmmming his battery-operated Thomas up her legs and over her shoulders, and in truth she was quite enjoying the sensation, except that Jack then brmmmed Thomas on to her head, where its four wheels promptly got horribly snarled up in Jane's hair.

It was stuck fast, she realized to her horror. In its refusal to budge even in the face of swearing, then pleading, then praying, it resembled the 07.53 Arriva train service from Leominster to Cardiff; Britain's hapless railway system is a subject I will revisit in a later chapter.

Then the inevitable happened; the front doorbell rang. Now, when you live in the countryside, a ring on the doorbell constitutes an event. It is not something you ignore, because it could be days, or even weeks, before it happens again. So Jane went to the door with Thomas the Tank Engine gazing with his cherubically sunny smile from the top of her head, hoping against hope that it might be a friend dropping round. But the other thing about the countryside is that friends, as a general rule, tend not to drop round. Visits from friends tend to be diarised, then underlined in triplicate on the kitchen calendar. At the very least, friends announce themselves with a phone call first. You can't take the risk, you see, that the person you're calling on might be out. Not when you've driven up a long bumpy lane and waited for twenty minutes behind a herd of cows being moved from one field to the next. Besides, Jane hadn't lived there for very long since moving from Birmingham; she realized with a sinking heart, as she opened the door, that there weren't many friends it could have been.

It was the postman, who didn't bat an eyelid to be met by a woman with Thomas the Tank Engine on her head. Maybe he'd seen stranger things on his rounds, although Jane couldn't imagine what. In retrospect she realizes that she should have made a joke of it, perhaps even asked him to lend a hand. But there was something about his countenance that discouraged this. She felt sure that, as she bent her head forward to sign for the package he was delivering, which Thomas appeared to be looking at too, he was thinking 'bloody stupid townies'. If

162

only he'd burst out laughing, and better still introduced himself as Postman Pat, her acute embarrassment might have been punctured.

Back in the sanctity of the kitchen, having overlooked the obvious solution of keeping her interesting headgear in place until Ladies' Day at Royal Ascot, and then passing it off as a Philip Treacy number, Jane very tentatively tried to cut Thomas out of her hair with scissors. But it couldn't be done. Every time she cocked her head to look in the mirror, all she could see was Thomas, smiling with what by now seemed to her to be a determined malevolence, like those toys in horror films that are possessed by the devil.

In the end she had to wait for several more hours until James came home from work, and then at least twenty minutes more until he had stopped laughing. If only she'd known then that he would one day be standing in the rain with a mouse clinging to the front of his underpants.

As for the indignities of parenthood, the worrying thing is that they don't seem to diminish much even as your kids get older. And, as always, the phenomenon is intensified by living in the country. Our friend Joanna, for example, would not have ended up being mistaken for a down-and-out had she not that morning driven from her home near Ludlow to Hereford, then the twenty-five or so miles back to Ludlow, then back to Hereford. When you live in the sticks you get to know certain stretches of road better than you know members of your own family. So it is with us and the five miles of the A44 between Docklow and Leominster; if we could invite it for Christmas, we would. And Joanna is even more intimately acquainted with the A49 north of Hereford. Maybe it's because she's on such good terms with it that she thinks nothing of trundling up and

163

down it four or even six times a day, although in so doing she takes her life in her hands, because like the A44 between Worcester and Leominster it is one of the most dangerous stretches of road in the country, especially over Dinmore Hill where fatal crashes occur with dismaying regularity.

Oddly enough, things weren't that different in 1148. While I was writing this book, Jane was reading a historical novel by Elizabeth Chadwick called *Shadows and Strongholds* in which Joscelin de Dinan, Lord of Ludlow, understandably eager to get home to Ludlow Castle and his fragrant wife Sybilla, set off from Hereford on what was obviously the forerunner of the A49. But just as he and his party were getting close to Ludlow, they were ambushed by men in the pay of the dastardly Hugh Mortimer and Roger de Courcy. Actually, I've just checked and it was Gilbert de Lacy not Roger de Courcy, who of course is a modern-day ventriloquist. I'm sure Nookie Bear had nothing to do with the ambush. Whatever, I suppose the deadly ambush was the twelfth-century version of the crash on Dinmore Hill; the unpredictable episode that could stop you getting home in one piece. According to Elizabeth Chadwick, Hereford to Ludlow in 1148 was 'a comfortable distance that could be covered in less than a day when it was high summer'. That would have been no good to Joanna.

On this particular day her 12-year-old daughter Sarah, who was at school in Hereford, had a late-morning dental appointment in Ludlow. So Joanna collected her from school, drove her to the dentist's, and then back down the A49. When they got back to Hereford there was still enough of Sarah's lunch break left to buy her a much-needed new pair of school shoes. So they rushed into shop A, where Sarah rejected everything Joanna liked, then dashed to the rather funkier shop B, where

Joanna rejected everything Sarah liked, then scooted into shop C, which had the right shoe but in the wrong size, then hammered across the road to shop D, which had the right size of the wrong shoe. They then decided to give shop B another try, and it was there that they finally agreed on a pair, which Joanna paid for and Sarah put on straight away. Sarah then trotted off to school, while Joanna stuffed the old shoes in a municipal rubbish bin and scurried back to the pay-and-display car park, anxious because her ticket had expired ten minutes earlier.

She was delighted to find that a traffic warden had not, after all, beaten her to it, but less delighted to find no sign of her car keys. She emptied her bag and checked every pocket, then repeated the process several more times, before deciding that she must have left the keys in one of the shoe shops. So she ran back to shop B, where the purchase had been made. Perhaps she had placed the keys on the counter while she fished out her purse? But no.

She then legged it in turn to shops A, C and D, but no, sorry madam, nobody had handed in a set of car keys. So Joanna flew back to the car park, now convinced that she must have dropped the elusive keys by the car. She hadn't. Then a thunderbolt of realisation struck her. She must have inadvertently dropped the keys into the same bin as the shoes. So she ran back to the bin, and with a grimace, peered in. This was not a straightforward operation. The litter bins in Hereford are fancy metal jobs with flaps, so peering in means getting your head through the flap. This she did, but found no shoes, and no keys. It was the wrong bin.

I wish I could say that she emerged from the bin with a half-eaten, three-day-old kebab on her head, but really it's a story that needs no embroidering. Joanna rummaged busily through three more bins, painfully aware of passers-by giving her a wide berth, before she finally found the discarded shoes, and with them – hurrah! – the unwittingly discarded keys. She then hurried back to the car certain that, the way her day was going, there would be a fixed penalty notice attached to the windscreen. Happily, there wasn't. And even more happily, she had not been tapped on the shoulder while she'd had her head in a bin by another parent from Sarah's school, sweetly offering to buy her a sandwich. She gamely concluded that her day could have been worse.

I roared when Jane told me Joanna's story, but of course, which of us has not had a broadly similar experience? It's not long since I searched high and low for a book I'd been reading and eventually found it in the fridge. My theory is that it's a side effect of middle age. The very young and the very old perhaps have feebler short-term memories, but it doesn't matter, because other people are not generally reliant on them remembering things. But the middle-aged have to remember on behalf of our children and sometimes our parents as well, and with all that on our plates it's no wonder that keys get put in bins and books left in fridges. In the country it's even more pronounced, because we're constantly criss-crossing the county getting kids to school, to football and netball practice, to parties, to sleepovers, to guitar lessons, as well as keeping the dogs walked, the chickens fed, the fire stoked, the compost heaped, the bills paid. It's a worrying, exhausting business. But you should see the views.

12

Tashi, and the Slacker

By the end of 2004 Eleanor, too, was at school in Hereford, indeed at the same school as Sarah. All three of our children had gone to a fine primary school in a village to which, in *Tales of the Country*, I gave the pseudonym Stamford Heath. The reason I did so was that I didn't particularly want to advertise where my kids went to school, not because I had delusions of celebrity, and thought that the paparazzi might turn up outside the school gate, but because of something that happened after I'd recorded in my newspaper column that the school took a coachload of pupils to Wolverhampton one day, for what was termed a 'cultural exchange'.

It had seemed like a perfectly admirable idea to me:

167

Stamford Heath is in one of the most mono-racial areas of Britain, with hardly a black or Asian face to be seen, and the headmaster thought it would be a worthy exercise to spend a day at a school where white kids were actually in a minority, so that the children could see another slice of English life.

With this in mind, Wolverhampton was a pretty obvious destination, and I thought of the Stamford Heath day out a few months later when I talked to a woman called Sandra Samuels, a black councillor in one of Wolverhampton's predominantly non-white wards. Miss Samuels was Labour's parliamentary candidate for the overwhelmingly white constituency of North Shropshire, rather evoking the old joke about the bigoted, redneck farmer in the American South who dies, and somewhat to his surprise is escorted to the gates of heaven, where St Peter confirms that he, Tyler B. Grudge, late of Pike County, Alabama, committed racist and misogynist, is indeed to be permitted entry.

'But before you go in,' St Peter adds, 'there's just one thing you should know about God.'

'What's that?' says Grudge. Or more likely, 'What's thayat?'

'She's black,' St Peter says.

Naturally I would not dream of comparing the good people of North Shropshire with the likes of Tyler B. Grudge, but even so, it would have been a notable first for such a rural constituency, for many years the Tory seat of the Right Honourable John Biffen MP, to be represented on the Labour benches by a black woman. Unsurprisingly, it didn't happen. In fact, the Labour share of the vote dropped from 35 per cent in 2001, to 25 per cent.

But before election day I talked to Sandra Samuels on the

phone, and she told me that in three months of canvassing in North Shropshire's five market towns – Wem, Whitchurch, Market Drayton, Ellesmere and Oswestry – she had encountered not one other black face, and just one brown one, an Asian newsagent.

Nor, happily, had she encountered any racism. 'Everyone's been very polite to my face,' she said. 'Whether there have been comments behind my back, I don't know. I have noticed a few raised eyebrows when I've walked into country pubs, but on the whole I think the main shock to people is not that I'm black and female, but that there's someone telling them to vote Labour.'

I could relate to that, because in North Herefordshire we had seen neither hide nor hair of our Labour candidate. Nor, along the eleven miles of road between Bromyard and Leominster, had I spotted a single Labour poster. Or even a Lib Dem one. There were loads of Vote Conservatives, and a couple of enormous boards proclaiming the virtues of the UK Independence Party, and a few rather desultory Green Party placards, and that was it. All of which was in stark contrast to our surroundings at the previous General Election. In our part of Hornsey and Wood Green it had been as hard to spot blue posters as it now was to spot yellow-and-red ones. And black faces were even scarcer. Scarcer, probably, than in North Shropshire, which at least had Sandra Samuels buzzing around, electioneering.

Slightly to my surprise, none of this bothered me in the slightest. In 2002 we had agonized, like the bleeding-heart north London liberals we were, about leaving behind such a vibrant, multicultural society. But in truth we hadn't missed it especially, despite the regular reminders that Herefordshire was anything but multicultural. The most sinister of these reminders came one evening in the early summer of 2006, when I went into a pub near Ledbury after a round of golf with a friend, and my friend saw a group of six blokes, most of whom he knew. They invited us to join them, which we did. They were a companionable bunch, and seemed like kindred spirits. I got on particularly well with one engagingly smiley guy, whom I'll call Bill.

Then, somehow or other, the conversation moved from sport to politics. David Cameron was too left-wing for many mainstream Tory voters and risked driving them into the arms of the British National Party, somebody ventured. I listened with interest. 'The BNP's the way forward,' said Bill. Curiously, my response was to laugh. I thought he was joking. Then it became clear he wasn't. 'Multiculturalism doesn't work,' he added.

My heart started pounding. I had never met a BNP voter before, still less shared a thus-far convivial evening with one. In my naive mind's eye, they were all heavily tattooed and bullet-headed, but Bill was a respectable-looking professional man of about forty-five. It turned out that he didn't know anyone in the group either, and had been brought along by his friend Dick, who quietly counselled him to drop the subject. 'Don't start,' Dick muttered. 'You don't really know these people.'

Later, as I drove home mulling the evening over, it struck me as heartening that Bill had been advised to keep quiet because he didn't know the company he was in. On the other hand, that somehow made it all the more sinister. After all, there was a time, in the cafés of the Weimar Republic, when it was dangerous for Hitler to be overheard. Maybe Dick was a BNP sympathiser, too.

A fleeting silence descended on the table. Into it I said, with as much scorn as I could muster: 'What do you know about multiculturalism?' Bill looked at me. The smile had faded. 'Only that it doesn't work,' he said, flatly. And that was it. That was my attempt at confronting a man of the Far Right. It was a pretty poor show, really, and in the car on the way home I thought of all the things I should have said, and how far from multicultural Crouch End I had felt.

As for other, less disturbing reminders that we now lived in an overwhelmingly white part of England, Joe brought home from school one day the interesting titbit of information that travellers, what used to be known as gypsies, constituted our county's biggest ethnic minority. This meant less that there were loads of travellers in Herefordshire, more that there were very few ethnic minorities. All the same, there was a travellers' site not far from us for a while, on Eyton Common, quite close to where our pony Zoe was now being regularly rogered by Vinnie. One day, while taking Jacob to see Zoe, I stopped the car by the travellers' site and bought a painted horseshoe, for £5, from a bright-eyed urchin who was also called Zoe, to Jacob's great amusement. She assured me that it would bring me luck, and the following day I won £10 on the Lottery, so she was right. I was a fiver in credit.

When I worked on the *Hampstead & Highgate Express* I had often reported on furious controversies concerning travellers, but I noticed that the good people of Eyton didn't seem remotely perturbed. Maybe this was because they were a picturesque band, with the kind of painted wooden caravans coveted by middle-class women driving past in their Saabs, saying 'Oh, that would look absolutely super in our orchard.' It was exactly the spectacle that you find romantically described in the works of Enid Blyton as a gypsy encampment, nothing at all like the miserable collection of mobile homes and mangy dogs that so outraged the middle classes of London NW3. And when I asked one of the residents of Eyton what she thought of the travellers, she said, simply: 'I just think it's nice that the common is being used as it has been for centuries.'

Despite having moved to a part of the world where a few caravans on Eyton Common was about the closest thing to a ghetto, I didn't for a second think that our kids would grow up with some skewed image of England. Also, and I don't want to sound condescending, I found that there was something beguiling about living in the sticks at election time, something reassuring in the awareness that the next harvest was far more important than any manifesto.

This was compounded on General Election Day itself, when Jane and I went to cast our votes at our local polling station, which was not a church hall as it had been in London, but the home of some charming people who lived a few fields away, Sue and Richard. We parked in their drive and there was Sue, behind a table in their hall, fishing out our voting cards and offering us a cup of tea and a piece of cake. We then had a conversation about their donkey, which had just died, making Sue a bit tearful. After composing herself, she told me that she'd been meaning to call me after reading in my column that Milo, our dog, had rolled in badger poo and that we simply couldn't get rid of the smell. When it happened to her dog, she said, she'd applied liberal quantities of tomato ketchup, then hosed down the fur. The smell had gone completely. We laughed, and said that we'd try it the next time Milo rolled in badger poo. After fifteen minutes of nattering about this and other things, we left, and it was only when we got home that we

172

realized we'd clean forgotten to cast our votes. That's all it takes to bring democracy to its knees – a nice cup of tea and a conversation about the best way of getting rid of the smell of badger poo.

I suppose that's fairly typical of the countryside. One day I flicked through a collection of Alistair Cooke's *Letters from America*, and in one of them he told the story of a poll conducted by the original pollster, Dr George Gallup himself, in 1940. While the Battle of Britain raged, Dr Gallup travelled round England asking people if they had ever heard of Winston Churchill. He reported that 96 per cent had. The 4 per cent who hadn't were all farmers, and all from one county. Alas, the identity of that county has never been made public. But I wouldn't mind betting it was Herefordshire.

To return to Eleanor's cultural exchange visit to Wolverhampton, it all went swimmingly and that was that, but when I wrote about it, the story was picked up by a national newspaper of a slightly bluer political hue than the *Independent*: I'll call it the *Despatch*. A reporter called me, and it was pretty plain that he was not after a story applauding the fact that a school in Herefordshire should spend public money on a cultural exchange visit to a school in Wolverhampton. I politely refused to tell him anything, still less to identify the school, and yet the school secretary phoned later that day in a state of some agitation, saying that she'd had the same reporter on wanting to speak to the headmaster, and he'd phoned back three times refusing to take no for an answer. I still don't know how he'd found out where my children went to school.

About a year later, funnily enough, a female reporter from the *Despatch* called, again picking up on something I'd written in my column. It was kind of nice to know that they were reading my stuff, and gratifying that it was generating occasional stories for them, but of course they had a very different agenda to mine.

This time she'd read in my column that on a half-term visit to London I had gone with Jane and the children to Madame Tussaud's and the Planetarium. It was, I should add, one of the least enjoyable family days out I can remember. We had decided that, as country bumpkins, we wanted to do something touristy, and Madame Tussaud's fitted the bill perfectly. Of course, we would never have gone when we were actually living in London. There are several sights in our great capital that make residents feel faintly superior to those merely visiting. One is people feeding and even having their photographs taken with the horrible, verminous pigeons that plague Trafalgar Square. Another is the mob waiting to get into Madame Tussaud's. I sometimes used to pass them while driving along the Marylebone Road, and think 'Suckers!' Although now it occurs to me that maybe they looked at me in my car progressing at four miles an hour and thought 'Sucker!'

Either way, since we were no longer residents, I was almost, in a masochistic way, looking forward to being part of that very mob. It didn't take long, however, for my cheerful anticipation to dwindle. We had bought our extraordinarily expensive tickets over the internet and were therefore entitled to stand in the pre-bought tickets queue, which meant queuing, in sub-zero conditions on a litter-strewn pavement, only for seventeen hours rather than the usual fortnight. Finally we made it inside and got to thaw out, although I was troubled to discover that the waxwork model beckoning us in was Tara Palmer-Tomkinson. Now, I wouldn't want to get too Victor Meldrewish about this, but it seemed to me that the 8 million people a day who visit Madame Tussauds – and that's a conservative estimate for the day we went – deserved someone slightly grander than Tara Palmer-Tomkinson welcoming them through the door: someone like Lord Nelson, perhaps, or Winston Churchill, or even Pierce Brosnan.

Of course, it could be that the queue, the cold, the expense, and the fact that inside the building everyone seemed to have been given a personal space allocation of one square yard, had made me grumpy and determined to find fault. But it did also seem to me that wax models in the twenty-first century could be made to do something other than stand around quite so waxily. There was, in fairness, a conversion-taking contest alongside a crouching Jonny Wilkinson, who not long before had helped to win the Rugby Union World Cup final for England. And there was a karaoke set-up presided over by a frowning Simon Cowell. But in terms of anything vaguely interactive, that was about it. I concluded that Madame Tussaud was sitting on her wax laurels. And my grumpiness increased when I realized that to get into the Planetarium – admission to which was included in the price of the Madame Tussaud's tickets, although if they really wanted to give value for money they should have thrown in dinner at the Savoy – we had to start queuing again.

It was then, however, that things perked up considerably, and this, rather than my ruminations on Madame Tussaud's being overpriced and overrated, was what later attracted the interest of the dear old *Despatch*. Jane suddenly whispered excitedly to me that right behind us in the Planetarium queue was the real Jude Law, with his two young children. Our friend Cathy, who'd come up from East Grinstead to meet us, was even more excited. Now, you can always tell provincial yokels in London because they're the ones hyperventilating at the sight of a celebrity. Had we still been living in Crouch End, where we got occasional glimpses of Victoria Wood and Maureen Lipman buying their groceries (although rarely, if ever, together), we might have taken the spectacle of Jude Law a little more in our stride. On the other hand, not even hardened Londoners can shrug off a sighting of a bona fide movie star.

As we shuffled into the Planetarium I realized that the way we were being directed into the rows of seats, Jude and I were going to end up sitting directly next to each other. As soon as we sat down I tried to establish friendly eye-contact, but that's not easy in the darkened auditorium of the Planetarium, and I didn't want him to think I was trying to kiss him. Also, of course, Famous People are trained to avoid eye-contact with the rest of us. Moreover, he had his hands full with his little daughter, who was raising hell, screaming that she was scared. 'Daddy wouldn't take you somewhere scary, poppet,' he kept saying, but she just screamed even louder until finally he barked 'right' and dragged both kids out even before the complicated commentary about the universe started up.

I described this brief encounter in my column, saying that I found it rather sweet that Jude Law should spend the Friday of half-term week taking his kids to the Planetarium and Madame Tussaud's, where he would be on nodding terms with many of the waxworks if only they could bloody nod. I wondered whether, while the rest of us were identifying the likes of Brad Pitt and Julia Roberts (which isn't always easy at Madame Tussaud's; it also has to be said that some of the likenesses are decidedly tenuous), his kids were saying 'Look Daddy, there's Uncle Brad and Auntie Julia'? And I declared it downright reassuring that although he could snog Nicole Kidman and get paid lavishly for doing so, Jude Law, like the rest of us, struggled to reassure a fractious child. In the end, I decided, his presence had just about made the visit worthwhile, even if my patience was tried again on the way home when 5-year-old Jacob repeatedly asked, 'Which was the woman with two swords?'

'No, there wasn't a woman with two swords, darling,' we repeatedly replied. 'It's called Madame Tussaud's because that was the name of the woman who started the waxworks.'

There was an 'oh' from the back seat. And then, 'So why did she have two swords?'

Young children, as my friend Jude knows, can be particularly demanding on days out in central London. But not many of them arouse the interest of the *Despatch*. After reading my story, the reporter phoned and talked to Jane – I was out at the time – wanting to know whether the distressed child had been calling for her mummy, Sadie Frost, from whom Law was separated. No? Was Jane absolutely sure? Didn't she seem as though she might have wanted her mummy there? Even for experienced journalists like Jane and me, it was a dispiritingly enlightening insight into the operational procedures of the Fourth Estate.

But all that has diverted me from Eleanor's move to a new school. She settled in quickly, made some excellent friends, and two years later Joe followed her. That left only Jacob at Stamford Heath, and after much consideration, we decided to do what my bad-tempered correspondent Mr Hall thought we should have done with all three offspring in the first place. For the last three years of his primary education we moved him from Stamford Heath and sent him to the tiny school in the nearby village of (another pseudonym) Spindle-bury. We felt that the reasons we had overlooked it in the first place, not wanting to move our children from a big urban primary in London to somewhere so diddy, had long since expired. Moreover, Spindlebury had acquired a new head-mistress since we'd looked at the school four years earlier, and she was a warm, loving woman with an aura of saintliness, almost. We knew that Jacob would respond to her kindness. We also knew that by cutting out the forty-four-mile daily round trip to Stamford Heath, our Volvo's petrol consumption would stop resembling that of a Boeing 747, and get nearer to that of a small Learjet. These things matter in the country.

The other benefit of our children starting new schools was that it meant new friends for us as well as for them. We soon got to know the parents of one of Eleanor's classmates, Charlie and Caroline Henshaw, a delightful couple who, with their two kids, had several years earlier spent two years travelling round the world and hadn't quite kicked the travel bug. One Easter holiday they went trekking in Bhutan and were so enamoured of their guide, Tashi, that they encouraged him to visit them in Herefordshire the following summer. I don't doubt that Tashi, a sunny-natured man in his early thirties, had received similar invitations before, but Charlie and Caroline do not say such things frivolously. With their financial assistance, and the help of the trekking company he worked for, Tashi got the fare together for his first trip on an aeroplane and his first trip outside Bhutan. The deal was that the Henshaws would give him free bed and board in return for his help in the garden.

Apart from Charlie and Caroline and their kids, the only person we knew who'd been to Bhutan was John H, our dear Luncheon Club mate, who'd been absolutely smitten both by the place and the people. They positively exuded contentment with their lives, he told us, which corresponded with a survey I had seen published in a newspaper measuring levels of contentment around the globe. It was discovered that the happiness of the populace had no correlation whatever with per capita wealth, car ownership, medical insurance, ease of access to Starbucks etc. If anything the correlation worked in reverse; Britain was near the bottom of the list of 178 countries measured for the happiness of their people, and humble Bhutan was near the top. Charlie had told me, moreover, that the Bhutanese king had declared his preoccupation to be not gross national product but 'gross national happiness'. What a marvellous philosophy. I think I might go and live there. If I can get Sky Sports, obviously.

As for Tashi, Charlie duly went to collect him from Heathrow Airport. He had stayed awake for the entire twelve-hour journey, not wanting to sleep in case he missed something. He was duly rewarded with his first sight of the sea, albeit from 36,000 feet, and was still buzzing with excitement when he arrived at Heathrow. Charlie then took him to London for three days, and introduced him to the Stygian hell of the Underground at rush hour, not out of sadism but because he thought Tashi would be interested. He was. The spectacle of so many people crowded into such a small space – which I must say never fails to amaze me, either – left him astounded. Nor had he ever seen escalators before, of course. Or traffic lights. Bhutan had recently got its first set of traffic lights, but they had been removed after a few days by public demand.

Once Tashi had been in Herefordshire for a few weeks, Charlie phoned me and asked if I could find some odd-job work for him. He thought it would be good for him to see a bit more of the county, and meet some other English people. The story of Tashi's visit to England would in truth make a book on its own. Or a film. And when Charlie filled me in on the details of the London visit, I made the inevitable comparison with Paul Hogan's Crocodile Dundee, who was similarly bemused by city life. He told me that it was more apt than I realized. Tashi, it turned out, was the Bhutanese national archery champion, as well as a former champion in the specialist Bhutanese sport of throwing gigantic darts at a distant target. While they had been out there, the Henshaws had witnessed his expertise. He took part in an archery competition in which each team aimed at a target 140 metres away, with the opposition team standing scarcely a metre to the side of the target, firing back. Clearly, the health and safety guidelines in Bhutan are not what they are over here, not that anyone copped an arrow in the forehead.

Whatever, it seemed to me rather a shame that Tashi was not called upon while in London to fell a runaway mugger by firing an arrow 140 metres over the heads of the multitude mooching down Oxford Street, Crocodile Dundee-style. It was also a shame that at the airport in Delhi, where he had boarded the plane for London, the security people had confiscated his present for the Henshaws, which he'd been carrying in his hand baggage. It was a set of gigantic Bhutanese darts, and one can only guess at his dismayed bewilderment as they were taken off him, and for that matter at their horror when they found them.

After the overwhelming experience of London, Tashi found that the Herefordshire way and pace of life was a little less alien. But only a little. Even having seen London, he considered Hereford to be a glittering metropolis, and spent hours wandering wide-eyed round the shops, in particular the chemists and the shoe shops, which for some curious reason seemed to him to provide the best-possible spectacle of frantic Western consumerism in action. He became quite a familiar sight in Hereford's shoe shops, apparently, and got to know most of the staff. I rather like to think that he might have been doing the rounds one day when a beleaguered woman – our friend Joanna – rushed in asking if anyone had found her car keys, and then later spotted her outside with her head in a series of bins. That would have been a good story to take back to Bhutan.

Which brings me to another tale Jane brought home one day after walking the dogs with Joanna. While in Ludlow the week before, Joanna had found two ceramic mugs in a shop selling quirky knick-knacks. One was marked 'Chef' and the other was marked 'Slacker'. Since Steve did most of the event cooking in their house, sweating over the Bearnaise sauce while delegating peeling and grating jobs to her, she thought they might provide the family with a laugh. Not that she was by any means a slacker, but she had never minded a joke at her own expense, and was often the first to crack them. She bought the mugs.

A week or so later, a man came to cut the lawn and weed the flowerbeds. He had been hired through a gardening agency and it was his first time at Joanna's house. It was also a warm day, and after an hour or so Joanna wandered into the garden to find him, quite understandably, resting on his spade. She asked him if he fancied a cup of coffee. He did, and you don't have to be Miss Marple to see where this story is leading. She made two mugs of coffee, took one out to him and sipped the other herself while she did the ironing. It was only on draining her coffee that she realized that the mugs she'd used were the ones purchased in the knick-knack shop in Ludlow, and that her mug was the one marked 'Chef'. Would the gardener notice that he had been handed the slacker's mug? When Joanna later spoke to the guy's boss at the agency, she found that he had, and had been duly hurt. It could only happen to Joanna.

13

Dennis, and the Duck

When we left Crouch End in 2002 we had been sure, perhaps naively, that the people we'd got to know there would remain our nearest and dearest friends, that the friends we would undoubtedly make in Herefordshire could never be quite as close.

That was partly because our London friends had seen our children grow up from the time they were newborn babies, and we theirs, establishing an unbreakable bond. We had been so anxious about leaving Crouch End, indeed, that we had hatched a plan with some friends there to whom we were not quite so close, the arrangement being that the two families would swap houses for the weekend once every three months or so. That way, they'd get a weekend in the country four times a year, and we'd be plunged back into the comfortable bosom (I'm not thinking of anyone in particular) of our old social circle.

It never happened, of course. Although our closest London friends remained dear to us, we realized pretty quickly that when you step into a new life, you can't keep one foot in the old. But it's natural enough to fret about uncertainty: when we thought of our London mates during the first few days after we arrived to set up home in Docklow Grange, we'd pictured faces, and voices, and remembered late-night laughter around dinner tables. Who might our friends be in Herefordshire? Would there be as much late-night laughter after good dinners?

As it turned out there was at least as much, possibly more. In our friend Jane, we even had an expert in what might be called the *faux-naïf* strain of humour, that in London had been supplied by our friend Ali. For example, when we told Ali that we were going to a highly rated North African restaurant, she asked what kind of food they served. 'I suppose it's Moorish,' I said. 'Oh,' she said. A perfectly timed pause. 'Do you mean like Pringles?'

At a dinner party in Docklow one evening, someone happened to mention that Viagra, though best known as a treatment for erectile dysfunction, was in America available for women, too. However, in Britain it was not, not even at the pharmacy where you could get it over the counter. Someone else, and I'm almost 40 per cent sure it wasn't my wife, then asked whether there were any products on the British market that enhanced pleasure for women during intercourse? 'Yes, a Farrow & Ball colour chart,' said our friend Jane, to screams of hilarity from the other women around the table, and slightly forced chuckles from the men.

While I'm on the subject of male and female perspectives on sex, I might as well relate the story of the man, let's call him Gerald, who is involved in a serious car crash and regains consciousness in hospital to be told that he is fine in almost every department, but that, unfortunately, his penis was severed in the impact and couldn't be found.

'But don't worry,' says the doctor. 'They make fully operational prosthetic penises these days. The only thing is, they're rather expensive. They cost £1,000 per inch, so you need to discuss the matter with your wife, and decide what length you want. Do you want to pay £4,000, or £8,000, or even £12,000?'

The following day, the doctor returns. 'Have you discussed it with your wife?' he asks.

'Yes,' says Gerald, a little glumly.

'And what did you both decide?' the doctor asks.

'We're having a new kitchen,' says Gerald.

The reason Viagra had popped up in our conversation, if you'll excuse the predictable popping-up pun, was that one of our dinner guests that night was a Viagra sales rep. That was something we had noticed about the rural dinner party that was different. Our guests that particular evening included the aforementioned rep, a head of English at a sixth-form college, a health visitor, a primary-school dinner lady, a dentist and a British Telecom engineer. By comparison, our dinner-party line-ups in the city had tended to be much more homogeneous. Five journalists and a barrister, that sort of thing.

The other difference we noted was that dinner parties in London quite often happened during the week, and sometimes even spontaneously, in the country they are almost always on

Saturdays – rarely even Fridays – and are invariably on the calendar for weeks and weeks beforehand, if not months and months.

After four years of living in Herefordshire we had become used to this convention, so were duly surprised to get an invitation from a couple called Annabel and Richard to go round for dinner one Tuesday night; an excitingly avant-garde prospect. To get there we had to drive out of Herefordshire, through Shropshire and into Worcestershire, which I suppose is the reason why socialising in these parts tends to happen mainly at weekends, when there are the same lanes to negotiate but no 6.30 a.m. alarm calls the next day.

The reason for this startlingly uncoventional invitation was that Annabel and Richard wanted us to meet their neighbour Dennis, and Dennis worked away from home from Thursdays to Mondays. He turned out to be a London cabbie, who had moved to the area a few years earlier with his wife Susie, and found that the tranquility of the Welsh Marches was the perfect antidote to sitting in traffic on Kensington Church Street. It was always tough for him to point the cab southwards down the M40 on a Thursday morning, he said, but he was generally back in the swing of it by the time he got inside the M25, and knew for certain whether it was going to be a good few days or a bad few days depending on whether or not he picked up a fare on Holland Park Avenue, which was always where he first switched on his 'for hire' light.

Over Annabel's excellent cheese soufflé, I pumped him for stories from his life as London cabbie. I know hardly any professions that yield as many good stories, as long as you get a decent raconteur telling them, I suppose. And if you doubt me, then consider the results of a survey published in November

2006, which revealed some of the things left on the back seats of black cabs, among them a bag of diamonds worth over £100,000, and a machine gun. Prosthetic limbs were also quite commonly left behind, apparently. And in the previous six months alone, 54,872 mobile phones and 3,179 laptops had been left in the back of London cabs. I'm almost proud that my own tally only amounts to three umbrellas and two pairs of gloves.

I asked Dennis the most embarrassingly clichéd question of all: which famous people had he had in the back of his cab? It's always worth asking, because sometimes you get memorable snippets of gossip, like the snippet I once got from a guy taking me to Heathrow Airport who assured me that a Very Famous Television Star had the week before been in the back of his cab necking with a Very Famous Sports Star, both of them, ahem, female. I was agog. Maybe I have more in common than I like to think with the pushy *Despatch* reporter who'd wanted some dirt on Jude Law. As it happened, the best Dennis could offer on celebrities in the back of his cab was Hugh Grant, who was 'chatty', and Nick Faldo, who was 'grumpy'. So I shared with him the story another London cab driver once told me, that he'd been sent to wait outside a central London hotel at midnight, to pick up a nun and take her to some address in Belgravia, and accordingly remonstrated with the four glamorous black American women who climbed in, telling them that he was waiting for a Sister Sledge. It occurred to me later, on the long journey home through Worcestershire, Shropshire and finally Herefordshire, that perhaps this was a standard London cabbie joke, and entirely apocryphal, but Dennis, bless him, did me the kindness of laughing.

Dennis and I agreed that it was a shame I hadn't encountered him first by climbing into the back of his cab, because if I'd asked him where he lived, how marvellous it would have been to be told 'Clee Hill, just outside Ludlow'. I would then have been tempted to bag a lift all the way home, and probably would have done so had his been the cab I'd clambered into after an alcoholic lunch in London just the day before. Instead, it took me to Paddington Station, where I thought I was pretty much sober until I needed three stabs at asking the woman behind the information desk: 'What time's the next train to Worcester Shrub Hill?' I now know it to be one of the trickiest of tongue-twisters after a couple of bottles of wine.

I arrived at Shrub Hill three hours later, after a sobering snooze – one of those embarrassing snoozes on trains from which you jerk awake with your mouth open, a little bit of drool hanging from it, and the woman opposite looking contemptuously at you – which left me feeling perfectly capable of driving my car. I'd left it in the station car park the previous afternoon, but now I wasn't sure whether or not I was over the drink-drive limit. Clearly, the sensible thing would have been not to drink at all at lunchtime knowing that I'd be driving even five hours later, but one glass had led inexorably to two, and two to four, and here I was, clutching my car keys and wondering what might happen if I were breathalysed.

So I had what I thought was a brainwave. I got into a cab and asked the driver to take me to the main police station in Worcester, where I explained my situation and asked them to breathalyse me. They wouldn't do it. Apparently the police don't breathalyse by request. But they did say that if there was the slightest doubt in my mind then I shouldn't risk it, which, of course, I knew anyway. So I got another cab to take me all the way home, twenty-odd miles. It cost me £40 and meant that

Jane had to drive me back into Worcester to pick up my car the next day, which she wasn't overjoyed about, but the further you live from London, the harder it is to get home on the same day that you've had an enjoyable lunch in Chelsea.

The further you live from London, too, the more you become aware of, and affronted by, the Londoncentricity of the national media. Their tendency to assume that England, to all intents and purposes, means London, I suppose affords us country bumpkins a small taste of what it must be like to be a Scot, sporran aflame with indignation when the word 'England' is used rather than 'Britain'. In 2005 I went to Lausanne in Switzerland to interview Jacques Rogge, the president of the International Olympic Committee, and a man who exudes worldly sophistication from every pore, yet even he referred to 'your recent English general election'. I had to suppress a smile, knowing how some Scots of my acquaintance would have given him a fearful earful.

Some years ago, in a Highland pub, I stumbled into conversation with a man so conspicuously Scottish that he might have stepped off the lid of a shortbread tin. He had a shock of unruly ginger hair, wore a heavy kilt even though it was midsummer, and the barmaid trilled 'good evening, Angus' as he settled on his stool, before handing him a double malt, no ice. It was an almost comically Scottish tableau, and I use the word 'tableau' out of respect for the Auld Alliance between Scotland and France of which the Scots are so proud, although it was a Scottish friend of mine who observed to me once that only in Scotland has he ever heard people talking about the Auld Alliance; when he refers to it in France nobody has a clue what he's on about.

Anyway, I bravely decided to engage the ferocious-looking

Angus in conversation. We swapped a few pleasantries, or rather, I sent a few pleasantries his way, and he sent a few grunts back. Then I asked if he had always lived in the area. He took a long, slow draught of whisky. 'No, I lived abroad fae six years,' he growled. I asked him where. A hint of menace entered his expression. 'Have ye ever heard,' he said, 'of a place called High Wycombe?'

I have often used that story as an example of the chippiness of some Scots, yet after a few years in Herefordshire I began to feel a similar kind of chippiness coming on. When a quality newspaper – OK, I'll own up, it was the *Independent* – listed the fifty best places for breakfast in Britain, I very chippily counted them to see how many were in the capital. It was thirty-one, which seemed wholly disproportionate, especially as the best eating in Britain was manifestly to be had in the Welsh Marches, not London.

I had reliable evidence that this applied to birds as well as to humankind. We knew someone called Jenny who had found a disorientated homing pigeon in her Herefordshire garden, and attached to its leg was a label with a phone number with an 020 8 prefix; the owner lived in outer London. Jenny phoned him and he explained that he had released the bird a few days earlier in the Lake District, and it had obviously lost its bearings. Could she please feed it, then take it a couple of miles down the road and release it?

She did exactly as instructed, but the next morning the pigeon was outside her kitchen window, tapping plaintively on the glass with its beak. It obviously wanted more corn, which she supplied, before shooing it away before her cats could get at it. About an hour later, to her astonishment, she found the pigeon standing behind her, actually in the kitchen. Delighted with the quality of the grub, it had wandered through the back door in search of seconds. This time she took it further afield, to Mortimer Forest, and set it free again. A couple of people walking their dog watched her do this, and when she told them what had happened, they said that the same thing had happened to them two years earlier. A pigeon, on its way to Greater London from Scotland, had wound up in their garden and they had repeatedly tried to send it on its way, taking it further and further each time, only for it to return repeatedly to them. In the end – and this is the bit of the story I love – they had sent it with Parcelforce. Can you imagine the humiliation a homing pigeon must feel as it is handed to its owner from the back of a Parcelforce van, its entire *raison d'être* demolished? On the other hand, the wretched creature had at least had a seductive taste of life in what people hereabouts like to call God's own country, especially those of us who have, as it were, flown the metropolitan coop.

On yet another hand, whenever I become too proprietorial about Herefordshire, there is always someone or something to remind me that I am, and will forever be, a blow-in. When I phoned an electrician one day and gave him our address, he said, in that wonderful Herefordshire accent that is somehow a hybrid of Wales, Birmingham and West Country: 'Blimey, I haven't been there since I was invited to a birthday party when I was seven, and I'm forty-nine now. The reason I remember it is that I was terribly sick. I threw up all over the place.'

I laughed, although I wasn't sure whether I liked the idea of someone associating our house with vomit. Still, better that, I supposed, than covering it with vomit. It can't have been very nice for the Manzoni family, who owned the house in the mid-1960s. I knew this because an enterprising woman had sent us a letter asking whether, as the present owners of Docklow Grange, we might like to buy a nicely mounted original advertisement from the property section of Country Life, dated 30 June 1966. This was what her company did, relying on people's interest in seeing their homes advertised in old issues of *Country Life*. It cost only £15, which seemed like a bargain to me but probably also represented a nice profit for her. Anyway, the advert was duly given pride of place in our downstairs loo, and that's how I know that the house was sold at auction in Leominster on 5 August 1966, by order of Sir Herbert J. Manzoni CBE, having been advertised in *Country Life* as 'a small country estate of 77 acres in a beautiful elevated position'.

By the time we bought the place, it hardly qualified as a country estate. Most of the seventy-seven acres had been sold off and reduced to fewer than five. As for Sir Herbert, I found that he had been the city engineer and surveyor for Birmingham from 1935 to the early 1960s, and as such had been responsible for Birmingham's post-war reconstruction, in particular the unlovely Inner Ring Road. Critics of his schemes joked that he did more damage to Birmingham's city centre than the Luftwaffe, which I'm sure was unfair, although I'm equally sure that he was entirely typical of city planners in the 1950s, returning from a hard day concreting over a city centre to a comfortable Victorian house in 'a beautiful elevated position' in the country.

When the electrician who'd attended the Manzoni birthday party turned up, he did not, as I'd feared, have a Pavlovian reaction and start retching. Instead he reminisced wistfully about what he remembered about the house, making me feel, as so often in the life we'd made for ourselves, like a Johnny-come-lately. At the bar of the King's Head it was worse. If you couldn't trace your roots in the area back to the Crimean War, then most of the pub regulars weren't ever likely to consider you truly at home in Herefordshire. In Crouch End it had been so different. There, your antecedents didn't need to go back much beyond the first Gulf War. If you could remember when the betting shop had been a Chinese takeaway, you were a local.

Still, by our own somewhat subjective standards, we had become Herefordians through and through. And one of the ways we calculated the degree of our assimilation was the declining number of times we visited London. Even though the arrangement to swap houses with friends in Crouch End had come to naught, we still, in our first couple of years in Herefordshire, went back six or seven times as a family, and Jane and I a couple of times for parties. But by year three that had become three or four times, and by year four, only once or twice. My mother lived in London but didn't have room for us all to stay, and so, like our friends, she came up to Docklow. The city played less and less of a role in our lives.

And yet the strange thing is that, several years after settling in north Herefordshire, with hundreds of newspaper columns and two books behind me recording more pleasures than pitfalls in country living, with our children happily settled in excellent schools, and with a new repertoire of skills, including the underrated ability to turn a sheep stranded on its back the right way up, even now I am frequently asked whether I ever regret moving out of London.

Let me here just take a short diversion to tell you about sheep. In Herefordshire, with them in the fields all around us, it seems important to know more than that they taste good with mint sauce; important to know, for example, that a sheep stranded on its back will soon die because its internal organs will cease to function, so it is vital to turn it upright. When I heard this I got our neighbour Roger to show me how. It seemed silly to have to phone him every time I saw a ewe upside-down.

Roger, like most of the farmers around us, had Herefordshire roots extending deep into the red-clay soil. Yet at shearing time, I learnt, much of the work was done by New Zealanders, marshalled by a Kiwi living in bucolic Much Marcle whose name, blissfully, was Shaun. A guy called Derek, a sheep farmer in Kimbolton, three or four miles from us, told me that Shaun and his two mates were the finest shearers he'd ever seen. He made them sound like shearing's answer to the Three Tenors, in the way they worked together in such harmony. 'Each man shears a sheep in a minute,' said Derek, admiringly. 'They started at nine, and they were in here having lunch by 12.30.'

For all I had known, sheep-shearing was done in the shower with a Phillips Ladyshave. But Derek brought me up to speed. Apparently, there was another New Zealander called Godfrey Bowen who in the mid-1950s pioneered a new style of shearing. The old style went from stomach to back, but according to the Bowen technique, the sheep is sat on its bottom, and sheared in single swipes along the entire length of its body.

I phoned Shaun, who told me that he and his two mates would between them shear about 22,000 sheep that summer, which amounted to between 700 and 900 per man per day. These were men who put the 'rug' in rugged. But they didn't fleece the farmer as well. Shaun charged between 75p and 90p per sheep, which seemed reasonable enough to me, and meant that everyone went home happy except possibly the sheep. Certainly, for Shaun and his pair of shearers it added up to a decent hourly income. He kept the full payment for those he sheared himself, but paid his men 55p per sheep. So even with a five-minute rest that was over £30 an hour, pretty good money given that these guys didn't consider it work. 'We think of it more as sport,' Shaun told me. 'There's a lot of teamwork, but also a lot of competition.'

He didn't just mean casual competition between mates, either. He told me about the official sheep-shearing championships, and explained that the Michael Schumacher, the Roger Federer, the Tiger Woods, the unassailable world champ for nigh on twenty years, was another New Zealander, named David Fagan. 'I've competed against him, but you just can't get near him,' said Shaun, in awestruck tones. 'His record is eighteen seconds.'

Not even Fagan could shear a Merino in eighteen seconds, though. They're the hardest, according to Shaun, although Ryelands are tricky as well because they have wool from head to tail and the skin is very soft. For ease of shearing the conditions have to be right, too. 'If it's wet then the wool doesn't lift, and you've got to get lift on it, otherwise it's hard to push the handpiece through. This year we've had a lot of rain and where you should get a nice white fleece it's been coming off yellow.' I commiserated, while making a mental note, next time I saw someone shearing a sheep, to ask about the lift. To feel at home in the country you've got to know the jargon.

You've also got to understand that, although to city-dwellers the countryside is a place where tradition is venerated and time stands still, in fact it is evolving faster than the skyline of the City of London, and is more at the mercy of market forces.

Two summers after I spoke to Shaun, I called him again, hoping to go and watch him at work. He told me that he had left Much Marcle and moved to Scotland to concentrate on agricultural fencing for the simple reason that he couldn't find enough shearers to work with him. There was a dire shortage, mainly because Kiwi shearers, for the first time in years, could make more money by staying at home. He was still in Herefordshire for the shearing season but, with one sidekick rather than the usual two, had only managed to shear 14,000 sheep, rather than the usual 25,000. Whether that meant that there were 11,000 unusually woolly sheep wandering around, I wasn't sure. I didn't ask. A wise old reporter once told me that the secret of good journalism is to ask the questions a child would, but you've got to draw the line somewhere.

Still, my ignorance about so much going on around me in the countryside simply increased my desire to know more. For that reason and many others I had never had a moment's doubt about whether we did the right thing by moving out of London. Jane and I had fretted about plenty of other things, such as whether we should have moved to quite such a scantily populated part of England's most scantily populated county, and whether we should have landed ourselves with quite such a high-maintenance property, and, indeed, how it was that sheep do end up on their backs, but never about whether we should have stayed in Crouch End.

If there had, in some remote nook of our minds, lingered one last atom of doubt, it was eradicated by our visit to the capital one weekend in the summer of 2005. It wasn't that we didn't have a nice time, or that we wound up seeing touristy London at its worst, as we had in the wretched Madame Tussaud's at least until we were joined by Jude Law. On the contrary, we had the nicest time imaginable. On the Friday we had dinner with twelve of our dearest Crouch End mates, and the following morning took the children on the amphibious wartime vehicle used in the Normandy Landings and known as the Duck, which was simply fantastic, especially when it plunged into the Thames without us having told the kids that it would.

Coincidentally, my mother-in-law later told us that her cousin Ralph, the man whose later demise I would confuse with that of a hamster, had driven a Duck during the war. That gave us another reason to like him, to add to his infallible memory for the children's birthdays. The Duck tour has gone down in Viner family lore as one of the best of all outings, enhanced by the spiel from the tour guide, who introduced himself to us, as we boarded this strange jalopy close to the London Eye, not knowing quite what to expect, as Roberto.

'I . . . Roberto, and I am . . . you guide,' he said, in hesitant, heavily accented English. 'I . . . friend of usual . . . guide. He sick. Please . . . be . . . patient . . . with . . . my . . . English . . . for . . . next . . . two . . . hour.' Jane and I exchanged a look. He then roared with laughter and in a broad Cockney accent said, 'Oh my gawd, you should have seen your bleedin' faces!' So, should you ever take a Duck tour, I've now utterly blown his cover. But he fooled us utterly for thirty seconds or so, and of course the subsequent laughter set the tone for the rest of the trip and, for us, the rest of the day. That evening, with the kids dotted around north London on sleepovers, Jane and I went to see a highly entertaining play at the National Theatre called *Theatre of Blood*. Afterwards we had dinner in a fine restaurant overlooking the Thames. It was a capital day in more ways than one.

Even driving around London was fun. You don't see many

197

people when driving around Herefordshire, which rather limits opportunities for playing one of my favourite car-journey games. This involves me inventing stories about the pedestrians we pass – or, in London, the pedestrians who pass us – for the children's delectation. That day, while sitting in a monstrous tailback on the Finchley Road, I spotted a tall, skinny woman wearing a white tracksuit. I told the kids she was going to a fancy-dress party as a snowflake, and was just about to elaborate, when Jane murmured, sotto voce, but not quite sotto enough: 'She looks more like a tampon.'

Unfortunately, she had temporarily forgotten that we had an 11-year-old daughter who was just becoming aware of such things. 'Mummy!' exclaimed Eleanor, pretending to be outraged. This ignited the interest of 10-year-old Joseph, who said, 'What's a tampon?' After a moment's hesitation, Jane decided to rise to the challenge and produced one from her handbag.

'This is a tampon,' she said.

'Can I taste it?' asked 6-year-old Jacob, who had a fairly one-dimensional view of the world, and believed that anything in attractive packaging must be edible.

Anyway, this gave us all a good laugh, which brings me to my point: that even Finchley Road tailbacks can be fun and educational, as long as you don't have to suffer them too often. Similarly, London is an absolutely wonderful city in which to take a thrilling tour on a 60-year-old amphibious truck in the morning, and go to a first-rate play in the evening. Obviously, you don't have to be a visiting bumpkin to do these things, yet as metropolitans, with supermarket visits and swimming lessons and whatnot to get on with at weekends, we hardly ever did. It was only after leaving London that our kids had been on the London Eye, visited the Houses of Parliament, skated at Somerset House ... all of which added up to one good reason why I didn't regret leaving Crouch End. Another is that we were all truly happy, on a balmy Sunday evening, with the sun setting over the distant Black Mountains, to get back to the sticks.

14

Parsley, and the Lion

Just as we as country-dwellers formed opinions of London, so, when they came to stay, did our mates from London form opinions of the countryside. These were not always especially positive. One Christmas holiday we had our friends Derek and Rebecca staying, with their sons Thomas and Benjamin. On the Wednesday afternoon of their visit, Derek offered to go into Leominster, five miles away, to get some provisions. Jane asked him to get some parsley. He duly went into the greengrocer's, a characterful place where a wonderfully lugubrious comedy act goes on between the two men behind the counter. I was in there once when the older of the two was complaining of a sore foot. 'Drop your wallet on it, did you?' muttered the other.

This was typical local humour: poking fun in drily acerbic fashion. Jane reported another example from a butcher's shop in Ludlow. The Ludlow Community Hospital was under threat and a campaign had been started to raise funds to save it. Jane was buying some sausages when a very tall, well-spoken man came in saying that he'd come to pick up the collection box for the hospital.

'I don't know anything about a collection box,' the butcher said.

'Oh, but I'm quite sure I brought one in,' the man said.

The butcher's mate then started in mock-realisation. 'I remember – wasn't that the box we emptied before we all went out last Saturday night?'

The butcher flashed him a look; the tall man simply looked bemused. There wasn't much of a gap between his scalp and the ceiling but this lovely burst of mordant Marches humour had still managed to sail over his head.

Similarly, in the greengrocer's in Leominster, in the days before we had our own chickens, Jane had asked whether their eggs were free-range. The grocer looked at her with an expression that managed to combine puzzlement, amusement and disdain. 'Well, the barn door's open, look,' he said. This was the guy Derek later asked for parsley, to be met with a slightly pitying smile. 'There'll be no parsley in Leominster until Friday,' he said. Derek, who lived in a part of London where you can buy kumquats at midnight on Christmas Eve, should you really want to, was greatly tickled by this. It seemed to confirm all his preconceptions about country living, just as it would have confirmed my worst fears when we first moved to Herefordshire. Indeed, I was in a queue at a farm shop, not long after we arrived, when a man walked in and asked the guy behind the till whether there was a B&Q nearby?

'A B&Q?' the guy at the till said, slowly. 'In Leominster? Don't be silly.'

At the time I'd gone home and nervously reported this to Jane, and yet I had come round to the charms of living in a part of the world where not everything was available all the time. I liked the idea of a town waiting for parsley. It reminded me of the one-horse towns in those old John Ford and Howard Hawks westerns, where folk were always waiting for stuff to arrive by railroad. 'There won't be no supplies, mister, until the weekly train from Phoenix passes through.' That kind of thing.

After the parsley episode I tried hard to persuade Derek of these charms. The need to go a little further for things we might need, or wait a little longer, had had an unequivocally positive influence on our lives, I said. With every day we spent in the countryside, the importance of instant gratification had receded a little further. He didn't seem convinced.

The next time he came to visit, eight months or so later over a bank holiday weekend, he again offered to go shopping in Leominster, and we assured him that he would have a much more successful experience than he'd had the time before. We had a large gang of London friends staying, and by the Tuesday, recognising that it was our fourth successive day of having to put a meal for thirteen on the table, Derek generously undertook to go into town to buy steaks, burgers and sausages for the barbecue. Now, Leominster might sometimes run short of parsley, but like everywhere in the Welsh Marches, it is a fantastic place for buying meat. We directed him to our favourite butcher. By the time he got there, however, the shop had closed. It was 12.15 pm. So Derek wandered across the road to the deli and asked the woman there if she knew why the butcher's was shut. 'Yes, he closes at midday on a Monday,' she said.

'Oh,' said Derek, and selected some cheese. Then a thought occurred to him.

'But it's Tuesday,' he said.

'Goodness, so it is,' she said. She thought for a moment. 'Ah,' she added, 'but it was Monday yesterday.'

When Derek came back and recounted this gnomic exchange, we decided that the point she'd been making was that even though the butcher had been closed the previous day for bank holiday, he was damned if he was going to forsake his half-day off. It was a retailing philosophy that had driven us mad for our first twelve months in the country, but as I say, we had come to value this air of unhurriedness.

Thinking about it now, it was rather ironic, given that Leominster was a town where butchers sometimes closed at midday and parsley was a commodity you had to wait for, that large swathes of the countryside around the town had been commandeered and covered in polytunnels by fruit farmers whose profits depended on year-round demand. To pick the fruit they hired a largely foreign workforce, such as the Poles Jane had picked up on the A49, and increasingly we saw whey-faced Eastern Europeans in Leominster, looking into shop windows as if the shops were repositories of plenty, which to them they were, unless they were looking for parsley, I suppose. Everything's relative. Which reminds me of a quotation that once ended the Radio 4 programme *Quote Unquote*, and was thought to be Eastern European in origin: 'If we had ham, we could have ham and eggs . . . if we had eggs.' I like that.

In truth, though, I am more of a Radio Five Live man

myself, and listened attentively during the week in November 2004 that Five Live spent broadcasting from rural England. As part of the exercise, listeners were invited to define the word 'countryside'. Some suggestions were sober – 'the countryside is any place with fewer than two people per square kilometre' – and some were wry – 'the countryside is where people have Save British Farming stickers in the backs of their German cars'. Some were sweet: 'I was a literal-minded child; I used to think the countryside was the coast.' But I decided that the definition I enjoyed most was that the countryside is where people's second vehicle is a 4×4, as opposed to Hampstead Garden Suburb, where it's the main family car. There was a lot of truth in that. There were also plenty of Herefordshire mums who delivered their kids to school in Range Rovers, but not as many as in the ritzier parts of north London, and at least in the country there's every chance that you might have to negotiate a mudslide or a snowdrift, which tends not to be the case in and around Hampstead.

I considered what my own definition of the countryside would be. Anywhere, perhaps, where you can hear mooing, baaing or clucking before you've got out of bed on a Sunday morning, but without having switched on *The Archers*. But it was Jane who came up with a nice definition of small-town country life when she came home from Ludlow one day, and reported a conversation she'd had with a chap at one of the market stalls in Castle Square. She happened to mention that she had overrun the hour she had paid for in the municipal car park, and was a bit anxious that a traffic warden might descend on the car. 'No, you'll be all right, my love,' he said. 'I've just seen him go home for the day.'

Shortly after this, Jane came home with an entirely different tale of men and motors. She had a strange confession to make to me, that she had just spent quarter of an hour sitting in our Volvo in the Stamford Heath School car park, with a man gazing into her eyes, fiddling with her hair and gently touching her face. She thought that she had better own up before someone broke the news to me, which they might, because the encounter had been witnessed by one or two other mums, who predictably had done a double-take at the sight of Jane apparently canoodling with a man not her husband. In the school car park! So brazen!

There was an innocent but curious explanation. The man had been Mark Richards, the father of two of the children at the school. Mark was a brilliant portrait sculptor, who the year before had moved from Brixton in south London to the small village of Richards Castle, aptly enough, on the Shropshire–Herefordshire border. A few weeks earlier, Mark had been commissioned to produce a bronze of Anna Lindh, the recently murdered Swedish Foreign Minister, which a Lebanese businessman, who had much admired her, wanted to present to the Swedish government.

There were two problems with the commission. One, it needed to be done in a hurry. Two, Mark normally required several sittings with his subject, but this subject, alas, was dead.

So there was Mark standing in his workshop one afternoon, probably smacking his palm against his forehead in the time-honoured fashion of frustrated artists everywhere, when his young daughter Nemone wandered in. Mark sighed and prepared to be distracted from his project. But Nemone looked at the photographs of Anna Lindh strewn across his desk, and said, matter-of-factly, 'that's Eleanor's mummy.'

It was a eureka! moment. Or perhaps, since the subject was

a Swedish woman, an Ulrika! moment. Either way, Mark swept Nemone gratefully into his arms, gave her a kiss, and then asked his partner Jo to phone Jane with an unusual request: could she meet him in the school car park the following morning, so that he could measure the distance between her ears, and from the tip of her nose to her chin. So now you know the story of the bronze head of my wife that you will see next time you venture into the Swedish parliament building. I would have told our neighbours Kerstin and Ingemar, except that by now their short tenancy of Limetree Cottage had finished, and they had gone back to Gothenburg, doubtless to be received warmly by friends deeply relieved that the Midsomer murderer hadn't claimed them. Still, I supposed there was a chance that they might one day see the head, and remark on how very much it resembled Jane from Docklow.

Meanwhile, sculpture was by no means the only branch of the arts flourishing in Herefordshire. I received a call from the news desk of the *Independent* one Friday morning in spring 2005, asking whether I would like to cover a concert that Sunday evening at the Lion Ballroom in Leominster, being given by the Birmingham Contemporary Music Group. The reason they wanted me there was that the concert's centrepiece, following Igor Stravinsky's relatively conventional String Quartet, was to be the American composer John Cage's controversial silent composition *4'33"*, an unusually avant-garde piece to be playing, or rather not playing, in a small market town in the Marches.

Even though we had counted our next-door-but-two neighbours Paul Cassidy and Jacky Thomas of the Brodsky Quartet among our closest friends in Crouch End, classical music had never really been my thing. I suppose someone on the news desk knew that I lived nearby and just thought that I might have some fun with it. But I needed to know a bit more about Cage. So I phoned Paul, who told me that *4'33"* had been conceived in 1952 after Cage spent some time in a sound-proof chamber where, he claimed, he could hear his own blood circulating.

That story rather reminded me, I told Paul, of a visit Jane and I had made to a health spa in Leicestershire called Ragdale Hall way back before we had children, and when I was still working for the *Hampstead & Highgate Express*. The owner of Ragdale Hall lived in Hampstead, and had invited me to spend the weekend up there, with a view to writing a feature about it. I wasn't then, and am not now, a health spa kind of guy. But for the purposes of the feature I had to sample lots of treatments, which was the reason I subjected myself to half an hour in a flotation tank. This was a dark chamber containing an epsom salt solution only 20 centimetres deep or so, but very dense. The idea was that the sensation of floating, in silence and darkness, would encourage a blissful feeling of weightlessness. To this end, I was advised to do it in the nude. All of which would have been pleasant, perhaps even bordering on blissful, had there not a) been a monotonous drip somewhere in the tank and b) had the flotation tank therapist, an eager young woman with a strong East Midlands accent, not given me a terrible start by once or twice calling out from her desk, not a metre from where I was lying naked in salty water, 'Are you all roight in there, Mr Voiner?' I was a nervous wreck when I came out.

Some years earlier, John Cage had emerged from his sound-proof chamber eager to prove that, as I would later discover myself at Ragdale Hall, there is no such thing as perfect silence, that there is always some ambient sound, whether it's the sound of your own blood circulating or a drip and a young woman calling 'Are you all roight in there, Mr Voiner?' He duly came up with *4'33"*, although probably never meant it to be performed, as it was that Sunday evening, within startlingly loud earshot of Leominster's bank holiday weekend May Fair.

It was a fairly spectacular collision of high culture and low culture, and as an exercise in showing there is always some ambient sound, the thing worked triumphantly. The group entered the room, took their seats, raised their instruments purposefully, lowered them again, then sat doing nothing for precisely four minutes, thirty-three seconds, except once turning over a blank page of music to reveal another blank page. Precisely as they did so, outside on the Mighty Waltzer, a youth cried 'Fuck off, Tazzer!'

I must say that I rather enjoyed myself, although I could understand why, even in the classical music world, there was considerable ambivalence towards Cage, who died aged seventy-nine in 1992, which come to think of it was probably the year I had my flotation tank experience. The French composer and conductor Pierre Boulez hit a resonant note when he said he loved Cage's mind but didn't like what he thought. And after the concert, as I gathered quotes for my newspaper article, a local woman called Hilda Stainrod seemed to agree with him. 'It went a little over my head,' she said. 'I find the twentieth century rather heavy going.'

For another concert-goer I talked to, *4'33"* would have been more enjoyable without the clicks of the *Independent* photographer's camera. It had been an annoying distraction, he said, which unleashed a pseudo-existential argument in which I advanced the proposition that Cage would have approved of the clicks; surely, background noise was what *4'33"* was all about?

'But it wasn't in the background, it was in the foreground,' he protested. I apologized, and emerged into the evening to find another pseudo-existential argument raging between a family beside the Hook-a-Duck stall on Broad Street. 'Mum, you owe me 50p,' wailed a child. 'Your mum don't owe you nothing,' barked his father. I debated for a while whether to show them the notes on *4'33"* in the BCMG programme, which read: 'Nothing. But there is no such thing as nothing. The word is already something. Try to imagine nothing without the word or the concept of nothing.' But I decided not to bother, and instead wandered away with my respect for Leominster reinforced. The small town had risen comfortably to the challenge of accommodating, simultaneously, the Mighty Waltzer and the Birmingham Contemporary Music Group, although it was only a concerted effort by the concert organiser, Alan Crumpler, that ensured that cider-fuelled youths did not wander into the Lion Ballroom to see what the silence was all about. He spent the evening as a bouncer, albeit a rather improbably thin and intellectual bouncer, and possibly the only bouncer in Herefordshire who made his own harpsichords.

Every small town should have a Crumpler. I didn't even know of his existence until I was leaving, and was button-holed by an *Independent* reader who recognized me. He told me that Crumpler would make an excellent subject for my column, since life in the sticks is greatly enhanced by the inexhaustible energy and enthusiasm of such people. I was well aware of that already, of course, from the example of people like Rob Hanson in Docklow. But Alan Crumpler, it turned out, was a different animal altogether. With his wife, Maureen, he had owned a shop in Leominster selling classical instruments, but they now devoted much of their time, unpaid, to running the Lion Ballroom.

This they did on a shoestring budget, and put on an admirably eclectic programme. 'Old and New Music from Wales and Finland', which had been the concert the month before, would probably not have had me hammering the five miles along the A44, even had I known about it. But for those whose bag it was, I'm sure it was a splendid evening, and I was assured that the acoustics in the ballroom were the envy of many a larger concert hall.

When I sought out Crumpler, he told me that the ballroom was the pride (my pun) of the Lion Hotel when it opened in 1840. But the Lion was a coaching inn, at the dawn of the railway era. In the *Hereford Journal* on 18 October 1843, it was gloomily reported that 'within the last week the only coach that was left on the road from Bristol to London ceased running. The railroad monopoly is now complete.' In 1851, the Lion unsurprisingly went bankrupt. This reminded me of the story of a pub I used to go to when I lived in a small flat in London near Lord's cricket ground, called Crocker's Folly. It had been built by a Victorian entrepreneur called Frank Crocker, whose folly was to site it directly opposite the proposed entrance of the soon-to-be-built Marylebone Station. Crocker then sat back and waited to make his fortune, except that some bugger then decided to move the station half a mile or so to the south. The pub duly went bust and poor Crocker killed himself by leaping off its roof. There must have been thousands of personal tragedies like that resulting from the advent of rail transport, which the history books tell us was such a triumph of the Industrial Revolution.

Anyway, despite the Lion Hotel's closure, the ballroom remained largely intact, and for years housed an ironmongery business. Thanks to the vision and dedication of Alan Crumpler and a small band of similarly selfless people, however, it had been restored to its former fleeting glory, and was being run much as the 1840 owners would have liked. I dare say, though, that those early Victorians would have been a trifle bewildered by John Cage's silent 4′33″. I know I was.

15

Al Pacino, and the Tip

Another admirable band of people, possibly even some of the same band, had also spent several years selflessly and tirelessly campaigning for Leominster's swimming pool to be rebuilt. Shortly before we moved to the area, the Leominster pool had been closed so abruptly for health and safety reasons that by all accounts there was a man doing lengths who got to the shallow end and found that the place had been padlocked in the time it had taken him to arrive from the deep end.

There didn't seem to be much municipal will to build a new pool but in June 2003, a stalwart group of townsfolk formed an organisation unambiguously called We Want Our Pool, and the following month, to its credit, Herefordshire Council agreed to splash out £2 million. The WWOP campaigners then agreed to find a further £250,000 to add a learner pool, and apart from the last £14,000 which was stumped up by a local benefactor, collected every penny with just about every fund-raising activity imaginable.

The official opening took place one Saturday in January 2006, preceded by a celebration aptly called 'Splashout' that filled the market square, not least with some comedy synchronized swimmers performing to *Swan Lake*, which I think was probably a first for Leominster. It was all extremely jolly, yet the triumph with the swimming pool rather underlined the sad fate of the town's distinctly unjolly post office, which stood overlooking the celebrations in the market square as forlornly as it is possible for a building to look. Not even with all that water-themed fun going on, was anyone able to throw the poor post office a lifeline. It was due to be shut down as part of the Royal Mail's disgraceful cull of rural and small-town post offices around the country, and rehoused in the newsagent's round the corner.

A couple of weeks before the planned closure, Jane was in there buying some stamps, and overheard the fellow behind the counter asking an elderly woman who'd just finished her transaction, whether he could interest her in a Post Office credit card?

She looked at him sharply. 'No you most certainly can't,' she barked. 'Not unless you stay put in this building. Then I might listen, but if you move then I doubt whether you can interest me in anything!'

And with that she bustled out, leaving the man behind the counter looking, according to Jane, as though he'd just been hit over the head with a blunt instrument. It was, of course, grossly

214

unfair of the woman to blame this hapless man for the Royal Mail's ruthlessness, the more so as he was probably worrying about his livelihood, yet her annoyance reflected the general feeling of frustrated impotence that prevails in rural England as post offices and even hospitals are shut in the name of that twenty-first century god, profitability. By November 2006, barely 25 per cent of villages in England had managed to cling on to a post office. When I was a local newspaper reporter, I was taught never to use the word 'axed' in relation to a disappearing service, but in these cases it seemed appropriate: as in all the best horror movies, what else but an axe would you use for violent, indiscriminate chopping?

Leominster was not actually stripped of a post office, of course. But a town of more than 11,000 people should surely have a dedicated central post office, and I huffed and puffed with everyone else, while privately conceding to Jane that if an enterprising restaurateur came in and opened up a lively pizzeria in the now-disused building, calling it The Old Post Office, then I might just get over my outrage. Apart from the usual small-town ration of chippies and curry houses, Leominster lacked anywhere decent to eat in the evenings, which was ironic, because Ludlow, a twenty-minute drive north except on mornings when you got stuck behind a potato lorry, in which case it could take anything up to a month, was considered one of the gastronomic capitals of England.

It was true that Ludlow's proud claim to have more Michelin-starred restaurants than any town or city outside London was, by the end of 2006, no longer valid. Shaun Hill's acclaimed restaurant, the Merchant House, had closed because Hill had tired of cooking in a kitchen the size of a telephone box. Claude Bosi at Hibiscus, one of only a dozen or so

215

restaurants in the country with two Michelin stars, had also announced his intention to leave.

But there were still plenty of good reasons for foodies to visit Ludlow, among them a fine delicatessen, Deli on the Square, which sold most of the delicacies that some of our visiting friends from London, clinging to the view that we had moved to some kind of culinary backwater, very sweetly brought us from posh places such as Harrods' Food Hall and Fortnum & Mason. These delicacies, I should add, sat in our pantry for months on end, more or less forgotten about, although they did come in useful on the day Joseph came home from school with a homework assignment to find foodstuffs of varying weights. Inexplicably, he ignored banal things like bags of sugar, and we could only imagine the raucous laughter at our expense when his list was passed round the Stamford Heath staff room the following day: duck pâté with armagnac (200g); rillons confit au Vouvray (450g), and figues moelleuses from Gascony (500g).

I will revisit Ludlow in this book, but for now let me stick with Leominster, which might not have been overburdened with good restaurants but still had some striking assets once you knew where to find them. The best and best-hidden of all these assets was the municipal tip just on the edge of town. I never thought that I'd become the kind of middle-aged man who enthuses about a good tip, but then the word 'tip' scarcely does the place justice.

There are separate skips for general rubbish, cardboard, scrap metal, wood and garden waste, as well as further recycling bins for bottles, newspapers, cans, plastic, shoes, tyres and even fridges. As you leave, a sign tells you how much waste was recycled the previous month, and how many tonnes were thereby saved from being landfilled. It's most heartening. I've had holidays in places that have pleased me less.

Leominster tip even had an energetic young woman in a donkey jacket who at peak times would help you unload your car – the domestic-refuse equivalent of those bag-packers you sometimes find in particularly busy branches of Waitrose. She seems to have moved on now, perhaps to a bag-packing job at Waitrose, but whenever she lent me a gauntleted hand, I was reminded of the Caroline Aherne character in *The Fast Show*, sitting at the supermarket till passing irreverent comment on the contents of people's trolleys. The woman at the tip must have seen all sorts coming out of the boots of cars. I was there once when I saw a man dumping a life-sized cardboard cut-out of Cilla Black, which begged a number of questions that regrettably I didn't have time to ask, since I was slightly behind schedule on the way to collect Joseph and Jacob from school.

I quite often called at the tip en route to picking the boys up from Stamford Heath. In fact, if I am brutally honest, I regarded the school run as a bit of a chore, yet a visit to the tip as an unalloyed pleasure, when it really ought to have been the other way round. The only explanation I can find for this curious mindset is that I arrived at school with an empty car, which was then filled with boys who were always hungry, sometimes a little bit smelly, and either tremendously over-excited or excessively grumpy, whereas I arrived at the tip with a full and often smelly car, yet drove away with it empty and much less malodorous. Also, there was something almost emotionally cathartic about chucking away a dozen bulging refuse sacks and dumping twenty empty bottles and a stack of old newspapers into recycling bins. Maybe it was a guy thing. Or maybe it was just me.

But I think it was the former, because I noticed that when certain male friends came to stay for the weekend, they were eager to come with me to the tip, whether I happened to be going or not. Chris, a friend from London, was particularly impressed with the woman who helped to empty the boot. In the capital, as a general rule, the only people who will help empty your car have got into it with a crowbar.

On the day of my accident at the tip, however, I was on my own. Normally there was a merry crowd of us there, recycling cheerfully and even chattily; rarely had I ever emptied a boxful of bottles into the bottle bank without someone jovially asking whether it was a good party (which admittedly could be disconcerting if you were just binning your usual weekly intake). But on this occasion I was alone, sorting my bottles into the brown, green and clear bins, when I somehow rammed the jagged edge of the single broken bottle into the back of my left hand, gashing it badly and drawing an alarming amount of blood.

I wrapped a handkerchief around my hand and drove myself to Leominster Community Hospital, which was so quiet that it reminded me of the hospital scene in *The Godfather*, when Al Pacino's character, Michael Corleone, turns up to visit his father, only to find the place deserted. But then a nurse appeared, just as in *The Godfather*, and promptly gave me four stitches, while we chatted – and this is where my experience diverged from Michael Corleone's – about her daughter's chemistry degree at Bath University.

She was a charming woman, and although it would be wrong of me to say that I can't think of a better way of spending a Saturday morning, the whole experience was about as pleasurable as it could have been, and of course exemplified

218

the benefits of living in small-town rural England. Had the same thing happened to me in the city, I would have ended up in the unspeakable hell of a jam-packed A&E, waiting for half a day between a man with an axe in his forehead and a woman holding a head under her arm. Yet it is the understretched community hospitals such as those in Leominster and Ludlow, where you can turn up, get treatment and be sent home some-times not just within the same morning but within the same hour, that politicians and bureaucrats want to close down. If it's true that we get the kind of governance we deserve, then we should probably take a long hard look at ourselves.

On the other hand, I wouldn't want to sound too smug about the advantages of requiring hospital treatment in the country as opposed to the city. I have already related the story of how, in London, there were paramedics at my dying stepfather's side within minutes. And Herefordshire hospitals weren't always beds of roses, either.

One Friday afternoon, Chris, the friend who so appreciated the pleasures of Leominster tip, arrived from Crouch End with his wife Ali (the woman who'd wondered whether Moorish food meant Pringles) and their children Lauren, Rosie and Jake. Their kids were almost exactly the same ages as our three, and devoted friends, but because they saw each other infrequently the general excitement very quickly reached fever pitch. By the time the four adults had consumed a couple of bottles of Merlot and were on to the third, which must have been almost an hour after their arrival, 6-year-old Jake had been injured in a game of try-to-see-how-far-you-can-jump-from-the-top-of-the-stairs.

He had hurt his arm but there seemed no need to take him to casualty. This was just as well, since none of us were sure whether we were within the drink-driving limit. I write those words with slight trepidation, incidentally, half-anticipating an angry letter from someone who, with six school-age children in their care, would decline alcohol on the off-chance that a car journey to hospital might be required. As I've already recorded, it's amazing what I get angry letters about. I once got one saying that it was insulting to call a snake Nigel. I started to compose a reply saying that it was even more ridiculous to anthropomorphise a snake by suggesting it might be vulnerable to insults, than it was to call it Nigel. But I gave up. There's no point arguing with such people.

As it happened, Jake's arm was still hurting the following morning, so Ali and Chris took him to Hereford County Hospital, about fifteen miles away. It was 9 a.m. when they arrived, having parked directly outside. They appreciated this, later pointing out that if you can park directly outside their nearest hospital, the Whittington in Highgate, then you have probably arrived by skateboard. In A&E, moreover, there was only one other person waiting, again in striking contrast to life at the Whittington.

An X-ray duly showed that Jake had a hairline fracture, so he was given a snazzy blue sling, of which he was understandably proud. The entire business took less than forty minutes, whereas when Lauren had broken her arm nine years earlier, they had waited at the Whittington for five hours. When they told me all this I swelled with pride – yet another example of the sticks triumphing over the city! – but they added that the nurse who saw Jake had coincidentally spent fifteen years working at the Whittington. She had agreed that there was an almost comical difference, ascribing it largely to the fact that the Whittington A&E got clogged up with people who do not have GPs, whereas in Hereford the NHS worked as it should, with GPs doing much of the work that in London gets dumped on hospitals. Even so, she still heard locals criticising Hereford Hospital for being busy and overstretched, which tickled her enormously. But – and this is where my smugness was well and truly punctured – Ali and Chris told the nurse that they might have brought Jake in the evening before, but had been worried about driving while over the limit.

'It's a good job you didn't,' she said. 'Friday nights are a nightmare in here, mainly because of all the binge-drinking that goes on in Hereford.'

'Surely not worse than Friday nights in the Whittington?' said Ali.

'Oh God, much worse,' the nurse said.

Much as I like to champion life in the countryside and rural towns, there is no point overlooking its many deficiencies, and binge-drinking, mainly by youths with not enough to do, is one of them.

Especially since Eleanor and then Joe started at school in Hereford, I had come to like it enormously. It is an attractive and characterful place, a city by name but a fairly small town by nature, with a marvellous cathedral, a picturesque river, the Wye, and a vibrant shopping area that miraculously has not been disfigured by the excrescences imposed on so many other English towns and cities in the 1950s and 1960s. But there is not that much else to divert youngsters from the dubious pleasures of blackcurrant snakebites, or whatever is the let's-get-pissed-quickly-then-vomit-on-the-pavement drink of choice these days. There is no multiplex cinema, for instance, and no ice-rink, not that ice-skating did me any good as an adolescent. I have gloomy memories of going on a sixth-form outing to the Silver Blades rink in Liverpool, and yielding vital ground to a boy I considered my rival for the affections of a girl in the Lower Sixth called Carol. When I saw him take to the ice like Robin Cousins, as I took to it like a Robin Reliant, I knew my chance was gone.

Again, I digress. In the *Independent*, a fellow columnist of mine, the comedian Mark Steel, made a fairly regular target of life in country towns such as Hereford and Leominster, or more specifically of people like me for hymning its praises.

One of his characteristically witty and pugnacious columns was headlined 'The unbearable smugness of country dwellers' and lambasted people who move to the sticks and then say 'we don't know how you put up with all that traffic and noise. While you're stuck on the Underground, we're out with the children identifying elderberries and hunting otters.' And who boast at how well they've integrated into the community. 'Last week the whole village turned out for the autumn fayre and it was wonderful fun because we all had to take part in the annual squirrel-catapulting contest. And Barbara got a big cheer because she almost landed one on the village's mentally ill person.' Mark reckoned that there was something 'disturbingly misanthropic' about these people. That by celebrating their retreat from a city they were really saying 'isn't it marvellous to not be near many people'.

He added that

one of the main reasons cited for moving into the country-side is 'it's a better place to bring up kids'. So they might grow up never mixing with anyone who's black, foreign or openly gay, but at least they can tell the difference between five different species of heron. And while there may be some advantages for small children, when they get to 15 it's unlikely they'll say 'thanks for moving out here, because however much fun there is in London, it can't be as good as spending every night hanging about in the bus shelter by the Spar'.

I confess that I recognized myself in much of what he wrote, indeed I wondered immodestly whether he might even have had me in mind, though I hoped I'd never been sanctimonious when writing positively about country life, and had been candid about its disadvantages. Whatever, I felt bound to use my own column to send a broadside back, and suggested that Mark had fallen into the common trap of deploying prejudice to attack prejudice. Which, I asked, was more ill-informed and patronising, the belief of some in the sticks that urban teenagers all end up doing drugs and mugging other adolescents for their mobile phones, or the urban conviction, championed by Mark, that teenagers in the country spend 'every night hanging about in the bus shelter by the Spar'? A dead heat, I concluded.

I also wondered whether, by implying that parents are wrong to bring up their kids in the country 'never mixing with anyone who's black, foreign or openly gay', but at least educating them to 'tell the difference between five different species of heron', Mark was not himself being just a teeny bit smug and sanctimonious? Another of his criticisms of former city-dwellers now removed to the country concerned their preoccupation with property values. He quoted them as saying: 'We sold our flat in Stoke Newington and without borrowing any extra we were able to buy the Peak District.' It was a fair jibe in many ways. My rejoinder, however, was that I couldn't recall having a single conversation with anyone in Herefordshire

BRIAN VINER

about property prices. And that was true. It was in London that they were an obsession.

The only winners in this argument are not the people who live in the city frequenting Portuguese cafés and Lebanese restaurants, and not those who live in the country watching heron, but the people who acknowledge the pleasures of life on the other side of the fence, while preferring to stay just where they are. While living in London I had been just as scathing as Mark Steel about proselytising ex-metropolitans, and had been particularly irritated by a friend who, visiting us in Crouch End from his home in remote Northumberland, stepped out into our tiny back garden, and said, 'What it's like being so overlooked?', before detailing all the wildlife he saw while driving his kids to school each morning over a particularly majestic moor. I've told all my London friends that if I ever say anything like that, they have permission to thump me, hard.

16

Proust, and the Smell

By the beginning of 2005 I considered myself sufficiently fully fledged as a country-dweller to have an opinion on the prospective fox-hunting ban, which would finally become law at midnight on 17 February, not that anyone ended up taking much notice. Eighteen months later, in November 2006, with hunts all over the country continuing as enthusiastically as ever, the Crown Prosecution Service still had not successfully prosecuted anyone under the Hunting Act. And the police, pretty much everywhere, and certainly in Herefordshire, were doing a fair impression of not caring whether the law was flouted or not. I heard that one local Master of Hounds was told by the police that they would only take an interest in the hunt if the anti-hunting activists turned up to disrupt it. Their over-riding concern was not fox welfare but public order. And that seemed rather sensible to me.

My opinion of the histrionic fuss about fox-hunting was that it had got out of all sensible proportion, that it was a disgraceful waste of parliamentary time, and a regrettable example of the way in which Britain, or more particularly England, was still blighted by class-related prejudice and misconceptions.

I found it dispiriting that factory farming did not inspire anything like the same degree of loathing. How could decent, intelligent urban folk simply register their opposition to factory farming by buying free-range chickens, yet angrily petition their MPs in the case of hunting? Actually, the answer wasn't very complicated. It was partly because nobody believed that factory farms were run by the landed gentry, the people (wrongly) considered to be the principal champions of hunting, and nothing inflames an issue quite like class prejudice. It was also because factory farming played a more tangible role in the economy, and even to suggest banning it would upset many vested interests. It was also partly because nobody keeps 10,000 chickens in a shed for enjoyment. What really stuck in the craw of the anti-hunting lobby was not so much that people went out intending to kill foxes, but that they did it for fun. But the main reason why nobody got their knickers in a twist about factory farming to anything like the same extent, was basically because the fox is a fine-looking creature with a fabulous bushy tail, and the chicken isn't.

So, while hunting was not my thing any more than shooting or fishing were, I sort of sympathized with the tally-ho brigade, although less because of the merits of their case than the lack of merit in opposition. In north Herefordshire my sympathies did not exactly place me out on a limb, of course. There were posters up and down the A44, paid for by the Countryside Alliance, most of which proclaimed that 59 per cent of people had said NO to a ban.

As effective campaigning messages go, I wasn't sure that this was quite on a par with, say, 'Labour isn't working' or even 'Go to work on an egg'. It was not, after all, a particularly striking percentage. Expressed in words, the posters would have said: 'Very slightly more than half the population oppose a hunting ban', which, however accurate, would have been distinctly wishy-washy. I was rather disappointed that the fox-hunting fraternity, so used to responding to the powerful blast of a shiny horn, had failed to come up with a more impressive rallying call. Had they been selling cat-food, would they have boasted that 'between five and six out of ten owners say their cats prefer it'? I seriously doubted it.

Our own cats Tiger and Sooty, meanwhile, supplemented their Kit-e-Kat diet by eating a variety of small mammals and birds, and leaving what they didn't fancy at the back door, as a generous present for the rest of us. Just about every day brought a reminder that nature is red in tooth and claw, quite often in the form of a decapitated baby rabbit deposited by Sooty, whose murderous instincts belied his sweet name. He was black but for white feet and a white chest, and a terribly refined woman who came to our house once said: 'Oh look, your cat is dressed for dinner.'

But that made him sound civilised, when, in fact, his name should have been Attila, or Genghis. It was rather satisfying to see him confounded by the pair of swallows which spent every night during the summer perched at the top of the electric light flex in our porch. He sat for ages trying to work out a way to get to the top of the light-fitting, but eventually the swallows departed safely for the Algarve, or wherever it is that swallows spend the winter months. I like to think that Sooty watched them go with a certain feline respect.

Tiger, although she had dispatched a few rabbits herself, seemed to have a more moderate taste for violence. Perhaps it was a gender thing. One Saturday morning, from my bedroom window, I watched a couple of pigeons performing a courtship dance. I am no lover of pigeons, except braised with red cabbage, but it was actually a very charming spectacle, a kind of quickstep with a lot of billing and cooing. I told Jane what was going on, and she said: 'They'd better get on with it, before Sooty arrives.'

These were extraordinarily prescient words. Suddenly, pouncing like a miniature panther, Sooty took out Romeo, or possibly Juliet. There were feathers everywhere, hanging in the air along with Romeo's last words: 'And so to thee I plight my tro—' It was the first time I had actually seen Sooty catch a pigeon, and I watched in horrified fascination. He didn't kill it, just maimed it horribly, relishing the sport as the stricken bird, no longer able to fly, tried to escape. Sooty watched these efforts with, it seemed to me, amusement, then pinned it to the ground again for a bit more cheerful disembowelment. By the time I got outside the pigeon was gone. I assumed Sooty had finally finished it off. But about five hours later I heard a rustle coming from a bush and there it was, guts hanging out, desperately flapping its one half-detached wing. I killed it by dropping a large stone on it, and reflected that, for true cruelty, no fox hunt could hold a candle to Mother Nature.

Doing the right thing by the stricken pigeon did not make me St Francis of Assisi – or even his modern-day equivalent,

Rolf Harris – but I did try to do my bit for damaged members of the animal kingdom. In the field next to our house I noticed a sweet black lamb one day, unable to stand. The rest of the flock had all legged it for some important sheepy reason to the next field up, so this little guy was left all alone, and there was a buzzard circling overhead with what looked like dangerous intent. So, whether or not it needed rescuing, I decided to rescue it. I clambered over the stile, picked up the lamb, clambered back out of the field and carried it into our kitchen, where the children fussed over it while Jane phoned Roger, the farmer.

Shortly afterwards I needed to go to the post office in Leominster – the inadequate new one, tucked away in the back of the newsagent's – where I noticed several people in the queue sniffing the air. Sniffing with them, I realized that there was indeed a pungent smell, and, while folk in the country are used to ripe aromas, they don't necessarily expect them while they're waiting to buy twenty first-class stamps. Gradually I became aware that the pungent smell was coming from me, the lamb having defecated copiously on to my trousers. Why it had taken me so long to realize this, I don't know. Nobody at home had pointed it out, even though I didn't knowingly make a habit of entering the kitchen stinking to high heaven. Perhaps, in all the excitement over the lamb, it simply wasn't noticed. Whatever, it was the first time in about forty-one years that I had been the source of a serious smell in a post-office queue, so in one sense it was an almost Proustian experience.

My next encounter with wildlife was remarkably similar. The very next day, at the bottom of the garden, Joe found a baby bird that had evidently fallen out of the nest. Again I carried it into the house and again I was crapped on; nobody ever tells you that there is a price to pay for saving birds and animals, and that it comes in the form of excrement. St Francis must have been covered in the stuff.

Anyway, we put the bird in a shoebox, following the advice of our neighbour Will, a professional wildlife consultant. He said that because it was nearly dusk, we should keep the creature indoors overnight and in the morning put it back on the grass where Joe had found it, in the hope that its mother would find it before the homicidal Sooty did. We duly followed Will's advice to the letter, making the tiny bird comfortable in a shoebox, and the next morning we released it, making sure that Sooty was nowhere to be seen. This was just after an unfortunate misunderstanding had narrowly been averted, when Jacob came down for breakfast, saw the shoebox, and asked if it was the shoebox containing the toys he'd been asked to take into school, to be sent to earthquake victims in Pakistan. I had horrible visions of small Pakistani children surrounded by rubble being handed out gifts: a kaleidoscope for you, a rubber ball for you, a dead fledgling for you.

Will also loaned us a book called *Care of the Wild: Family First Aid for Birds and Other Animals* by W. J. Jordan and John Hughes, which advised on first-aid procedures for wild animals and birds. We didn't really need it, but afterwards I leafed through it, fascinated. It was first published in 1982, but it might almost have been 1882, so exquisitely dry was the style. Apparently, if you ever have cause to handle an incapacitated stoat, weasel, polecat or pine marten, 'a pair of fairly stout gloves would be distinctly advantageous'. Invaluable advice, I'm sure you'll agree.

Another useful addition to my natural history library, around the same time, was a book called *A Bird in the Bush:*

A Social History of Birdwatching, by Stephen Moss. Some friendly publishing PR sent it to me, and while I didn't exactly read it cover to cover, I did dip my beak, as it were, and surprised myself by being enthralled. If you think a social history of birdwatching sounds boring, as I might have done before leafing through it, then consider this: the world's most prolific bird-spotter was Phoebe Snetsinger, of Missouri, who in September 1995 reached the coveted 8,000 mark by spotting a Rufous-necked Woodrail at a mangrove swamp in Mexico. This was after a thirty-year bird-spotting career in which she survived shipwrecks, earthquakes and a gang-rape in Papua New Guinea, only to die in a minibus crash in Madagascar, minutes after spotting a Red-shouldered Vanga. That, I think, is information worth having.

It is rather humbling, actually, to think of people like Stephen Moss, hundreds if not thousands of them, sitting at keyboards all over the world enthusiastically bashing out stuff like that, and indeed about far more esoteric subjects than birdwatching. Another book I was sent out of the blue was called *The Hare*. The publisher, Merlin Unwin, was based in Ludlow, and wondered whether I might give *The Hare* a plug in my column. He explained that it was the first biography of the hare to be written for twenty-three years, which, in all honesty, didn't greatly surprise me. The surprise was more that another book about the hare had been written as recently as twenty-three years earlier. So why had this one been produced? It was hard to picture publishing types sitting around a table stroking their chins, saying, 'It's high time there was another biography of the hare', as they might have done about Franco or Tolkien or Isambard Kingdom Brunel. What was there to say about the hare?

A hell of a lot, was the answer. The author, Jill Mason, had been a gamekeeper for thirty years, and tackled the subject from every imaginable angle. My favourite bit was the section on superstitions concerning the hare. When planning which route her army should take, Queen Boudicca is said to have produced one from under her gown (which must have given her generals something to talk about) and released it, insisting that the hare would choose the direction. Maybe, come to think of it, that's why she ended up buried under one of the platforms at King's Cross station, or so legend has it. Maybe that's what comes of letting a hare lead the way. You wind up at King's Cross, of all places.

Because traditionally, as I knew after reading Jill Mason's book, the poor old hare has been associated with bad luck. In what anyone other than my children might call the olden days (for them, somewhat distressingly, the 'olden days' refers to the years before the introduction of colour television), a belief prevailed that if a pregnant woman saw a hare, then her child would be born with a harelip. In northern England, if you dreamt about a hare, then it was taken to mean that someone in your family was about to die. And in Cornwall it was believed that a girl who had died of grief after being betrayed by her lover would turn into a white hare and return to haunt him. I don't suppose there were ever that many Cornishwomen who expired with grief after being let down by errant lovers – even in those olden days I was talking about it can't have been a particularly common cause of death – but maybe the very thought of being haunted by a white hare was enough to keep their chaps faithful.

The story also cast an interesting light on an encounter I had almost every time I took Milo for a walk across the farmland adjoining our house. The same thing happened again and again; whenever we reached a particular spot in a particular field, a hare leapt up in front of us and ran hell for leather for the sanctity of the hedgerow, with Milo in hot, but always vain, pursuit. Milo, the big, daft lump, was taken by surprise every time. But I had a hunch that the hare was expecting us, almost lying in wait, looking forward to the thrill of a chase it knew it would never lose.

What I did not have a hunch about was that Milo – the lovely, lovable golden retriever we'd bought as an 8-week-old puppy on our first full day in Docklow Grange, and who was consequently part of our life in Herefordshire no less than the house itself – was about to turn into the most notorious animal for miles around, a Dog-of-Docklow version of the Beast of Bodmin.

17

Milo, and the Carnage

With hindsight, the seeds of disaster were sown when we added Paddy the long-haired Jack Russell to the menagerie. It would be easy enough for me to crow that I was the only member of the family who opposed Paddy's arrival, which is true enough, but it is also true that within a few days I was as smitten as anyone. He was an adorable little creature, who had a way of looking at people, with a quizzical cock of his head, that secured him all kinds of indulgences. Milo had never been allowed upstairs, for example, but Paddy was welcomed into our bedrooms from the start. Not that Milo was resentful; the two of them got on like a house on fire, although that wasn't quite the disaster the pair of them unleashed. In some ways this disaster was worse.

In all honesty I can't claim that Milo was ever perfectly behaved, even before Paddy arrived to lead him astray. For instance, he had a predilection for humping people's lower legs that was particularly embarrassing when strangers came to the door, especially, as in one memorable instance, the stranger had been sent by the English Tourist Board to determine what ranking our cottages deserved. We finally realized that we had to take drastic steps to stop Milo's sudden bursts of randiness on the eve of the 2005 Docklow fête, when the twenty-something girlfriend of the son of one of Docklow's parish councillors, who'd been helping to erect a marquee, suddenly got more of an erection than she'd bargained for.

She was down on her hands and knees playing with Paddy when Milo, seeing what he considered to be an inviting bottom, thundered over, pinned her to the ground and started frantically humping her until I furiously dragged him off. If ever there was a very public sexual practice that really did deserve the name dogging, this was it. But we'd never met this young woman before, which made it all the more horrifying. To her great credit she managed to see the funny side, and the situation was further defused by the parish councillor himself, a dry-humoured Brummie who brushed away my appalled apologies, saying: 'It's all right, just give us first choice of the puppies.'

But something clearly had to be done, so the very next day we booked Milo in to be castrated. When Jane told our friend Angie about Milo's impending operation, she expressed the hope that he would recover more quickly than I had done from the same procedure. This tickled Jane no end. 'But Brian wasn't castrated,' she said. 'He had a vasectomy.'

'Oh,' said Angie, looking both puzzled and embarrassed. 'Isn't it the same thing?'

This reminded me of a story another friend, Jonny, had recently told me about his seven-year-old son, who coincidentally had the same forenames as our 7-year-old, Jacob Alexander – and even more coincidentally, at least as far as both Jacobs were concerned, had the same Shrek pyjamas.

Jonny's son Jacob had come home from school one day, and told his parents that his teacher had related to the class the story of Joseph, he of the Technicolour Dreamcoat. The story had obviously made a big impression on him, because he remembered all the details vividly. He explained solemnly that Joseph had been put in jail by the Egyptians, but was released because he was the only person in the land who could interpret Pharaoh's strange dreams, which included one about seven thin cows eating seven fat cows. Joseph was able to tell Pharaoh that this dream meant that Egypt would enjoy seven years of plenty, followed by seven years of famine, and that to survive the long famine the people must put aside plenty of grain during the time of prosperity. So impressed was Pharaoh that he made Joseph his Prime Minister, and sure enough the next fourteen years followed exactly the pattern that Joseph had predicted.

According to Jonny, young Jacob told this story beautifully, and seemed to understand every nuance of it. But that night, as he was going to bed, he said that he was puzzled about something. 'What's that darling,' said Catherine, his mum. 'You know Joseph in the Bible,' said Jacob. 'Well, I still don't understand why his family were badgers.'

Catherine suppressed the urge to laugh. 'I don't think they were badgers, darling. What makes you say that?'

'Because that's what Mrs Jackson told us,' replied Jacob, indignantly. 'Joseph told Pharaoh that his people would have seven good years, followed by seven badgers.'

It was tempting to file this story under the cute things children say, along with my own Jacob's innocent query one day when he was looking at Eleanor's copy of the James Blunt album, *Back to Bedlam*. 'Why,' he asked us, 'is it called the same as what you say to me when I sometimes come downstairs at night – "back to bed, lamb"?'

But actually it struck me that it was an example of something more profound than that, an example of a condition that grows less acute with age but never really leaves us. It is the impression we give of understanding a subject thoroughly, and yet our knowledge turns out to be built on foundations of sand, based on a whopping misapprehension. Thus it was with young Jacob, who heard the story of Joseph and pictured a badger, and thus it was, too, with Angie, a woman in her forties, with three children, yet who heard about me having a vasectomy and pictured a eunuch.

Milo's operation, meanwhile, really did make a eunuch of him. But our fears that he might somehow undergo a personality change proved groundless. He was the same as before, just not as much of a liability in the vicinity of young women on their hands and knees. He had another personality trait, however, which we hoped the operation might have curbed; Milo had developed a fondness for chasing sheep.

His motivation for chasing them was entirely playful, but once, while Jane was walking him on Bircher Common, a beautiful stretch of heathland not far from Ludlow, he disappeared for ten minutes and returned, to her dismay, with some blood round his mouth. She could find no evidence of a wounded sheep, and putting two and two together, gratefully made five: he had perhaps just cut his tongue, she concluded, or at worst found an already injured pheasant or rabbit.

But not long after Paddy was introduced into the mix, he and Milo started disappearing from our garden together, initially for only ten or twenty minutes at a time, but then for an hour or two. Naively, we thought this was rather sweet. They always came back when we whistled and we rather liked the idea of them having little doggie adventures on their own. One Friday, however, they had not returned by nightfall. We were desperately anxious about them, and the only moment of levity was when we stood in the back garden yelling their names. Our friends Paul and Jacky, the Brodsky Quartet musicians, had arrived that afternoon to spend the weekend with us, and because they quite often worked with Elvis Costello, Paul pointed out that two of Costello's roadies were also called Paddy and Milo. He said he kept expecting a pair of hefty Irishmen to emerge from the trees, explaining that they'd 'just been moving the feckin' amps'.

To our great relief, just after 9 p.m. we heard a little Jack Russell yap – Paddy – followed by the basso-profundo bark of a golden retriever – Milo. They seemed delighted to be home and almost as relieved as we were, so we foolishly thought that it wouldn't happen again. But it did, only three days later. They took off from the garden in the afternoon and this time weren't back even by the following morning. We were frantic. We reported them missing to the police and the Hereford Council dog warden, and called Roger, who farms 1,000 acres alongside us. He hadn't seen them, he said, although he had found a bloodstained ewe, which had obviously been attacked by a powerful creature, very possibly a golden retriever. Shit! Milo had spent hours in our garden gazing benignly at Roger's sheep; the thought had never occurred to us that he might attack them.

A few hours later, Roger phoned with a doom-laden tone in his voice. He had come across a whole field of slain and wounded ewes and lambs, although they weren't his own. There were men out with shotguns looking for the miscreants, he reported. Shortly afterwards, we got another call, from a chap who lived in a hamlet a couple of miles away. Was it true that we were missing a retriever and a terrier? Yes, it was. And did we know that they had apparently attacked some sheep? Yes, unfortunately we did. 'Well,' he said, 'I have your dogs. I've hidden them in my barn because I don't want to see them shot. My wife and I are dog-lovers, and we think you should decide what is to become of them, not farmers with guns.'

This added a surreal espionage quality to the whole unfolding drama, with this chap surreptitiously loading Milo and Paddy into the back of a truck and driving them back to the Grange, while armed men hunted for them in neighbouring fields. It was practically the plot of a Frederick Forsyth or Len Deighton novel. Not that our two dogs much resembled spies. When their benefactor threw open the back of his truck they looked, of all expressions, distinctly sheepish. And much as we yearned for them to be innocent of the crime, their guilt was plain. They carried an unmistakable ovine stink, and Milo also had blood on his fur. He was bang – although mercifully not BANG! – to rights.

However, Roger was with us when they arrived back, and suggested, as sensitively as he could, that Milo at least might have to be destroyed. Once a dog has tasted the warm blood of a sheep, it will reoffend, he said. We tried desperately to think of alternatives. We could put up electric fences, or confine them to a run, or perhaps give Paddy away on the basis that two dogs act as a pack. But we had chosen Milo from his mother's litter; he'd been a bribe, a real-life cuddly toy, to make the children less upset about leaving behind their friends in London. They adored him. So did we. How could we have him put down?

Roger looked as aghast as we did. No matter what the circumstances, he wouldn't feel comfortable knowing that Milo was living near his livestock, he said. We understood. We had lived in Herefordshire for long enough to know that in sheep-farming country, it is a stigma to own a sheep-killing dog, as much of a no-no as it would be for a bank to employ a known embezzler, or a school to hire a convicted paedophile. What to do? Even if we were to give them away, it might merely be handing the problem to someone else. With a heavy heart, I phoned the vet in Leominster to make an appointment for both dogs to be destroyed. If the dreadful deed could be done before the children got home from school, then perhaps we could tell them that Milo and Paddy had been taken away to live happily somewhere else. We knew we had to do the right thing: by the farmer whose livestock had been killed and, indeed, by the farming community in which we lived, but also by ourselves and our children, and for that matter by the dogs, who had not turned overnight into crazed killers. They were still the sweet-natured pair we had raised from puppy-hood; they had just been acting as dogs sometimes will in a pack situation.

But when you live in the country, it is important not to be constrained by townie sensibilities. The townie way would be to compensate the farmer and make damn sure such a thing never happened again. The country code dictated other-wise. We had a friend, another local farmer, who had shot his beloved family dog simply for chasing sheep, let alone attacking them. He was a tough man, but he told us that he had cried as he loaded his shotgun and put a bullet through the hapless mutt's head. Yet he hadn't hesitated. Sheep-worrying, as it is known, is considered a heinous business in the country. In lambing season especially, people's livelihoods are at stake. We didn't want the slaughter to cost us whatever reputation we had built up, on top of the £1,500 that it turned out we owed the farmer, a Mr Jones (which, almost miraculously, was coughed up by our admirable insurers, Petplan).

I loaded Paddy and Milo into the back of the Volvo. Jane, understandably, had declined to accompany them on their final journey. But just as I inserted the key in the ignition, my mobile phone rang. It was the vet, Mr Tunney. He said he'd heard the story and didn't think that either of the animals should be destroyed. Bluntly, he said, the blame belonged with us for letting them escape our garden, not with the dogs. I thought about volunteering to be put down myself, but it was no time even for gallows humour. Mr Tunney explained that a terrier's brain and a retriever's brawn had been a combustible combination. 'It's like teenagers,' he said. 'One on his own can be very polite and charming, but several together can get up to all sorts.'

He was a beacon of measured common sense in what could fairly be described as an emotional maelstrom. We might have to consider getting one or both dogs rehomed, he said, but killing them wasn't the answer. In fact, he would refuse to do it.

In the meantime, there was still the question of the farmer's loss to deal with. Anxious to do whatever I could to help, I drove to the scene of the massacre and offered my assistance. Milo and Paddy had killed five sheep outright and fatally wounded 18 more. A further 20 or so were bloodied. It was not, to put it mildly, a pretty sight. I helped manoeuvre one distressed ewe into the back of the farmer's truck; its throat was ripped and its guts were trailing on the grass. None of this hardened me against Milo and Paddy – the country code that demands tough measures against rampaging dogs also dictates that nobody should get sentimental about sheep. But it did make me realize that there must not be an iota of possibility of either dog reoffending. If the vet wouldn't destroy them, then they would both have to be rehomed well away from sheep country.

The children, when they arrived home from school, were predictably distraught at this news. Joe, then aged ten, started emptying his money box to help pay the farmer, in the belief that it would make things better. Eleanor sobbed into Milo's sheep-scented fur for most of the evening. But the next day, we put the dogs into kennels while we could find them new homes, and started to call people we knew who might want them.

About a fortnight later, our friends Jonny and Catherine – whose son Jacob had thought that Joseph in the book of Genesis was a badger – agreed to take Paddy. They lived in my home town of Southport, seventeen miles north of Liverpool. And they also found a home for Milo, with some friends of theirs, the Mitchells, who lived just a few miles from them. It was an area conspicuously short of sheep, in fact the only chance of either dog reoffending would be by bringing down an elderly man wearing a sheepskin coat.

Fortuitously, I had an impending interviewing assignment for the *Independent* in Wigan, which wasn't far away from Southport. I was to interview the manager of Wigan Athletic Football Club, an engaging Scouser called Paul Jewell, at eleven one Tuesday morning, at the club's training-ground. So I phoned Catherine and said that I would drive over afterwards with the dogs. The only problem was that to be sure of getting to Wigan by 11 a.m., I needed to set off by 7.30 at the latest, and the kennels didn't open until nine. I would normally have taken the train to Wigan rather than run the gauntlet of the dreaded M6 on a weekday morning, but for obvious reasons this was not a trip that I could undertake by train. So I had to fetch the dogs the night before, except that I didn't want to take them home even for a night, because it would have been distressing for the children to see them, only to be separated again. I duly called on my friend Alex, of Broadfield Court vineyard, who lived on a farm. She kindly offered me the use of her stable.

The dogs would be secure overnight, she said, and I could collect them as early as I liked the following morning. She showed me to the stable, which, if they were ever to remake the epic 1977 mini-series *Jesus of Nazareth*, would make a perfect location. Incidentally, I once read somewhere that when the director Franco Zeffirelli got to the Last Supper scene in *Jesus of Nazareth*, Ian McShane, playing Judas, slipped shiftily out of the room with Zeffirelli's camera carefully following him, but couldn't resist popping his head back round the door and saying: 'Now, have I got this right? Eight cod and four haddock, all with mushy peas?'

It was 6.45 a.m. and still dark when I got to Alex's stable the following morning. In the nearby farmhouse, there was no sign of life. Alex's husband, Mark, was probably already out milking the cows. I opened the stable door, and was greeted with wild, slavering excitement by Paddy and Milo, who seemed less appreciative than I was of their New Testament setting, and were anxious to get out, cock their legs, and then climb into the back of the Volvo, which to them meant walkies. I gave them each a Bonio, put them on leads, and then turned to find that the stable door had shut behind me. I was locked in.

I am pleased to say that the surrealism of this situation – being shut in a cold, dark Herefordshire stable with a pair of dogs, all three of us desperate for a pee, when I needed to be on the M6 heading for Wigan and an interview with Paul Jewell – did not escape me. But after I had chortled awhile, I began to weigh up the seriousness of my predicament. After all, it might be some time before anyone heard me yelling to be let out. I might shout myself hoarse after the stable door had bolted, so to speak. Thankfully, the power of prayer, combined with some sustained door-jiggling, eventually got me out.

On the M6 I stopped at some godforsaken service station to let Paddy and Milo have a brief walk, and then drove on to Wigan, where I arrived just in time for my interview with Paul Jewell, having first tied up my two sheep-murdering dogs to a drainpipe on the outside of the Wigan Athletic treatment room. That evening, swapping stories of our respective days, Jane and I agreed that country life is unpredictable, to say the least.

For while all this was happening, she was having an altogether different but similarly bizarre day. Her friend Rosemary was soon to get married and Avril had decided that it might be a laugh to buy Rosemary some sex aids. Somehow or other, Avril knew about a sex shop just outside Church Stretton, in Shropshire, and if that's not the oddest place for a sex shop, then I don't know what is. So, while I was tying up the dogs at the Wigan Athletic training-ground, and still picking bits of straw off myself left over from my unexpected

245

sojourn in the stable, Jane and Avril were waiting in the reception of a rural sex shop, having been told that they couldn't yet go in to look at the toys because 'there's a man in there who wants privacy'. Eventually he emerged, and what a conclusion it would have been to this story had he happened to be a vicar or magistrate of their acquaintance. Regrettably, they didn't recognise him, hard though they scrutinised him while both, of course, pretending to look the other way.

Up in Wigan, my interview with Jewell over, I loaded the dogs into the boot again and drove to Southport. Catherine met me at the Mitchells' house, and I handed Paddy to her, before introducing Milo to them. They seemed like a friendly, warm family, and I stayed there for half an hour or so, trying to memorise all the details I would need to pass on to Jane and the kids: the age and names of the children, the size of the garden, as much as possible to give them a mental picture of where Milo had gone to live. I confess that I drove away with a tear in my eye. It seemed like the end of a chapter.

18

Fergus, and the Shanties

As it turned out, Milo did not stay for long with the Mitchells. Mrs Mitchell had told me that her elderly parents, the Cunninghams, who lived in Cheshire, might decide to take him. They'd had a succession of retrievers over many years, and their latest one had recently died, so if they took a fancy to Milo, he might move to Cheshire.

In the event, that's just what happened, and in the meantime we decided that we needed another family dog. The consensus was that we should get another retriever puppy, so Jane looked on the puppy sales register on the Kennel Club website and found that there was a litter not far away in Kidderminster. I later wrote about this in my column, and was taken to task by a reader for buying a pedigree puppy rather than taking in a rescue dog, which in her words would have meant some good coming out of something bad. It was an entirely fair criticism, but we were all fixated on repeating the Milo experience, except for its miserable denouement, of course.

So off we went to Kidderminster and paid £475 for an 11-week-old puppy. We called him Fergus in keeping with the Gaelic theme established by Milo and Paddy, and also in the hope that Fergus might be the name of another of Elvis Costello's roadies. Fergus, we decided, would end up with the equivalent of a PhD in leaving sheep alone, no matter how much it might cost, although several people had told us that the lesson could be cheaply taught, simply by confining a puppy in a barn for an hour with a ram. It never fails, apparently, except when the puppy is killed. If it survives, then it understandably never goes near anything woolly ever again. Were your Uncle Horace to enter the room simply wearing a pure new lambswool sweater, even then it would cower in a corner.

We decided to opt for the less brutal tactics of Bert Harris, a gently spoken Scotsman who ran a dog-training operation twenty-odd miles away called School for Scoundrels. We told Bert that we were keen to stop Fergus developing some of Milo's less appealing habits, such as jumping up at people, occasionally attempting to bonk them, and randomly slaughtering sheep, and he was full of good tips. Interestingly enough, he said that 90 per cent of those who sought his advice did so with their second dogs, anxious not to repeat the mistakes they'd made with their first. He also said that with patience you could train a dog to go to the fridge, open it, and fetch you a bottle of beer. I quite liked that idea.

Fergus soon helped lift our sadness over Milo; he was an equally delightful creature, although with one deficiency. Where Milo only ever had to see an open boot to leap into it, knowing that it probably meant a good long walk somewhere along the line, Fergus was intractably opposed. He simply wouldn't jump in, which, as he grew, became a problem. Hoisting a heavy, muddy, reluctant retriever in and out of a car was nobody's idea of a good time.

Then, one day, we happened to bump into the wonderful Bert Harris again. We told Bert about the car thing, and he advised us to starve Fergus of both food and affection for twenty-four hours, then put a bowl of Chappie in the open boot, perhaps with a special treat on top, such as cheese. He also said that the entire family should sit in the car chatting and laughing and generally appearing to have a good time. The lure of the food, combined with the feeling that he was missing out on the fun, ought to tempt Fergus into the car, said Bert. And so it did, at the third attempt, just as we were all beginning to feel a little foolish for throwing a mock party, in a Volvo, for the benefit of a dog.

But then, dogs lead human beings into doing some funny things. On Christmas Eve 2005, three months after we had parted with Milo, the phone rang. 'Is that Mr Viner?' came a voice. I owned up. 'This is Mrs Cunningham from Cheshire, Milo's new mummy. I just wanted to wish you a merry Christmas and to tell you that Milo is a tweetie-pie.'

I agreed that he was an extremely lovable, good-natured and well-behaved dog, apart from when he was ripping out sheep's throats. 'He's a tweetie-pie,' she reiterated. 'And I don't think he's capable of killing sheep. I heard the story, but think they were already dead, killed by a fox.'

I assured her that I would not have accepted a £1,500 compensation claim from Mr Jones the farmer had I not been absolutely certain that Milo and Paddy were jointly responsible for the carnage that I saw for myself and indeed helped to clear up, hauling scarcely alive ewes with their entrails hanging out into the back of a Land Rover. Moreover, we would hardly have given up an adored family pet, subjecting ourselves to the abject spectacle of our 12-year-old daughter sobbing into Milo's fur for an hour, had we not been convinced that it was the correct course of action. To keep him and risk the same thing happening again would have put Milo at risk of a bullet, I explained, and it also would have been intolerably provocative to our neighbours, most of whom were farmers. So, I said, no matter how remote they considered the possibility of him harming another creature, they should never, ever take him into sheep country and allow him off the leash. 'Well,' she said, having digested this dire warning. 'All I can say is that he's an absolute tweetie-pie. In fact my husband's just come in from a walk with him. I'll put my husband on, I'm sure he'd like to talk to you.'

Mr Cunningham came on the line. 'Yes, he's a grand dog,' he said. 'Absolutely grand. Would you like a word with him?'

I politely declined, but Mr Cunningham insisted. 'No, no, I'll put him on.'

And so it was that I found myself, sotto voce in case anyone should overhear, talking to a golden retriever on the telephone, and for want of anything better to say, wishing him a merry Christmas and a happy new year. 'I don't suppose he knew what on earth was happening,' I said, when Mr Cunningham mercifully returned the phone to his own ear. 'Oh, he knew all right,' came the reply. 'I could tell he recognized your voice.'

These calls from Milo's new mummy, and daddy, continued periodically. It was very sweet of the Cunninghams to give us progress reports, but also slightly unsettling to be kept posted on Milo's new life. Mrs Cunningham called one evening and told me that Milo was about to go to the local dog-grooming parlour. She expressed surprise when I said we had never had him professionally groomed. 'What, you never had him tootsied up?' she cried. I came away with an unshakable image of Milo in curlers, reading *Marie Claire*. But I decided that maybe an effete new image would be good for him, that maybe his blood lust was diminishing with his tootsying-up sessions. He might not want to chase any more sheep in case he broke a nail.

Milo's new mummy also said that they were about to take him to the Lake District for a week. I reminded her again that we had deliberately sought a new home for him in an ovine-free zone and warned her to be especially careful if there were sheep anywhere in the vicinity. But she remained implacably convinced that Milo would never do such a terrible thing on his own, now blaming the incident all on wayward Paddy. She quickly changed the subject. It was like telling a disbelieving mother that her adored little boy, a paragon of good behaviour at home, had threatened someone with a flick-knife at school. I wished that I'd taken photographs of the carnage, but that probably wouldn't have persuaded her, either. Still, it was good to know that Milo was being treated well. By the sound of it, there had been Ming dynasty emperors treated worse.

Meanwhile, with Paddy also gone, Jane started agitating for another small dog, and in particular a West Highland terrier. Let the record show, as they say in legal circles, that I was dead against this, just as I had been against Paddy's arrival. And this time my case was bolstered by the knowledge that adding a terrier to a retriever had been as explosive as adding plutonium to nitrogen, or however it is that you make a bomb; I've already admitted that my chemistry skills were never up to much. But Jane, who'd had a much-loved Westie as a girl, argued that it would be different now that we were aware of the dangers. When some people turned up to Manor Cottage with an admittedly very sweet pair of Westies called Finlay and Crawford, she became resolute. And not long afterwards, a mother at Stamford Heath School happened to mention that her Westie had just had a litter. Thus it was that one day in August 2006, we acquired Bonnie.

We felt that the name Bonnie kept the Gaelic connection alive, even if Bonnie Prince Charlie was more garlic than Gaelic, having grown up in France. And Bonnie went quite nicely with Fergus; together they sounded like a couple who might have run the village pub in *A Ring of Bright Water*.

While Bonnie quickly made herself at home, weeing and pooing with abandon all over the house, I was reminded of what an amazing stench could be generated by the smallest puppy excretion. When my mother came to stay with us for a few days, she announced one night, shortly after 10 p.m., that she was going to bed. This seemed a little early, but seconds after she had left the room, Jane and I were hit by an olfactory howitzer that had clearly been launched from just behind the sofa where my mum had been cheerfully reading her book. She was first in the line of fire. However, she was too polite to say that she was going upstairs to escape the disgusting smell, so she feigned tiredness. And what was responsible for the offending pong? A tiny bit of poo about the size and shape of a jelly bean, not that there was much chance of confusing the two.

Fergus's excretions, although performed out of doors, were also becoming a problem. Desperate to keep him well away from sheepy temptation, we had invested in a £700 piece of kit called a Freedom Fence, basically a boundary wire with a low electrical current running through it which, via a transmitter on his collar, first issued a bleeping noise and then administered a small shock if he got too close to it. Not everyone approves of these things, but it certainly seemed to work. The only problem was that Fergus could no longer amble into the wood where he had done most of his pooing, so instead he started squatting on the lawn. Before every game of family cricket I had to go round like a bomb disposal officer, identifying toxic piles and carefully removing them from the field of play.

Nor was Fergus the only creature leaving piles in the garden. We also had a serious molehill problem, which one morning led to me listening with interest to a debate in the House of Lords, something that had never happened before, and would almost certainly never happen again.

As usual, the clock radio had woken us up, tuned, as usual, to the *Today* programme. There had been a period when Jane rebelled against the *Today* programme, and, very daringly for a former Radio 4 producer, retuned to Radio 1. It was actually quite refreshing to wake up to a rapper singing 'You and me baby, we ain't nothing but mammals/So let's do it like they do it on the Discovery Channel.' That's not a sentiment you ever hear from John Humphrys. But in due course we returned to Radio 4, lying there just before 6.30, which on winter mornings meant pitch blackness, with Humphrys discussing more deaths in Iraq, or James Naughtie stumbling over the latest starvation statistics from Africa.

At least such topics reminded us that there were greater

challenges in life than having to exit a blissfully warm bed when it is minus ten outside. And I don't mean outside the house, by the way, I mean outside the bed. Yet hardly anything seemed harder during those first few moments of our day than pushing back the duvet. Jane was better at it than I was; she was usually downstairs releasing Fergus and Bonnie for their long morning pees by the time I was vertical and ready for mine. Before that, I would lie there as the *Today* programme seeped slowly into my consciousness, attempting to work out who was talking about what and why.

Sometimes, this sleepy confusion lent the news a decidedly surreal dimension, as it did on this particular morning when the 'Yesterday in Parliament' segment reported a debate in the House of Lords about moles. It must have been at least a minute before I realized that their lordships were anxiously considering the pernicious effect of moles, in the sense of tiny, tunnelling mammals (and possibly not the mammals that had been in the mind of the Radio 1 rapper), rather than moles, in the sense of spies. Even once I was fully awake, it still seemed bizarre that they should have the former kind of moles on their noble minds, and yet reassuring, because I was all for a government crackdown on molehills.

Let me save you the trouble of looking up the debate in Hansard, the parliamentary chronicle, and simply relate that when Lord Bach – who was Parliamentary Under-Secretary of State for Environment, Food and Rural Affairs – explained that chemical means of reducing the mole population were being looked at, Viscount Montgomery of Alamein offered an alternative.

'My Lords,' he said, 'is the minister aware that another good method of control is old-fashioned traps? My wife some years ago became a considerable expert on this matter and was very successful too. However, as we now have no grassland, she has retired and is not available for advice.'

'My Lords, I am sorry to hear that,' said Lord Bach, followed by Lord Crickhowell, who said: 'My Lords, I declare an interest as one who employs a professional mole killer to try to deal with the plague of moles that do grave damage to the land around my property, then advance like a Napoleonic army into my garden.'

Lord Bach was again sympathetic. 'My Lords,' he said, 'there is no doubt that they cause a lot of inconvenience to a lot of people. On the other hand, many people find them very agreeable animals, although sometimes more at a distance than close to. There are alternative methods, however; one is phosphide gas, which I am told is used widely in northern Europe to achieve the same rather grisly end.'

Lord Lawson of Blaby, the former Chancellor of the Exchequer and father of the fragrant Nigella, then entered the fray. 'My Lords, is the minister aware that it is a genuinely European question. My noble friend Lord Kimball mentioned the explosion of moles in England. My experience at my home in France is that there is a similar phenomenon there this year. It has never been as bad as it is this year, so what effort is the minister making to get French support for this important derogation?'

And so it went on, with further important thoughts on the subject offered by several more noble friends, and me thinking how wonderful it was to live in a country in which our legislators talk about exterminating the velvet-clad monsters that advance into our gardens 'like a Napoleonic army'. My only regret was that none of their lordships appeared to have read *Tales of the Country*, for if they had they would have known about the technique for discouraging moles that I was told about in the King's Head not long after we moved to Docklow. 'Place a fresh turd on the top of a fresh molehill,' said Owen, 'and you won't have no more problems from the little bastard.' I couldn't help wondering how Viscount Montgomery of Alamein might have conveyed that advice.

Still, apart from the contributions of Fergus and the moles, the garden of Docklow Grange seemed to have benefited from our four years as owners. This owed less to us than to Alan, our fortnightly gardener, who took particular interest in the vegetable garden, compensating with careful expertise for my cheerful amateurishness.

It wasn't that I didn't try to learn how to tend a vegetable garden. For a while I consumed almost every book there was to read on the subject, and threw myself, very nearly literally, into the exciting business of composting. In fact, we were staying with our Crouch End friends Ali and Chris one weekend, when, during the preparation of Sunday lunch, I did something that even I recognized as weird. As Chris was scraping the vegetable peelings into the bin, I asked whether I could take them home. For our compost bin, obviously, but Jane thought I'd gone mad, carefully decanting someone else's unwanted broccoli stalks into a Sainsbury's bag, then clutching it tightly as we said goodbye, like a toddler leaving a birthday party. But that's what having a compost bin does for you, or at any rate what it did for me.

Similarly, I exulted when the Marshalls' vegetable seed catalogue arrived. Its pages soon became as grubby and dog-eared as had been the pages of the *Health and Efficiency* magazine that I traded for fifty Bazooka Joes and two Curly-

Wurlies in my first term at grammar school, circa November 1973. Indeed, if it is possible to look lasciviously at pictures of Glen Ample raspberries and Stockbridge Arrow rhubarb, then that is exactly what I did.

My newfound passion for growing vegetables was faintly troubling even to me, let alone to people whose homes I left carrying vegetable peelings. For example, it occurred to me one morning in the summer of 2005, while pottering among the broad beans and listening to *Test Match Special* on my headphones, that I had become thoroughly diverted from a particularly fascinating passage of play, in which the Australian wrist-spinner Shane Warne was bamboozling England's batsmen, by the discovery of black bean aphid. When vegetables get between a chap and his cricket, I decided, it was time to take stock. Or in my case, to make stock. While Warne continued to torment Andrew Flintoff and co., I picked a head of fennel, a carrot, an onion, some slightly scabby broccoli, cabbage and watercress leaves, and took comfort in the kitchen in the production of a top-notch vegetable stock.

The black bean aphid did not appear to have affected the flavour of the vegetables, ditto the flea beetle that had nibbled through all my rocket. Yet around that time there was a story in the press claiming that Britain's farmers were being forced to throw away as much as a third of their fruit and veg, because supermarkets wanted it cosmetically perfect. My rocket would scarcely have got into the Tesco car park. And Somerfield, of which there was a branch in Leominster, reportedly had a three-page document relating only to cauliflowers, which had all to be of uniform size and colour, with no more than two spots per leaf. No cauliflower grower could afford not to meet these regulations. One said that he didn't even bother to harvest about 20 per cent of his crop, knowing that it wouldn't pass muster. For the same reason he threw away another 10 per cent or so during processing, then had more returned by the packers for being sub-standard.

So there were all these perfectly good cauliflowers being left to rot, just because they didn't look perfect. I wondered what would happen if people were judged along the same lines, and realized gloomily that in some areas of human endeavour, they already were. Meanwhile, Patrick Holden, the director of the admirable Soil Association, rightly pointed out that 'the supermarkets want food that looks like it never came out of the ground'. We certainly weren't guilty of that ourselves; our home-grown food quite often reached the plate still containing the odd morsel of soil or small green creepy-crawly. Or sometimes both, if you were very lucky.

Assiduously as I tended the vegetable patch, and collected the eggs in the laying months, we were, alas, never remotely close to being self-sufficient. But at least we didn't have to venture far to buy food: some of the finest produce in the country was being grown on farms all around us, and sold in some wonderfully enterprising farm shops. And because we lived in the middle of nowhere we were visited every couple of months by a man with a refrigerated van, selling frozen food. That makes it sound like a slightly dodgy enterprise, but actually it was classy stuff: huge Dover soles and Thai gambas, and excellent salmon-and-broccoli fishcakes called Shanties, which the children adored, hence their excitement when 'the shanty man' pulled up in front of the house. We even wrote a family song in celebration of his arrival, wholly inventing the following lyrics:

Who can take a sunrise,
Sprinkle it with dew? Cover it in broccoli and a miracle or
  two . . .
The shanty man, the shanty man can,
The shanty man can 'cause he mixes it with love and makes
  the world taste good . . .

After a while, confusingly, we acquired two shanty men.
One represented a company called Good Taste, based in
Bristol; the other an outfit called Clever Cuisine, operating out
of Stratford-upon-Avon. Their wares and prices, as far as I
could tell, were identical. So it was understandably frustrating
for one shanty man to turn up, to find that the other had
recently been and that we had all the Shanties we needed for the
foreseeable future. One of them tended to deal stoically with
this disappointment; the other would throw a bit of a hissy fit. I
was reminded of the film *Tin Men*, in which Richard Dreyfuss
and Danny De Vito played feuding aluminium sidings sales-
men, and cruelly hoped that they might one day turn up at the
same time, and square up to each other, flexing their mussels.

Slightly more challenging than waiting for the shanty
man, but more rewarding and certainly a damn sight cheaper,
was foraging for our own food. I can't claim to have done much
of this beyond the occasional burst of blackberrying in the
hedgerows around us, and the odd unsuccessful stab at making
nettle soup, but I was aware that if only I knew how to spot a
mushroom that was safe to eat, I really could start calling
myself a backwoodsman.

Then, at the 2006 Ludlow Food Festival, I was introduced
by Merlin Unwin, the man who had published the first biography of the hare for twenty-three years, to a fellow called

Alexander Schwab, a jolly mushroom expert from Switzerland who had written a book called *Mushrooming without Fear*.

Alex, keen for me to publicise his book, offered to come over to Docklow to take me out mushrooming in my own garden and the surrounding fields. Such are the perks of journalism: as a sports writer I've had golf lessons from Seve Ballesteros and Nick Faldo, a snooker lesson from Steve Davis, a tennis lesson from John McEnroe, a darts lesson from Phil 'The Power' Taylor, and a spin-bowling masterclass from Shane Warne. But none was quite as enjoyable as a private mushroom forage with Alex Schwab, which ended up with me sitting at my own kitchen table eating an enormous cep fried in butter at 10.15 a.m. That's the sort of thing I got into the profession for.

The cep, alas, was not one we found. In fact, we found practically nothing. I had taken a large wicker basket with me, which turned out to be absurdly optimistic; it had recently been far too dry for mushrooms to prosper, and all we spotted was something alarmingly poisonous called *Lepiota josserandii*.

Nevertheless, it was a highly educational expedition. Alex told me that in his village, Biglen in the Emmenthal region of Switzerland, there was an official mushroom inspector. I told him that I liked the idea of a mushroom inspector and thought that Docklow should have one. This he considered very funny; whoever said the Swiss have no sense of humour? Biglen's mushroom inspector, he added, was a woman called Monika Lehmann. People would gather all sorts of mushrooms and take them to Monika for a thumbs up or down. Speaking of thumbs up or down, he also told me that the Romans tested mushrooms by letting slaves try them first, which wasn't very nice of them.

As we walked through the fields, I listened attentively to

260

Alex's tips on how to become a reliable mushroom forager. But I knew I had a long way to go before I became an entirely safe pair of hands. 'Here's an interesting mushroom,' I called to Alex as we skirted a copse of trees, not far from where Milo and Paddy had gone on the rampage. He came over to take a look. 'Zat,' he said, 'is a dried-out cowpat.'

The prize find for mushroom-hunters is the cep, and Alex looked with approval at the beech and oak trees round the pond at the bottom of the field next to our house: ceps thrive underneath beech and oak and he advised me to get out there after some steady rain. Then we returned to my kitchen where Alex produced the whopping cep that he had found the day before in Mortimer Forest. He cooked it in about half a pound of unsalted butter, explaining that I should freeze what was left of the cep-flavoured butter and use it to fry meat in, or to pour over rice or pasta. The cep itself we ate on toast and extraordinarily delicious it was too. 'It has to be cooked in unsalted butter,' said Alex, sternly. 'To cook a cep in olive oil is a crime.' I nodded, gravely, trying to look as though I could hardly think of anything worse.

The cep, he added, is known as the king of mushrooms. And the fly agaric, what most of us would call a toadstool, is known as the queen of mushrooms. Fly agaric is a hallucinogen and best avoided unless you want to have a particularly wild evening, but mushroomers have a saying, that wherever you find the queen, nearby you will find the king. According to Alex's book, the phrase 'to go berserk' derives from a particular band of Viking warriors called the Berserkers who were known for fighting like mad dogs, apparently because they'd dosed up beforehand on fly agaric. Which is another conversation-stopper, I think you will agree.

19

Ozzy Osbourne, and the Bordello

In September 2005, Merlin Unwin, who through his books would thoughtfully furnish me with enough valuable information about hares and mushrooms to fill a lifetime of awkward silences at dinner parties, also sent me a volume called *The Temptation and Downfall of the Vicar of Stanton Lacy*, by a man called Peter Klein. It was the fascinating tale of a seventeenth-century Shropshire vicar called Robert Foulkes, and was further confirmation of what could be ascertained simply by reading the property pages of the *Hereford Times* every week, that the Welsh Marches is a fascinatingly historic part of England.

Strictly speaking, of course, every part of England is as old as every other part, but there are still some regions where you feel the weight of history. That is true in spades for Herefordshire and Shropshire. A few miles from us stands a castle called Hampton Court, not to be confused with the Johnnie-come-lately Hampton Court on the banks of the River Thames. This is a place with even more history, on the banks of the less fêted River Lugg. It was built by Sir Rowland Lenthall, who, on 6 November 1434, was granted licence by King Henry VI 'to crenellate, turrelate and embattle' his manor – the fifteenth-century version of getting planning permission for some stone cladding, I suppose. But its origins go back even further; its foundation stone is said to have been laid by King Henry IV, when he was plain, or plain-ish, Henry Bolingbroke, Earl of Hereford.

Sir Rowland did a fine building job; the house has retained its grandeur through civil war, numerous changes of ownership and occasional penury. It enjoyed one of its grander periods in the time of Thomas Coningsby (1656–1729), a favourite of William and Mary, although a bit of a nutter, whose quick temper was satirised by the Ian Hislop of the day, Jonathan Swift. As it happened, Coningsby's father-in-law, Ferdinando Gorges, was the nephew of Sir Ferdinando Gorges who (I hope you're still with me) was known as 'the father of colonisation in America' after signing the charter by which the Pilgrim Fathers were allowed to set sail in 1620.

So it was fitting that Hampton Court had ended up in American hands. It was bought in 1994 by Robert and Judith Van Kampen, of Michigan, who spent a fortune restoring the house and more especially the grounds, which they opened to the public. When Robert Van Kampen died the place was put up for sale, and there was no doubt that, had it been in the Home Counties, there would have been a right old hue and cry about saving it for the nation. As it was, hardly anyone outside Herefordshire had even heard of it, let alone cared about its future.

In this neck of the woods, however, folk cared very much. Hampton Court is a magical place, thanks largely to the vision of a chap called Ed Waghorn, the estate manager, who over a ten-year-period had masterminded the transformation of featureless meadows into gardens of immense charm, complete with a yew maze, a wisteria tunnel, a sunken garden, a kitchen garden, and a water garden with an elegant waterfall that children, notably my children, could stand behind and get utterly saturated without having any dry clothes to change into afterwards. Still, while the little darlings played (some would say rampaged) to their hearts' content, parents could take sustenance in one of the finest country-house cafés I know.

I regretted but respected the Van Kampen family's decision to offload Hampton Court, which can't have offered them much return on their huge investment. It was, oddly enough, more of a religious investment than a financial one. They ran an organisation called Sola Scriptura, its lofty purpose 'the affirmation of the authenticity, accuracy and authority of God's Word, the Bible' – and Hampton Court was run accordingly. Those who hired the place for weddings, for example, were permitted to serve only strictly limited amounts of alcohol.

With the money from the Hampton Court sale, the Van Kampens wanted to extend their religious theme park, the Holy Land Experience in Orlando, Florida. I love the idea of a religious theme park, by the way, and can only pray that it has a Holy Ghost train. Whatever, dark rumours circulated for months after the estate was put up for sale: that the grounds were to be parcelled up and sold off to local farmers; that the golfer Ernie Els was part of a consortium hoping to turn the place into a golf and country club; even that Ozzy Osbourne had, in one of his more lucid moments, expressed some interest.

I followed the Hampton Court saga in the pages of the *Hereford Times* with great interest, but I had only to look in the paper's property section to be reminded of the amount of local history. A sixteenth-century house called Vauld Farm, for example, on the market for £625,000, was described as 'dating back to 1510, although parts could be earlier, the property was owned by King Henry VIII, who gave it, and the parish of Marden, to his Queen, Catherine of Aragon. More recently, Roy Harper extensively renovated the property.'

I loved that seamless combination of the portentous and the prosaic: Catherine of Aragon – later to lose favour with Henry, who, desperate for a male heir, forced a schism with the Roman Catholic Church when Pope Clement V declined to sanction a divorce, which in turn led to the king's excommunication and the dissolution of the monasteries – did her bit with the house and then, give or take a few centuries, it was over to Roy Harper. I presumed that this was the same Roy Harper who had enjoyed flickering fame as a singer-songwriter since the mid-1960s, but even so, it was a hoot to find him, as a former owner, given the same billing as Catherine of Aragon.

St Peter's church in Stanton Lacy, I learnt from Peter Klein's book, had an even more fascinating past than Vauld Farm, and an eerier one than Hampton Court. In 1968, a man popped in to take some photographs for a historian friend but was so over-come by a 'feeling of terror' that he scarpered. He then went back with his wife, but again got a bad case of the willies, so contacted the vicar, the Reverend Prebendary L. J. Blashford

Snell, who accompanied the man into the church and, reportedly, witnessed his hair standing on end.

This was simply by way of a preface to the story of the Reverend Foulkes, vicar of Stanton Lacy from 1660 to 1678, who had an extramarital affair with a parishioner, Ann Atkinson, and in January 1679 was hanged at Tyburn having been found guilty of the murder of their illegitimate child. Klein had uncovered a cracking story and told it brilliantly. In fact, it had all the elements of a really good *News of the World* splash – an adulterous 42-year-old vicar, his long-suffering wife, a 26-year-old mistress, an unscrupulous publican, prurient villagers, a murder, even a Peeping Tom – with the added bonus, not available even to the News of the Screws, of redemption on the scaffold. 'You may see in me what sin is, and what it will end in,' Foulkes told the assembled crowd.

He was certainly pretty sinful, reportedly carrying on not only with Ann but also behaving 'very ymodestly, rudely and undecently' with 'severall loose, idle, and incontinent persons of the female sex, att unseasonable and unfitt houres'. Whether there were perfectly seasonable and fitt houres in which to behave ymodestly, rudely and undecently, the book did not record. Whatever, the vicar's fate was sealed by the testimony of one Somerset Brabant, who swore that at the Talbot Inn in Worcester – which is still there, incidentally – he had peeped through a hole and watched Foulkes and his lover 'stirring and labouring as in the very Act of uncleanness' and later 'kissing and clipping with much vigour and earnestness'.

There had already been an unsuccessful attempt to prosecute Foulkes, but Brabant was the witness that the prosecuting lawyer, Richard Cornwall, had been praying for. Nor was Ann's increasingly obvious pregnancy good news for the vicar, so, in desperation, he seemingly killed the baby soon after she had given birth. Both he and Ann were then brought to trial, but she did a nifty bit of plea-bargaining and got off, while he was hanged. Even without any mention of Roy Harper, it was a heck of a yarn.

Buildings tell all the best yarns. In 2005 I learnt that a shop in Ludlow called Bodenhams was about to celebrate its sex-centenary – 600 years, all spent as a retail outlet, which must be some kind of record.

Journalists are incorrigibly fond, when writing about historical events, of evoking the era by informing the reader who was Prime Minister at the time, which famous people were born or died in that year, what you would have paid for a semi in Esher ... you know the sort of thing. But in this case it's irresistible. In the year that Bodenhams first started trading, Henry IV was on the throne, Owen Glendower seized Harlech Castle, Chaucer had been dead for only five years, the Battle of Agincourt was ten years in the future, and a semi in Esher cost, at a rough guess, less than 100 groats.

You wouldn't want to try saying it after a couple of pints of cider, just as I struggled when slightly intoxicated to ask the time of the next train to Worcester Shrub Hill, but Bodenhams is a phenomenon. An almost tear-jerkingly lovely, half-timbered building on the corner of Broad Street and King Street, it was purpose-built as a shop, opened in May 1405, and has remained a shop throughout every one of the subsequent 600 years or so. As the big anniversary approached, its owner, Muriel Curry, the great-granddaughter of William Bodenham who took over the premises in 1861, understandably thought that all this was worth a bit of media attention, so she sent a press release to every national newspaper informing them that on 16 May there would be a blessing of the timbers by the rector of Ludlow. Not a single national newspaper, to their collective shame, gave the story even an inch of coverage. And although a BBC Midlands television crew was dispatched to cover the celebrations, the item failed to make that day's bulletin which was dominated by West Bromwich Albion's achievement in avoiding relegation from the Premier League.

I heard about the sexcentenary a month later, but reckoned that a month wasn't much to worry about after 600 years. So I went to Bodenhams – still a clothes shop, as it was in 1405, although the sackcloth cowls have regrettably been discontinued – to meet Mrs Curry, a splendidly feisty woman pushing eighty, and her son Roger, a rather dashing, piratical-looking fellow with an earring.

Mrs Curry told me that the building had been commissioned by the Palmers' Guild, and that to be eligible to join the guild you had to have made a pilgrimage to the Holy Land and brought back a palm leaf. She speculated perfectly reasonably that some of the soldiers who fought at Agincourt in 1415 would have ridden off from Ludlow Castle and would therefore have worn longjohns under their chain mail bought from Bodenhams, or whatever it was called in the fifteenth century. Her son added that he was keen to diversify into furniture, which the shop last sold just before the First World War, and I went away thinking how thrilling it was that an institution with so much past plainly had plenty of future.

Even by Ludlow's venerable standards, the story of Bodenhams was quite something, but the rest of the town, too, is suffused with history. A retired architect called Michael Phillips contacted me one day to say that extensive renovation work on his house in Corve Street had exposed ancient oak timbers bearing clear scorch marks, apparently a legacy of the Great Fire of Ludlow of 1645, which began when besieged Royalists in the castle started firing on the Parliamentarians below. If the cannonballs had carried another 50 yards, they would have hit Tesco.

Coincidentally, Mr Phillips's letter arrived in the same post as another one telling me that a former London madam was setting up a discreet bordello in a Herefordshire farmhouse. I could only assume that my anonymous correspondent meant Miss Whiplash. Whatever, his letter enabled me to crack a joke that delighted me at the time and delights me still, that it pleased me to learn, on the very same morning, about scorched beams and debauched schemes.

However, if it was Miss Whiplash to whom he referred, his information was incorrect. I phoned her and asked her outright. I was also interested, I said, in reports that she was about to put up for auction some of the macabre memorabilia that she had collected while she was working as a dominatrix and madam.

I had read in the good old *Hereford Times* that she intended to flog, so to speak, three letters from the poisoner Dr Crippen that she had bought at Christie's in the mid-1980s. She told me about the letters: one was a simple diagnosis of a patient's ailment; one was written from his prison cell and addressed to his lawyers, asking them to dispose of his effects but to keep a particular suit (probably because he wished to be hanged in it); and one was to the Lord Chief Justice purporting to be from his wife, Belle Elmore, who had disappeared in February 1910, saying that she was alive but in hiding. It was later proved to have been forged by Crippen, who had in fact decapitated Belle and hidden her corpse in his cellar. Nice chap.

Miss Whiplash told me that she bought the letters because

she had loads of money back then and nothing better to spend it on. 'I had my boat and my Rolls-Royce,' she said. 'I had property. So I started buying things for my dungeon and torture chamber. People who collect china teapots start with one and build up a collection, and that's what I did. I had a hangman's rope, an execution warrant from Louis XIV, stuff from Newgate Prison, all sorts of things. It was something for my clients to look at while they were on the rack, or in the stocks.'

As far as you can tell over the phone, Miss Whiplash kept a straight face while she was telling me this. She added that she had been offered fortunes by the tabloids over the years to reveal her clients' identities, but had not succumbed – and never would. 'I liked all my men,' she said. 'There was one in particular, a Labour politician who's now a Lord. He was the one I liked most. I don't want to ruin his life, upset his family, by revealing his name. I wouldn't enjoy spending the money, anyway.'

I told Miss Whiplash that she was a woman of great moral rectitude, and did so without cracking a smile, as far as she could tell over the phone. 'Yeah, well, I come from an old East End gangster family,' she said. 'My mum used to play bingo with Violet Kray. And I was brought up never to grass.'

Then I asked whether someone had grassed on her, whether it was true that she was setting up in business again, having retired as a madam when she came to live in Herefordshire in 1999. She laughed and said it was cobblers, but added that she would cheerfully start up in business again if prostitution was ever legalised. 'I've got a four bedroomed-house so I'd have three girls, one of twenty-five, one of thrity-five, and one of forty-five,' she told me. She had it all worked out. 'You need different ages. I had an escort on my books in London who was seventy-five; very popular, she was. The girls would have a room each, they'd keep half the money themselves and half would go to the house. That's how it works. I'd have a minder to look after us, but it would all be very discreet, out in the country, high hedges and all that. I'll tell you what, there's already more escorts out here than you would ever think.'

She then told me of a tiny hamlet very close to my own home out of which an 'escort' was operating with notable success. As this place consisted of only about fifty people, this meant that if Miss Whiplash was right, 2 per cent of the population worked in the sex industry. Yet again, I realized that there was more to the countryside than met the eye.

To return to the far more wholesome matter of Mr Phillips' scorch marks, I visited his house to find out what it might be like to touch timber that had felt the lick of fire 361 years earlier. Rather stirring, was the answer. It also increased my respect for oak. I'm told that even today, if you happen to find yourself in a burning building, better it should be oak-framed than steel-framed.

It's a truism to say that they knew how to build things to last in those days. From the street, Mr Phillips's house looked classically Georgian, but its frontage dated 'only' from 1788. The same is true of many old properties in Ludlow. Broad Street, which our old friend Pevsner regarded as one of the most striking thoroughfares in England, is full of free-standing Georgian façades hiding much older buildings. You can see this clearly from the rear and Mr Phillips was able to tell me that the Georgians 'weren't worried about back elevations, only front elevations'. I couldn't help wondering whether the same principle might apply to the prostitutes should Miss Whiplash ever get her farmhouse bordello off the ground.

Anyway, after leaving Mr Phillips's fascinating house I wandered across the road to the offices of South Shropshire District Council, and asked for Colin Richards, Ludlow's conservation officer, who also happened to be the father of one of Joe's old classmates at Stamford Heath. Colin was due to receive the MBE for his services to conservation in the area, and it didn't take long chatting to him to understand why. He had spent sixteen years encouraging local craftsmen to learn traditional building skills so that when repairs to ancient properties are carried out, they are done so not only sensitively, but also in a manner that might last another 400 years. He had even overseen the export of these skills to places as disparate as Romania and Sweden, overseeing exchange schemes whereby experts in oak carpentry from Shropshire worked alongside Swedish timber-framers, all learning from each other. I didn't want to embarrass him, so I didn't say so, but it occurred to me that if it was the arch-conservationist Prince Charles who ended up giving Colin his MBE, he might just give him a kiss as well.

As for Mr Phillips's house, Colin said the burnt timbers showed that the fire – tackled by townsfolk passing pails of water along a human chain from the River Corve – had extended much further along Corve Street than had been thought, another reminder that tranquil Ludlow had known intense trauma. He also said that the demolition of the auction rooms next door had enabled him to organize an archaeological dig, and that one of the items unearthed had been a comb made out of bone. 'The Romans had bone combs,' he said, his eyes sparkling as only those of a conservation officer mentioning the Romans can. 'But actually we think it dates from the eleventh century. We also found pits full of bones, which was quite worrying, although they turned out to be animal bones.

Obviously some kind of butchery took place there, although the strange thing was that one pit was full of front legs, another full of back legs. At first we thought we'd found evidence of some kind of ritualistic slaughter.'

In Ludlow? Never!

20

Dido, and the Rennies

In *Tales of the Country* I wrote more about Leominster than Ludlow, trying in my small way to redress the publicity imbalance, for while Leominster has many charms, Ludlow, only twelve miles up the A49, gets a great deal more attention. And yet it's easy to see why.

Much of this attention concerns its reputation as the Santiago de Compostela of gastronomic pilgrimage, upon which I have already touched in this book. But it's worth examining further, because it pretty much all started with Shaun Hill's decision to set up business in the town, creating, with the Merchant House, what would eventually be rated the fourteenth-best restaurant in the world by none other than *Restaurant* magazine, aptly enough. You wouldn't want to be voted fourteenth-best restaurant in the world by *Asian Babes* magazine, say, or even by *Caravanning Monthly*, which you might recall was the magazine sitting on top of the pile when my friend, to check on the success of his vasectomy, was ushered into a small room at a hospital charged with providing a small sample of sperm.

It would be stretching a point to say that the Merchant House was the making of Ludlow. I imagine that the town was quite a nice destination for 1,000 years or so before Shaun Hill first blanched a leek in Lower Corve Street. But he certainly put it on the culinary map of modern Britain, and I was thrilled to find, while waiting to catch a British Airways flight to London from John F. Kennedy Airport in New York early in 2005, that the dish of the day in the Supper Room, a gleaming new restaurant for Club World passengers, was haddock with lentils 'created by Shaun Hill of the Merchant House in Ludlow'. It was nice to find BA flying the flag for Ludlow, although I did wonder how bright it was to give lentils to people about to get on a long-haul flight. Unless it was an initiative to get the plane home more quickly.

When I heard that Hill was selling up, I phoned him. He'd been a useful contact of mine over the years whenever I was writing about the restaurant industry, and was always as wise and eloquent as you might expect from a man who, as well as being a leading chef, was also a Research Fellow in Classics at Exeter University. In fact, he told me that he was writing a book about food in antiquity, examining the parallels between food hang-ups now and food hang-ups in ancient Rome. I only called to ask his reasons for selling up, and suddenly he was telling me why the Romans didn't eat lemons.

He was as amazed as the eating-out classes of Ludlow and its environs were dismayed, that he couldn't sell the Merchant House as a going concern. For £550,000 – the cost of a bog-standard terraced house in Dulwich – the buyer could have owned a mostly Jacobean property with a ground floor dating from 1430, and of course a kitchen with a formidable reputation. For goodwill alone, he'd been told that he could have stuck a further £150,000 on the asking price. He chose not to. 'I didn't want to piss about,' he said, saltily.

I ventured that, in a strange way, his reputation might have been the problem. Maybe nobody wanted to take on the Merchant House knowing they would have, forgive me, such big choux to fill. 'I think people are more conceited than that,' he said. 'Besides, there's no doubt that they would get reviewed by every major newspaper, and for attention like that, there are public relations firms paid £4,000 a month.'

In the end the fourteenth-best restaurant in the world was turned back into a private home, and Hill's every subsequent burp and twitch were analysed by people in the industry who wondered where he might go next. I contributed to the speculation myself, for he told me that it had always astounded him that affluent Malvern did not have a number of good restaurants. This line caused a bit of excitement in the industry, although probably not in Malvern. Nothing got them too excited in Malvern, from what I had seen of the place. It was there that I saw two extremely elderly women inching across the road, one inching slightly faster than the other. 'Sybil,' snapped the woman lagging marginally behind. 'I said "walk", not "run"!'

While I'm on the subject of Malvern, I should report an episode that unfolded on New Year's Day 2007. We had arranged to go for a long, hangover-busting walk with our friends Claire and Tom and their four children. We had suggested going to Bircher Common or Croft Ambrey near Ludlow, but Tom was underwhelmed by that idea, explaining that they'd walked there a million times before. I suppose his sniffiness showed just how absurdly spoilt we are for scenic walks in this part of the country. Bircher Common and Croft Ambrey are two of the loveliest spots imaginable. But Tom thought we should have a go at the Malvern Hills, to which we readily agreed. Even though we lived scarcely half an hour away from Malvern, the only time I had worked up any kind of sweat there was when accelerating towards the wine section in Waitrose. A walk in the Malvern Hills represented a huge gap in our country-dwelling CV, and the first day of a new year seemed like a good time to put that right.

When we arrived at Claire and Tom's house in the early afternoon, however, the rain was absolutely sheeting down. I legged it from the Volvo to their front door feeling certain – and if I'm honest, hoping – that they would want to knock on the head the whole idea of going for a walk, and invite us straight in for tea and muffins. But they were made of sterner stuff than us. 'We're still going for it, aren't we?' said Tom, with his trademark sunny smile, when he opened the door. The rain was still monsoon-like. 'Of course,' I said.

By the time we all reached the top of British Camp, an extraordinary Iron Age hill fort, I felt no drier than I had in the shower that morning. But the discomfort was drowned by the exhilaration: the rain had at last begun to ease, and the view eastwards was spellbinding. Everyone was having a good time, not least the dogs – our two, Fergus and Bonnie, and their two, Lucy and Widget. After a couple of hours we got back to the car park, and there realized that Widget, their young Jack Russell, was missing. The light was by now starting to fade quite quickly, so everyone apart from Tom and me piled into their Land Rover and headed home for those muffins. Manfully, the pair of us turned back to start searching for Widget. We decided to split up, but after forty-five minutes I had found no sign of the missing dog, while occasionally hearing the hopeful cry of 'Widget!' from the other side of the hill. Evidently, Tom hadn't managed to find her either.

I trudged back to the car park, thinking despondently that their children would always remember their New Year walk with us as the day they lost their beloved little Widget. When I reached the car park, however, there was Tom with Widget in his arms. 'She was in the pub,' he said. Like me he had been on the point of giving up hope, but had gone into the bar of the Malvern Hills Hotel to ask if anyone had by chance handed in a missing dog. He was promptly handed a delighted Widget, who had seemingly wandered into the building on his own, and had subsequently been cared for behind the bar. We put Widget in the car with Fergus and Bonnie, whereupon Tom kindly offered to buy me a fortifying drink before we headed back. Rarely had the thought of a large brandy seemed so appealing. So we phoned Claire to break the good news, then crossed the road to the hotel. But just as I was removing my muddy boots by the door, the woman who had handed Widget back to Tom – whether the landlady or the barmaid I wasn't sure – approached us. 'I'm sorry,' she said brusquely, 'but if you're wet you can't come in.' We admitted that we were indeed wet. 'Sorry,' she reiterated.

The Malvern Hills Hotel, I should emphasise, stands at the foot of the Malvern Hills, across the road from a car park that is used predominantly by walkers. I was literally speechless.

A damp dog had been given shelter and hospitality; two damp human beings, eager for alcoholic sustenance, had been turned away. From a pub. On New Year's Day. In fairness I should add that when I recorded all this in my newspaper column, I got an e-mail from the manager of the Malvern Hills Hotel, inviting Tom and me back for dinner sometime, which was a generous gesture. All the same, there are times when this seems like the maddest country on earth.

To return to Shaun Hill, as I sit here writing this book speculation continues to follow him around the country. But even without him, Ludlow retains a great reputation for food, with the Food Festival indelible in the calendar of all self-respecting foodie types. The only trouble with the Food Festival is the relentless sampling. There is so much to taste and it all looks so delicious that you start forgetting to say no; I can still practically feel the indigestion I suffered several years ago, when a morsel of smoked pilchard came far too soon after a small plastic spoonful of raspberries in Drambuie, which itself followed a sliver of Ragstone goat's cheese log. And that was only the start. Some venison, port and garlic sausage, sir? 'Why not?' Like to try some basil-infused olive oil? 'Yes please.' A slice of chocolate mint fudge? 'Oh, I think so.' How about a thimbleful of curried goat? 'It would be a shame not to.' If only there'd been a stall offering organic dried Rennies, the day would have been an unqualified success.

In 2004, Ludlow's gastronomic reputation was officially endorsed when it was declared Britain's representative in the Cittaslow movement. Cittaslow had originated in Rome in 1986, when a journalist named Carlo Petrini lost his rag, or possibly his ragu, on seeing a branch of McDonald's near the Spanish Steps. As a protest against fast food, he started a Slow

Food campaign, and from that grew Cittaslow, which by the turn of the new century was established in thirty-five towns and cities around Italy, and had spread to ten other countries. Cittaslow campaigns for such things as bicycle lanes, and against such things as car alarms. It promotes local produce and opposes GM foods. And it selected Ludlow, over Penzance and Totnes, to be Britain's first Slow City.

All this was the subject of a rather mealy-mouthed article in *The Times*, written by a man who had been dispatched to Ludlow to write about its new status, yet had been impervious to its enormous charm, as well as downright disdainful of the tendency of local motorists to observe speed limits. As unofficial Ludlow correspondent in the national press, I then got a call from a woman with the fabulous name of Dido Blench, who handled public relations for the town's Assembly Rooms, my favourite place, you will recall, to see films.

The man from *The Times* had been not remotely enamoured of the Assembly Rooms, however. He had called in twice, once to find a table-tennis tournament for the over-50s in full swing, and once to find that he was too late for the tea dance. No wonder Dido blenched. She asked me if I might perhaps write a counterblast. I was happy to, although I acknowledged, as had been touched on in *The Times*, that Ludlow did have a sizeable contingent of disaffected youth and, away from the genteel market square, some serious social problems. Speed, if not speed, was not unknown in Britain's first Slow City. And Ludlow, like Leominster, could clearly do with a place for those teenagers too young to go to the numerous pubs, a place for them to hang out in the evening, where they could eat fairly cheaply, or just sit around making a coffee last for hours. I wondered whether Cittaslow had a problem with Pizza Express?

For all that Ludlow had its social problems, though, it was undoubtedly a magnet for the affluent middle classes. But how much of a magnet I didn't realize until one day at Ludlow racecourse. Any romantic notions I'd had of desert life had receded some years earlier, when I read that a Bedouin tribe had delayed the date of its annual migration across the Sahara, a date enshrined by a thousand years of tradition, in order to watch the last episode of *Dallas*. But on that day in Ludlow I realized that cultural practices do not only travel from west to east, as I watched the upper-middle classes of Shropshire and Herefordshire descend, in a veritable caravan of four-wheel drives, upon the racecourse. For the next two days the main pavilion became a noisy and unruly souk, full of jabbing fingers and frantic, ululating women. The occasion was the Boden sale.

21

Walter, and the Boden Sale

The Boden sale is a truly nomadic phenomenon, the legendary mail-order clothing entrepreneur Johnnie Boden having realized that the nation's Jocastas and Gileses do not all live within an easy drive of the company's warehouse in the wastelands of north-west London. In fact, most of them don't. So he put the show on the road, and it has become one of the hottest tickets in – or rather out of – town. It is easy to poke gentle fun at Boden shoppers, but I have to confess that there is a Boden flavour to my own wardrobe, even if I have always felt faintly disappointed, having slipped on my olive-green moleskin trousers and harlequin polo shirt, to look in the mirror and see not a svelte 'Piers, actor' or a tanned 'Hamish, wine buyer', as in the celebrated catalogue, but 'Brian, could lose half a stone'.

Actually, I would need to have lost a lot more than half a stone to have found much to fit me at Ludlow racecourse. There were excellent bargains to be had, but by the time Jane and I got there, they were mainly for the skeletally thin or the abnormally large. Having said that, we had missed the frenzy of the opening morning. I was rather sorry about this. There are few spectacles as compelling as ordinarily genteel folk engaged in an unseemly stampede for a beige corduroy jacket reduced to £30.

Our friend Susan (a woefully plebeian name for someone at the Boden sale) told us that some truly unscrupulous tactics had been deployed. Not least by her. She was inspecting the left half of a nice pair of brogues when she noticed a man alongside her admiring the right half. Surreptitiously, she slipped it into her basket and wandered away, watching from a safe distance, only a little guiltily, as the poor chap launched an energetic but ultimately forlorn search for the missing shoe. Defeated and disillusioned, he eventually put his shoe down and twenty minutes later she sidled back to claim it. Despicable.

Occasionally, I'm told, people go to Ludlow racecourse not for brogues and beige corduroy jackets but for the races. But they don't always get there. In 2004, after I had interviewed the BBC's former Voice of Racing, the great Peter O'Sullevan, at his flat in South Kensington, he asked me where I lived. When I told him that we were about equidistant between the racecourses of Ludlow and Hereford, he complimented me for having the good sense to live in such a splendid part of the world, and invited me to listen to his favourite Ludlow anecdote. So very happily I sat down again for a further dose of that marvellous voice.

In 1941 – having been refused by the armed forces for medical reasons, 'and even by the Merchant Navy, which I found very embarrassing' – O'Sullevan received a telephone call from a jockey friend of his, a Belgian called Nobby Sawers. Later that week, said Sawers, he would be riding a horse called Niersteiner in the two o'clock at Ludlow. It would be an outsider, yet stood a good chance of winning. On the strength of this information, O'Sullevan drove to a garage he knew on the road to Cheltenham, and there sold his car, a Flying Standard, for £60. With this considerable sum of money in his pocket to bet with he set about hitchhiking to Ludlow racecourse.

'I was first picked up by a commercial traveller and his girlfriend, who drove me into the middle of Cheltenham,' he recalled. He then took a bus to Gloucester, but was advised not to try hitchhiking in the city centre, on the basis that nobody would pick up a man out of uniform. 'So I walked out of Gloucester, and after about an hour picked up a short ride with a farmer and six pigs. When we started drifting off any semblance of a main thoroughfare, the odds of making Ludlow in time for the two o'clock race were about 50-1 against.'

Instead, he decided to place the bet over the phone with William Hill, so went back to the farmer's house to use the phone. Unfortunately, it was out of order, so 'fortified by a pint of home-made cider' which he remembered having the strength of Calvados, he persevered with the journey, and three rides later found himself just outside Hereford, by which time the race was over, the result still unknown. He consoled himself with a 2/6 cream tea in a nearby farmhouse. 'Cream was unheard of in London, and jam was rationed, so that was an unbelievable treat,' he said.

He then began the long hitch back to London, eventually

steaming into Hammersmith Broadway the following morning in a huge truck, having offered to stand the driver the finest breakfast money could buy. 'So while he tucked into toast, dripping, spam and egg powder, I went to buy a morning paper, and found the racing results.' Which is why the very word Ludlow transported him over six decades back to a London pavement, where he read: 'First in the two o'clock, Niersteiner, trained by Percy Arm, ridden by N. Sawers, 20/1.'

As I walked away from O'Sullevan's mansion-block flat along the mean streets of South Kensington, I considered how Ludlow, for such a small place, meant so many different things to people: racing, food, architecture, history, cut-price clothing, and even, for the underwhelmed man from *The Times*, table tennis for the over-50s. It was, by any yardstick, a town with personality. Moreover, I always think that you can tell something about a town from the person chosen to switch on its Christmas lights, in which case Ludlow was shortly to cover itself in glory. As a rule, B-list towns get B-list celebrities; C-list towns, C-list celebrities. In the year that Cirencester, a town with front, chose the former topless model Melinda Messenger, football-obsessed Newcastle chose Sir Bobby Robson. And High Wycombe, not quite sure whether it was Thames Valley swanky, Chilterns genteel or Middle England bland, chose Frank Bruno, who had identity issues of his own.

Almost everywhere that year – and I know because I looked into it – the person hitting the switch or pulling the lever was, to a greater or lesser degree, famous. Wrexham went lesser, with former Steps star Lisa Scott-Lee; Birmingham went greater, with Jasper Carrott. Northampton gave the job to actor Brian Blessed; Plymouth, to the comedian Brian Conley. And where it wasn't a celebrity, it was a local dignitary, such as the mayor or a prominent councillor. But not in Ludlow. To its enormous credit, Ludlow chose Walter to switch on the lights. Walter was one of Ludlow's most familiar landmarks. He seemed to have been around for about as long as the castle, and had a similarly medieval countenance. He was out, cloth-capped, in all weathers, dispensing homilies and good cheer, and was known to have been, seventy-odd years ago, an alarmingly premature baby. His first bed was said to have been a shoebox.

Many towns have a Walter but few of them would hand him the honour of switching on the Christmas lights. For Ludlow to have done so suggested a generosity of civic spirit, as well as robust self-confidence. Not for Ludlow a bout of celebrity one-upmanship. Moreover, in honouring Walter it honoured a man most places would be more inclined to disown. Needless to say, Walter himself was thrilled. He stood on a dais and made a short speech which I am told by those who heard it was extremely moving.

All of which brings me to my own short, extremely moving speech, delivered from the dais at Hereford Magistrates' Court.

22

Annie, and the Magistrates

First, let me share with you the paradox with which anyone
who has moved from the city to the country will be familiar.
You leave behind traffic hell, only to enter a different kind
of purgatory – an unhealthy reliance on the car. In London we
had just one car. In Herefordshire we needed two, mainly for
all those mornings when Jane had to get the kids to school, and
I had to get myself to the station twenty-two miles away in
Worcester. In neither case was public transport an option.
Buses were rarer than the splay-toed armadillo, and the Great
Western Railway's east–west branch line service had been
discontinued before I was born. I have a 1944 timetable, which
I look at forlornly from time to time. It tells me that there used

to be four trains a day between Worcester Shrub Hill and Leominster, with eight scheduled stops and two halts. I love the idea of a halt, sticking out an arm to make a train stop in the days before the wrong kind of leaves on the line did the same job.

Further details of what trains were like in 1944 were supplied by the admirable Severn Valley Railway, the steam line from Kidderminster to Bridgnorth run by a small army of devoted volunteers, which in the early summer of 2004 was given a Second World War makeover. The army of volunteers dressed up as troops and ARP wardens and even spivs selling watches, and local schools participated, too, sending pupils along dressed like 1940 evacuees, with gas-mask containers, and cardboard labels with their names on, around their necks.

Joe's class from Stamford Heath made the trip, and a few days beforehand he brought home the following list detailing what he could or couldn't take in his packed lunch. 'Packed lunches: for authenticity, food should be packed in greaseproof paper and brown or white paper bags and carried either in cereal packets or tin lunch boxes of the period. Sandwich fillings (sandwiches made with wholemeal bread and margarine): Spam, pork luncheon meat, haslet, brawn or corned beef, jam, golden syrup, fish or meat paste, Marmite or cheese. Biscuits: morning coffee, plain digestive, malted milk, ginger nuts or Nice. Fruit: Apples, pears, plums or cherries (no bananas or oranges). Drinks: orange squash, lemon barley water, lemonade or fruit cordials.'

Where all else had failed to induce Joseph to eat wholemeal bread, the war succeeded. He loved his day as an evacuee (although Jane and I did gently point out to him that real evacuees weren't home in time for tea and half an hour in front of *The Simpsons*), and for the rest of that week barely stopped talking about what it was like in an Anderson shelter, and the smell of the sandbags.

Actually, he had been interested even before the outing in the Second World War, as rapidly became clear to the nice man at Bewdley station who asked if any of the kids could explain why the war started. According to Joe's teacher, Joe put his hand up and delivered a kind of A.J.P. Taylor lecture, going back to the First World War, German reparations and the Weimar Republic, before explaining the rise of Hitler, and then whisking through the consequences of Germany's invasion of Czechoslovakia and Poland. 'There's nothing I can add to that,' said the nice man, looking mildly taken aback.

I later related all this to my mother, to whom I felt able to blow my 9-year-old son's trumpet – in the style of Glenn Miller, naturally. She was duly proud. 'And because he's good at football,' she said, 'his classmates won't think him a swot.' The teacher might have done, however, if he had pointed out to her the Spam anachronism my mother, who was fourteen at the outbreak of war, pointed out to me. Apparently it shouldn't have been on the list of sandwich fillings because it didn't arrive in England until after Lend-Lease was arranged in 1941.

In all other respects, period authenticity was spot on. A sign at Kidderminster station declared that 'identity cards must be shewn when requested', complete with old-fashioned spelling of 'shown'. I learnt that because an acquaintance of mine, Nick, happened to see it. Nick, who is about the same age as me, told me that he remembered 'shewn' from signs on the buses in East Anglia in the 1970s. Not all on-the-buses recollections from the 1970s need involve Reg Varney.

Anyway, the reason Nick told me about all this was that on

the very day of Joe's trip, late in the afternoon, I bumped into him on the platform at Worcester Shrub Hill. He was on his way home to London following a business meeting, he told me. And someone in his company had had the bright idea of hiring a compartment on the Severn Valley Railway steam train, rather than the usual room in a Holiday Inn somewhere. But nobody at the Severn Valley Railway had mentioned the Second World War theme. So as if there were not novelty enough in climbing on to a steam train for a business meeting, Nick was startled to find himself fighting his way through lots of excited evacuees, including Joe, being directed by members of the Home Guard. I said I hoped that someone had had the wit to call the meeting to order with the reminder that careless talk costs lives.

I was at Worcester Shrub Hill because I, too, was on my way to London, yet sixty years earlier, according to my old timetable, I would not have needed to drive. I could have cycled a couple of miles from Docklow to Steens Bridge and caught the 7.17 a.m. train, arriving at Shrub Hill at 8.28. That was no longer possible, thanks to the ruthless culling of branch line services in the 1950s and 1960s. On the other hand, in 1944 I might have been getting killed in the Battle of Monte Cassino. That's life, I suppose; a series of swings and roundabouts.

By 2004, a more literal series of roundabouts, the ring road in Worcester, was positively festooned with speed cameras, in much the same way as Blackpool promenade over the winter months is festooned with illuminations. The only difference was that the speed cameras were more fun to look at. I send my apologies to Blackpool if the lights have been tarted up over the past few years, but the last time I went, they were depressingly humdrum. As Bill Bryson put it in *Notes from a Small Island*:

'I suppose if you had never seen electricity in action, it would be pretty breathtaking, but I'm not even sure of that.'

Back to Worcester. It was there, driving my little Volkswagen Polo to and from Shrub Hill, along a non-residential stretch of dual carriageway, at speeds of 37mph, 37mph and 38mph, that I accumulated nine penalty points and found myself perilously close to disqualification, which would have been a tolerable prospect in the city, but was unthinkable in the countryside. Unthinkable for a working journalist and father with three children, at any rate.

Consequently, after reaching nine points, I drove as anyone would with the sword of Damocles hanging over them; like an 88-year-old myopic vicar (retired), not merely observing the speed limit, but staying comfortably beneath it. Then, shortly before Christmas 2004, we all set off to see the musical *Annie* at Malvern Theatre, and as we passed through Bromyard, with the children squabbling on the back seat, and me at the wheel, reading the riot act, there was suddenly a horrible, unequivocal flash.

My heart lurched. I had somehow crept up to 35 m.p.h. in a 30 m.p.h. zone. I subsequently sat through *Annie*, wondering whether Miss Hannigan, the heartless superintendent of the orphanage, would throttle the ringleted ginger wretch before I did. After I had accumulated the first nine points, I moaned about the speed camera system in my newspaper column, and was vehemently abused in letters and e-mails, some of them quite alarmingly unpleasant. Nonetheless, I simply couldn't agree that being clocked for speeding four times in three years, once on a bypass and three times on an empty dual carriageway late at night, not in residential areas and never at more than 37 m.p.h., should have landed me before the beaks, facing a driving ban. It wasn't that I approved of reckless driving. On the contrary, I frequently saw acts of lunacy along the A44, had once been forced off the road by a moron overtaking on a bend, and I was all for those drivers being disqualified on the spot, and then tarred and feathered.

But there was no point arguing that there should be one law for the teenage idiot trying to impress his mates and another for the respectable family man taking his children to a Christmas show. And so I prepared to face the British judicial system, absolutely dreading the prospect. After all, I had been a law-abiding chap ever since I stopped shoplifting the odd can of Cresta in my early teens, so it was horrible to receive a court summons. A summons, moreover, which said 'Brian Viner vs the Chief Constable of West Mercia'. That seemed worryingly one-sided to me, like Dagenham & Redbridge vs Chelsea.

Worse than anything, though, was the likelihood of losing my licence. Just the idea that I might be legally prevented from fulfilling my responsibilities as a husband and father was emasculating. I developed eczema on my shin that was plainly stress-related.

I also needed to consider the mechanics of the court appearance itself. Should I hire legal representation, hopefully by Hereford's answer to Perry Mason? Some people advised me that I should, that it would show the magistrates I was treating the business seriously. Others told me that magistrates are impressed by people who represent themselves, if they are eloquent and persuasive. Feeling certain that my eloquence would give way to huge racking sobs if I tried to talk myself about the impact a ban would have on my poor wife and kids, I took the Perry Mason option.

The court case – on 22 February 2006 – was almost as much

of an ordeal as I thought it would be. I had taken along some supportive documentation, which my solicitor had said might come in useful. There was a map, with a neat red cross indicating that I lived in the middle of nowhere. And there were three letters, one from the deputy editor of *The Independent* saying that I needed to be able to drive to carry out my journalistic duties; one from the headmaster of Stamford Heath confirming that I frequently did the twenty-two-mile school run; and one written by Jane Lewis, who worked for Herefordshire Tourism and had organized the Flavours of Herefordshire lunch in Much Marcle. She wrote to say, bless her, that my newspaper column gave some decent publicity to Herefordshire and that to gather material for it I needed to be able to get around the county from time to time, which was true enough. I hoped that this might be my trump card.

These documents were duly handed up to the three magistrates, whom I had been carefully scrutinising. There were two women who looked, to me, like strong proponents of hanging and flogging even for minor parking offences. But between them was a rather twinkly-eyed, benign-looking chap, who gave me what I fancied was a reassuring smile. He was the chief magistarate, too. I thought that he might be a restrain-ing influence on his two stern, unsmiling colleagues. With him in charge I might have an outside chance of leaving court without a ban.

The three of them studied my map and read my letters, then the twinkly-eyed man said, benignly, that because one of them had been written by Jane Lewis, an employee of Herefordshire Council, he would have to stand down. It turned out that he was Leader of the Council, and as such, felt that the letter compromised him.

This left me in the hands of the two women who I'm quite sure were charming, caring individuals, but had by now metamorphosed, from where I was standing, into a Rottweiler and a bull mastiff, unfed for several days, with me about to become their breakfast. I was then ordered to stand in the dock, where I was cross-examined by a chap who asked me a few questions and then said: 'That's all, thank you', with a satisfied smile, as though I had just fallen into a massive legal trap and implicated myself in the Birmingham pub bombings, the Brinks-Mat bullion robbery and the murder of Lord Lucan's nanny. When my own solicitor questioned me and I talked about the impact a driving ban would have on my family, I just about managed to contain the huge racking sobs, but my eyes welled up with tears. And this was just a speeding case. I could only hope that I would never have to take the stand at the Old Bailey.

My solicitor concluded by reiterating the law, which says that anyone who has twelve points on their driving licence must be disqualified for at least six months, unless such a ban will cause them or others 'exceptional hardship'. He argued that I qualified for the exceptional hardship clause, while the prosecuting solicitor suggested that, while I might at times be seriously inconvenienced by a ban, that did not amount to exceptional hardship. At this, one of the two remaining magistrates nodded vigorously, while the other applauded and yelled 'Hear, hear! Send the wretch down!', albeit only in my doom-laden imagination.

They then left to consider their decision, a process which seemed to take hours, while I sat there wondering how much all this was costing the state and whether it could possibly constitute value for money. Eventually, they came back in. I was told to rise, which I did, on unsteady legs. I know that this must seem like a melodramatic description of a somewhat trivial episode in the long history of the British judiciary, but at the time it bore down on me like one of those cartoon 'one tonne' weights, squashing away all thoughts of anything else. The bull mastiff spoke. She told me that she and the Rottweiler had decided that I was indeed an exceptional hardship case, that I would be fined £80 but not banned. I thanked her profusely and marvelled at how two ferocious, slavering dogs could, in an instant, turn into a pair of enormously attractive and sweetly fragrant fairy godmothers. I'd assumed that even if I was let off, the fine at least would be punitive, running to several hundred pounds. But £80 and no ban seemed like the best result imaginable. I celebrated by continuing to drive like that myopic, retired vicar. I didn't want to go back to court in a hurry. For quite some time, I didn't go anywhere in a hurry.

23

Sebastian, and the Hindenburg

If for a while my life seemed, if only to me, like an episode of *Perry Mason* (or *Kavanagh QC* for the benefit of younger readers), then there were other times when it felt more like an extended version of *The Vicar of Dibley*. In fact, our development as country folk from the day we moved to Docklow in July 2002 equated to a series of analogies with television programmes: we had started out as characters from the Simon Nye series *How Do You Want Me?*, which starred Dylan Moran as an outsider regarded with the utmost suspicion by villagers, and we had ended up in Dibley.

In 2005 we felt as though we were sufficiently assimilated to offer to hold the Docklow summer fête, at which we had felt like such ingenues three years earlier, in our garden. Even then, we weren't at all sure how this offer would be greeted. As far as we knew, the summer fête had taken place in the grounds of Broadland, a big house a couple of miles away, since Methuselah was a boy, although in fact the nearest thing Docklow had to Methuselah, a sweet old man called Walter (not to be confused with the Walter who switched on the Ludlow Christmas lights), assured us that the fête always used to take place at the Grange. 'I think the last time was in 1955,' he said, drawing on his pipe.

Anyway, I made the offer tentatively to the Coopers, who lived at Broadland, wondering whether as relative newcomers we were yet entitled to muscle in on post-1955 tradition, only for the Coopers to say a loud 'yes' in perfect unison before I had quite finished my sentence. It seemed that it was rather a responsibility, hosting the fête.

As it turned out, the great and the good of Docklow (which amounted to only two great and three good, it being such a small place) took most of the responsibility off our shoulders. Rob Hanson from the Parish Council turned up on the eve of the fête with a platoon of helpers, and before we knew it there was a ring of trestle-tables round the garden for the first time since 1955, which might have been the year someone said, 'I think we need new trestle-tables', and then forgot to do anything about it for half a century. I've sometimes heard people asking, as they ponder the mysteries of the universe, why you never see baby pigeons. My own question is: why do you never see new trestle-tables?

The unfolding of the trestle-tables was briefly interrupted by our dog Milo humping the girlfriend of the son of one of the parish councillors, an episode already chronicled in these pages, but in due course we were able to repair to the King's Head, and then start again the following morning. The fête that afternoon was a huge success, and was blessed with warm sunshine, which we assumed had been organized by Rob Hanson. The man is a marvel. As someone said afterwards: 'Everyone else brings problems to meetings, Rob just brings solutions.' I seemed to remember Margaret Thatcher saying that of Cecil Parkinson, or maybe Norman Tebbit, but I bet neither of them had Rob's level-headedness in the face of a seemingly intractable problem, like where the folk arriving at the fête were going to park their cars. The obvious place was the field adjoining our drive, but it was bounded by a rather forbidding iron fence. 'No probs, we'll take a section of fence out,' said Rob. 'As long as we remember to put it back before you have 200 sheep in your garden, that'll work fine.'

Jane and I smiled weakly, but, of course, scarcely had the fête finished than the fence was back in place, with not one ewe chewing our cabbages. However, I mustn't give the impression that it was a one-man show; the usual 10 per cent of the Docklow community – 9.3 people – gave their usual copious time and sweat without the slightest fanfare. Two hours before the fête was due to start, Jane and I fretted that things weren't going to come together in time, but when we next looked, there was a tea-urn in the conservatory and a marquee on the lawn.

I suppose all rural counties are full of people like this, but human beings, unlike cowpats, are so thin on the ground in north Herefordshire that there must be a larger proportion of them here.

By the time the 2006 fête came around, the Grange was firmly established as the venue again. And again, Jane and I wondered whether it would all come together in time. By

11 a.m., with festivities due to start at two, only the portable loo was in place, halfway down the drive. Moreover, far from the early erection of the loo constituting one less thing to worry about, it had already been mistaken for the ticket booth by a Mrs Clayton from Essex, who was staying in one of our holiday cottages, and whose two West Highland terriers, Finlay and Crawford, would later inspire Jane to buy Bonnie.

The portable loo, in fairness, was a rather salubrious-looking structure mock-Tudor in appearance, so I could see what Mrs Clayton meant. But would others make the same mistake? I didn't want a line of people building up outside it, only for someone in the queue to give the door a tentative push and be greeted by a faint smell of urine. Anyway, by about ten to two, just like the year before and as if by magic, a large tea tent had appeared on our sun-baked back lawn. It really was as if someone had waved a wand and said 'Let there be a fête.' Suddenly there were trestle-tables groaning with home-made cakes, jams and chutneys, enough bric-a-brac to fill Steptoe's yard, a tombola, a skittle alley, a pig roast, a chocolate fountain, and a twenty-five-piece brass band had taken up residence in the (very necessary) shade of the old cedar tree. We had pinched the idea of having a band from the Yarpole village fête, the king of village fêtes hereabouts.

Unfortunately, the good people of Yarpole had chosen the same day for their fête, which was a shame because I'd been asked to open theirs. As I have recorded, a smidgen of notoriety goes a long way in north Herefordshire, not that anyone had asked me to open the Docklow fête, indeed the very suggestion would have caused much merriment in the King's Head, where Owen still knew me not as 'journalist and author' but as the daft incomer who once hired a hitman to kill a cockerel. Not going to Yarpole also meant that I couldn't be roped in, all too literally, to their tug-of-war, which had caused me such flatulence.

At our fête we didn't have a tug-of-war, but it was rather wonderful to have Dvorak's 'Hovis' music wafting round the garden, as the Teme Valley Band got into their stride. At the bottom of the garden, meanwhile, Joe did a cracking job of running the penalty shoot-out competition, not in the slightest bit diminished by the fact that he proceeded to win it. We were ever so slightly embarrassed when Fergus then won first prize in the dog show, not that it compared with the embarrassment caused by randy Milo the year before. Joint runners-up in the dog show were Finlay and Crawford, the two Westies. Mrs Clayton, who'd mistaken the portable loo for the ticket booth, said it was the proudest day of her life.

But if that was the highlight of her day, the highlight of mine was seeing Tashi, the trekking guide from Bhutan, wandering around the fête in a kind of silk dressing gown, which was his national costume. 'Who's the guy in the kung-fu get-up having a go on the skittles,' asked Tim, the dog-show judge. 'A Bhutanese trekker,' I replied. I felt secure in the knowledge that the Yarpole fête wouldn't ever have one of those.

The day after our fête we went to the annual Richards Castle Soapbox Derby on Hanway Common. It was one of those summer weekends when every village in Herefordshire seemed to have something exciting going on, at least if a soapbox derby fits your definition of excitement. It did ours. The thing had been organized by Avril's partner Ian, another person who, in our four years in the country, had become a friend for life. Ian's own 'soapbox' was a tank constructed out of, among other things, a wheelbarrow. It was a proper, working tank, too, at least as proper as anyone is ever likely to see on Hanway Common. On his descent, Ian stopped, swivelled the gun turret, and fired at a distant hut on which was painted the words 'Staff Toilet'. The first two 'shells' exploded left and right, but the third scored a direct hit, whereupon the sides of the hut collapsed to reveal Ian's mate Richard holding a white flag.

It was very funny and beautifully done, and particularly resonant for those of us who didn't really know Richard but already associated him with lavatorial difficulties. Apparently, on a visit to France a few years earlier, he had stayed in a small auberge where he was assailed by a terrible dose of diarrhoea. To make matters worse, there was a problem with the cistern, so that when he flushed the loo, the water rose and – *horreur!* – overflowed. It was not, as you can perhaps imagine, a pretty sight. Nor a particularly fragrant smell. Aghast, Richard sought out the owner, a woman who spoke no English, just as he spoke hardly any French. He took her to his room, opened the toilet door, and summoned the only two French words he could think of that seemed remotely appropriate, accompanied by an involuntary flourish of the arm. 'Voilà madame,' he said.

I enjoy that story whenever I hear it, which is not to criticise Ian for retelling it. Ian, who has lived in Richards Castle all his fifty-odd years, has a fine repertoire of stories, although his most outstanding party piece, about which I enthused in *Tales of the Country*, is an uncannily fine warble fly impression. He is a man of many parts, just as his is usually a soapbox of many parts. For the inaugural Richards Castle Soapbox Derby, in 2004, he built a tiny replica of a Midlands Red bus, which was driven, on one of its three timed descents, by Richard of 'Voilà madame' fame. We were standing with Ian as the bus hurtled past, although in truth it was less of a hurtle, more of a trundle. Even at trundling speed, however, it ran into trouble round the final bend, and almost in slow motion started falling to bits.

We had been looking forward for weeks to seeing Ian's bus in action, and here, before our very eyes, it was falling apart. There is some famous old footage of the Hindenburg disaster, when in front of an excited, then horrified crowd, the great airship bursts into flames, passengers start leaping to their deaths, and the announcer begins to cry. This was Hanway Common's own Hindenburg disaster, except that there were no flames, nobody died, and the announcer began to laugh. As, indeed, did Ian. He laughed and laughed and laughed, and we all took our cue from him.

Coincidentally, the event took place on the same day as the British Grand Prix at Silverstone, but was infinitely more exciting. There were some truly weird and wonderful contraptions, all engine-less according to the strict competition rules, including one painted to look like a giant slab of cheese. 'Oh no,' exclaimed the announcer, as this contraption veered off the track towards another local beauty spot. 'The cheese is heading for the Goggin!'

The announcer, a plummy chap called Sebastian with a voice that evoked a 1950s BBC radio broadcast, did an absolutely superb job, retaining his enthusiasm from first descent to last, over many hours. 'Wibble, wobble, wobble, wibble!' he cried, as a souped-up go-kart looked vulnerable round the bend where the Midlands Red had expired. And then, 'wobble wibble, wibble, wobble!', as a box on pram wheels looked shaky down the straight. As a study of the English at play on a July day, the first Richards Castle Soap Box Derby could not have been bettered. A patrician announcer, capable middle-aged women dispensing tea and walnut cake, a hot-dog van, a bouncy castle and leaden skies. It was marvellous.

24

Abba, and the Scotch Egg

One Saturday lunchtime early in 2006, my old mate Chris married his lovely girlfriend Sarah. This on its own was cause for great celebration, but for us there was an added frisson of excitement because the wedding took place in a diddy place called Llantilio-Crossenny, which is bang on the Offa's Dyke trail. So bang on it, that it would not have been surprising if Sarah had been preceded up the aisle of the church by a stout-booted couple wearing his'n'hers cagoules, heads down, Ordnance Survey maps around their necks, oblivious to the congregation around them.

Llantilio-Crossenny is about half-way between Monmouth and Abergavenny and therefore – here's the exciting bit –

scarcely an hour's drive from our house! It was strangely satisfying to know that almost everyone else, including even the bride and groom, had to make a longer journey than us to get there. To attend gatherings of relatives and old friends, we had become used to being the ones having to set off at the crack of dawn.

This time, however, we were able to treat ourselves to a leisurely home-cooked breakfast before casually pointing the Volvo down the A49, and even though it then had to negotiate the A465, the B4233 and several miles of tricky country lanes, it was nice to know that all those city slickers had been on the road since shortly after dawn, with hardly enough time to dust the tops of their lattes with cinnamon at the services near Reading.

You probably think that I'm making too much of this, and I probably am. But, as you might have gathered by now, you get oversensitive living in the sticks. We once had some London friends staying with us, and on a walk through Mortimer Forest we met some Herefordshire friends, to whom we introduced them. 'Can you see yourselves doing what Brian and Jane did, moving out of London?' asked our Herefordshire friends, guilelessly. 'OH NO!' cried our London friends in exact unison. 'WE LOVE VISITING BUT WE COULD NEVER LIVE HERE. THE CHILDREN WOULD HATE IT!!! WE'D HATE IT!!!'

'Don't mind us,' muttered Jane, but I was the only one who heard her.

Maybe it was partly my fault. The rise of what might loosely be termed lifestyle journalism, doubtless helps to fuel a peculiarly modern phenomenon: the nagging feeling that the human condition might be a little improved if you lived in the country next to a field full of grazing bullocks, or for that matter in the city next to a Lebanese restaurant. Paradoxically, I can't get too het up about the subject myself. I don't particularly want to live in London again but I know that if we'd stayed there we'd still be perfectly happy. There are many wonderful things about city life, and many drawbacks about living in the country.

I don't want to get competitive about it; it's just that for us, country life works better. In 2004, at the British Film Institute, I watched a film called *Sunrise* – made by one F. W. Murnau in 1927 and re-released by the BFI – which dealt among other things, with the contrasts between city and country.

The film tells the story of a farmer, who has his head turned by a scheming city sophisticate, so much so that when she encourages him to murder his gentle wife, he very nearly does. He and his wife (a performance for which Janet Gaynor won an Oscar) then jump on a tram in the sticks and a few seconds later turn up in the city. Rural transport links were obviously much better in 1927 than they are now. Anyway, surrounded by traffic and general frenzy they recover their love for one another and their zest for life, not to mention a runaway pig.

Once you stopped applying twenty-first century sensibilities to 1927, and realized that just because the farmer held a knife to the throat of a man who eyed up his wife it didn't make him a homicidal maniac, it was all rather sweet. And the message of the whole enterprise, displayed in a caption at the beginning, was a profound one. 'Wherever the sun rises and sets – in the city's turmoil or under the open sky of the farm – life is always the same, sometimes bitter, sometimes sweet.' That just about sums up our experience of moving from north London to north

Herefordshire. Life has its pleasure and its pain with or without chicken shit, but on the whole we prefer it with.

For instance, I like the fact that I have just watched a pair of buzzards circling over our couple of acres of woodland more than I am troubled by the absence, within less than half a day's walk, of a convenience store selling a medium-sliced loaf. But, of course, it's an invidious comparison to draw. After all, you can't make a sandwich out of a buzzard, not unless you're Ray Mears. Incidentally, I never knew, until I heard them calling each other just now, that buzzards have a high-pitched plaintive cry. It sounds all wrong coming from such a macho bird, although I've long been aware of the same thing happening in sport, where the hardest and most pugnacious guys often have the silliest voices. The footballer Alan Ball and the cricketer Graham Thorpe spring to mind, and apparently the legendary Victorian cricketer W. G. Grace talked like Joe Pasquale. I'd never have been able to compare a buzzard's cry with W. G. Grace's voice if I'd stayed in the city, but as you know, I really don't want to get competitive.

A vague frisson of competition, however, seems ever-present. Our old friends in London divide roughly into two categories: those who are perfectly happy for us to live the rural idyll but would no sooner do it themselves than unicycle naked along Oxford Street; and those who remain faintly unsettled by it, not so much because they yearn themselves to look out on heifers and hedgerows, but because it seems like a mild affront to the order of things – we, who seemed so urban, growing several different types of bean within sight of the Black Mountains.

This latter band occasionally try to remind us just how utterly swell it is to live in London, although, frankly, they're wasting their time. We need no reminding of the pleasures of living within ambling distance of a Greek grocer, a French confectioner or a Lebanese restaurant, or of trawling *Time Out* for any film that takes one's fancy, because we enjoyed them and we still miss them. It's just that we have a different set of pleasures now.

Not necessarily better, just different. And come to think of it, not necessarily different, either. I thought about all this one evening when I got a text message from a mate, informing me that he was having a fabulous evening at an Elvis Costello concert at Kenwood House, beside Hampstead Heath, with a few friends and a lavish picnic. Coincidentally, we were at that very moment picnicking at another outdoor concert, in the grounds of Ludlow Castle. I texted him straight back, writing 'bet there's enough hummus to sink the *Ark Royal*' but I didn't tell him where we were, because the headline act at our concert was not Bob Dylan or Eric Clapton, but the Abba tribute band Björn Again. Even I could see that going to see Bjorn Again was a little more provincial than Elvis Costello, and I didn't want them laughing at us over their stuffed vine leaves.

Still, for the record, we had a wonderful evening at Ludlow Castle. The concert traditionally brings the curtain down on the annual Ludlow Festival, and in a way, the headline act is incidental (although I'm not ashamed to say that Björn Again were splendid).

Moreover, this was followed by a firework display as spectacular as any I've ever seen. At the end, as the smoke plumed up from the battlements into a clear night sky, it was illuminated by red light, which made it look as though the castle had been torched by marauding medieval chieftains. Or was it just that my imagination had been ignited by Björn

Again's rendition of 'Fernando'? Whatever, our picnic would certainly not have disgraced Kenwood, and there was probably enough hummus within the castle walls to account for the *Graf Spee*, if not the *Ark Royal*.

By the way, I love that English habit of glancing at neighbouring picnics to see whether theirs is better than yours. One or two passers-by were actually moved to comment on the magnificence of our spinach quiche, while I confess to gazing longingly at a handsome raspberry pavlova being carefully divided up by a busty woman wearing Abba satin. Maybe this business of us all obsessing about the virtues of city over country, or country over city, is a magnified version of the same thing. It's natural enough to be bothered by the thought that someone else is enjoying their picnic more. But if more of us contented ourselves with our mini-Scotch eggs, and stopped looking enviously at other people's smoked salmon parcels, the world, I think, would be a better place.

Acknowledgements

I owe a sizeable debt of gratitude to several people for their help in ensuring that this book was completed on time, and indeed that it was written at all. At Simon & Schuster, Andrew Gordon is everything one could hope for in an editor, calm and reassuring, and it was a particular pleasure to welcome him and his family to Docklow one weekend in autumn 2006 so that he might finally see for himself what has unleashed so many thousands of words.

My thanks too to Rory Scarfe for his excellent desk-editing, and to everyone else involved in the complex chain between me tapping out the first paragraph and the final product being carried by a customer to the till. On which subject, it is

313

probably unwise for an author to pick out an individual retailer, but Diana Ryan at Books Books Books, a small independent bookshop in the lovely Worcestershire town of Tenbury Wells, really deserves a mention for selling my books like men in North African souks sell tablecloths, practically not letting anyone out of the door without encouraging them to buy *Tales of the Country*. She sold many hundreds of copies, and I hope she'll do the same with *The Pheasants' Revolt*.

I must also thank some colleagues at the *Independent*, especially Christian Broughton, who edits my countryside column, his predecessor Madeleine Lim, and the irrepressible Deborah Ross, who allowed me to quote her account of keeping chickens for a week. Alan Brownjohn was similarly generous in allowing me to reproduce his poem, 'Farmer's Point of View', and I thoroughly recommend the excellent volume in which it appears, *Alan Brownjohn's Collected Poems*, published in 2006 by Enithamon Press.

I am indebted too to all those friends who have so cheerfully put up with me embarrassing them both in *Tales of the Country* and again here. In one or two cases I have used pseudonyms, but mostly I have called them by their real names, and they are better mates than I deserve.

As for my wife Jane, I can't imagine a wittier or more stimulating companion on life's journey, or anyone more likely to snort when they read this sentence. She is the source of much of my inspiration and, as she is first to remind me, many of my best lines. I thank her, and our beloved children Eleanor, Joseph and Jacob, for coming to Herefordshire with me and sharing the adventure.

Brian Viner
Docklow, spring 2007